SOCIAL PROBLEMS IN INDIA

M. D. Allen Selvakumar did M.Sc., Criminology and Criminal Justice, at Manonmaniam Sundaranar University, Tirunelveli-12, Tamilnadu. He was an ICSSR fellow when he was doing his doctoral programme. He had also cleared UGC NET for two times. Currently he is working as an Assistant Professor in the Department of Criminology and Police Administration, J.H.A. Agarsen College, Madhavaram, Chennai-600060, Tamilnadu. He has made assortment of presentations and publications which are credentials to his career. His areas of specializations are child sexual abuse and Human Rights.

I. Jenitta Mary is an USRF Research Fellow in the field of Maternal and Infant Health Care at Department of Sociology, Manonmaniam Sundaranar University, Tirunelveli-12, Tamilnadu. She was a gold medalist in post graduate level and university rank holder in under graduate level. She had cleared UGC NET and worked as a guest lecturer in the above institution. She had made assortment of presentations and publications which are credentials to her career. Her areas of specializations are population studies, women, child, and health.

C. Chidambaranathan is an UGC JRF Research Fellow in the department of Sociology, Manonmaniam Sundaranar University, Tirunelveli-12, Tamilnadu. He was a gold medalist at UG and PG level. He had worked as a junior research fellow in the BRNS Kudankulam project. Then he continued as a guest lecturer in the above institution. He had several presentations and publications under his credit. His areas of specializations are epidemiological studies, health, rural, studies, industry, and education.

SOCIAL PROBLEMS IN INDIA

M.D. Allen Selvakumar

I. Jenitta Mary

C. Chidambaranathan

Pointer Publishers

Jaipur 302 003 (Raj.) India

Distributed by
Prem C. Bakliwal for
Aavishkar Publishers, Distributors
807, Vyas Building, Chaura Rasta
Jaipur 302 003 (Raj.) India
Phone : 0141-2578159
e-mail : aavishkarbooks@hotmail.com

2016

ISBN 978-81-7132-650-1

Published by
Mrs. Shashi Jain for
Pointer Publishers
807, Vyas Building, Chaura Rasta
Jaipur 302 003 (Raj.) India
Phones : 0141-2578159, 2708286
e-mail : pointerpub@hotmail.com
Visit us at : www.pointerpublishers.com

Price : ₹ 1350.00

Printed at
Sheetal Printers
Jaipur (Raj.)

Foreword

"We the people of India..." have made tremendous progress, from that 'Midnight' to the present 'Millennium'. We, as a country, have developed infrastructure in all essential areas of social development and have made indigenous inroads into space technology and rocket science. Though being a pluralistic melting pot of varied cultures, we were able to achieve significantly. People in the know reiterate that economic growth jumped to 5% of GDP to 8.7% and is about to touch 10% of GDP. India's dynamic growth, averaging 5.9 percent annually at the cusp of the millennium and rising to 8 percent by 2007 with talk of even 10 percent in the next 5 years and India's gross domestic produce is rising so rapidly that it increases each year by amount that exceed the total GDP of Portugal or Norway. The other significant fact is that India's foreign reserves in 2007 exceed 140 billion dollars enough to cover fifteen months worth of imports, even though some years ago, the country had to mortgage its gold in London because the foreign exchanges were dry. Documenting these benchmarks, along with the pains of social development, hence, assumes much importance.

Books on contemporary Indian conditions are rare, and a multi disciplinary approach to the modern day India, is even more a rarity. It is in a constant dance with the past and the present, yet plans for a rendezvous with the future. It had a 'Buddha' and also a 'Buddha is smiling'. When India gained independence in 1947, its ethnic, caste, and religious conflicts, its security considerations, and its poverty, illiteracy, and other social woes caused many experts to predict that the country was bound to disintegrate. India, however, has proven otherwise.

Since, India is both a Marvel and a conundrum, capturing its moments is not an easy task. The book is deftly handled by its editors. This book is divided into five sections of strategic importance. The first section is on social occurrences covering a range of subjects like children with AIDS, people's religious experience, the impact of mass media, RTI, rights of disabled persons, a sociological appraisal of elderly people, and a socio-psychological perspective on modern India.

The next section on social evils covers areas like child sexual abuse, human trafficking, cyber addiction, and drug abuse. The third section on impact of education envelops areas of higher education and its impact, learning & education, and women empowerment through education. The fourth section on environmental reality focuses on the actualities of modern India like sea water intrusion, sustainable development, fresh water crisis and water management. The last section on Health, zooms over malnutrition, child mental retardation, neglect of women's health, well being of the elderly and the health decision making of SHG members.

In a world of monotony, no one knows the secrets of the next second - what surprises the next unfolding second will reveal...Every educator yearns for the pleasure of being surprised, by their students. When your students suddenly demands a foreword for a book, which they have edited. You become ecstatic. I am glad my students gave me that pleasure. The editors of the book – M. D. Allen Selva Kumar, I. Jenitta Mary, C. Chidambaranathan, have productively used their time at their departments, by producing this intellectual creation, apart from vigorously pursuing their doctoral goals. I congratulate the editors, on their efforts to plan for a book of this sort and to publish it in time. I wish and pray that they will join together, in life, and contribute such publications in future, too.

With three editors, 237 pages, 26 contributions, and 30 authors, this book will have a long shelf life, in many households, in the years to come. This books makes interesting reading and will be useful for social scientists, sociologists, social workers, criminologists, Jurists, lawyers and the like.

Dr. P. MADHAVA SOMA SUNDARAM
Head
Department of Criminology and Criminal Justice
Manonmaniam Sundaranar University
Tirunelveli-627012 India

Preface

Our world had come across against several threats and dangers from nature, environment and even socio-economic evils. Many countries had survived and attained it to good position, while some countries had still fighting against those threats to develop their nations. On the other hand few countries were surrendered to the social threats and it cannot cope up with that situation.

India is a developing nation. It had many struggles, obstacles and challenges to attain the status of developed nation. So it was still on the way to make the dream true "India as Developed nation in 2020" as said by the former President and Scientist Dr.A.P.J.Abdul Kalam. One full decade is remaining for our achievement. Why we can't achieve the target within five years or whether we can achieve in 2020 or not. For these questions, we have to see the present scenario of our nation in all fields. It might give the answer. We need to know the past as well as current issues and challenges of India in different sections. In that health, economy, education, environment, social occurrence and social evils were considered as one of the most significant one. So the real scenario of health, education, environment, social occurrence and social evils of India were analyzed to know the reality. Mainly all the sections focused the issues and challenges in a longitude manner. It would help the people of our nation to know the position and status of our nation. Moreover, it will be very useful for the administrators, academicians, research scholars, students, policy makers...etc. of different disciplines. Beside all it will help for people of our nation irrespective of their region and position.

M. D. Allen Selvakumar

I. Jenitta Mary

C. Chidambaranathan

Contents

Part-II

SOCIAL EVILS AND ITS COLLISIONS

Part-III

IMPACT OF EDUCATION IN INDIA

Contributors

Arunachalam, P.

Faculty Member, Head (2004-07), Department of Applied Economics, Cochin University of Science and Technology, Kochi-22. Kerala.

Cherian, P. Renu

Doctoral Research Scholar, School of Social Sciences, Mahatma Gandhi University, Kottayam, Kerala.

Chidambaranathan, C.

Doctoral Research Fellow (JRF), Department of Sociology, Manonmaniam Sundaranar University, Tirunelveli – 627 012, Tamilnadu.

Devi, S. Ramya

M.Phil Research Fellow, National University of Educational Planning and Administration, New Delhi.

Gayathridevi, S.

Doctoral Research Fellow, Department of Criminology, University of Madras, Chennai, Tamilnadu.

Hubert, M. R.

Founder and Director, Shabnam Resources, Chennai – 600 024, Tamilnadu.

Irudayaraj, V.

Senior Lecturer, Department of Plant Biology and Plant Biotechnology, St. Xavier's College (Autonomous), Palayamkottai, Tirunelveli, Tamilnadu.

Jeyasuresh, B.

Naturopath Specialist, Palayamkottai, Tirunelveli, Tamilnadu.

Kumar, S. Sampath

Assistant Professor (Sr), School of Social Sciences and Languages, VIT University, Vellore, Tamilnadu.

Mary, I. Jenitta

Doctoral Research Fellow (USRF), Department of Sociology, Manonmaniam Sundaranar University, Tirunelveli – 627 012, Tamilnadu.

Murugesan, T.

Doctoral Research Fellow, Department of Sociology, Madurai Kamaraj University, Madurai - 21, Tamilnadu.

Paramasivan, K. M.

M.Phil. Research fellow, Centre for Study of Social Exclusion and Inclusive Policy, Manonmaniam Sundaranar University, Tirunelveli – 627 012, Tamilnadu.

Rai, Anamika

Doctoral Research Fellow, Department of Psychology, University of Delhi, New Delhi.

Ramakrishnan, P.

Lecturer in English, National Engineering College, Kovilpatti, Tamilnadu.

Ramesh, S.

Doctoral Research Fellow, Sri Paramakalyani Centre for Environmental Sciences, Manonmaniam Sundaranar University, Alwarkurichi, Tirunelveli – 627 412, Tamilnadu.

Sacratees, J.

Assistant Professor, Department of Economics, Manonmaniam Sundaranar University, Tirunelveli – 627 012, Tamilnadu.

Sadananthan, M.

Professor and Head, Department of Education, Manonmaniam Sundaranar University, Tirunelveli – 627 012, Tamilnadu.

Saranya, P.

Doctoral Research Fellow, Department of Economics, Manonmaniam Sundaranar University, Tirunelveli – 627 012. Tamilnadu.

Sathya, M. V.

Administrar, Web Cable Network Services, Nagercoil – 629 001, Kanyakumari District, Tamilnadu.

Selvakumar, M. D. Allen

Assistant Professor, Department of Criminology and Police Administration, Jayagovind Harigopal Agarwal Agarsen College, Madhavaram, Chennai-600060, Tamilnadu.

Senthil, B.

Senior Research Fellow, Department of Life Skills Education, Rajiv Gandhi National Institute of Youth Development (RGNIYD), Sriperumbudur- 602 105, Tamilnadu.

Sethurajakumar, P.

Doctoral Research Fellow, Department of Sociology, Madurai Kamaraj University, Madurai-21, Tamilnadu.

Singaram, I.

Senior Professor, Department of Sociology, Madurai Kamaraj University, Madurai-21, Tamilnadu.

Sukumaran, N.

Professor and Head (Rtd), Sri Paramakalyani Centre for Environmental Sciences, Manonmaniam Sundaranar University, Alwarkurichi, Tirunelveli – 627 412, Tamilnadu.

Thirumalraja, D.

Doctoral Research Fellow, Department of Sociology, Madurai Kamaraj University, Madurai-21, Tamilnadu.

Umarhathab, Syed

Assistant Professor, Department of Criminology and Criminal

Justice, Manonmaniam Sundaranar University, Tirunelveli – 627 012, Tamilnadu.

Veliappan, A.

Faculty, Department of Education, Manonmaniam Sundaranar University, Tirunelveli – 627 012, Tamilnadu.

Vijayalakshmi, V.

Assistant Professor (Jr), School of Social Sciences and Languages, VIT University, Vellore, Tamilnadu.

Viswanathan, V. N.

Associate Professor, Department of Political Science, Presidency College, Chennai-5, Tamilnadu.

Yuvaraj, T.

Assitant Professor, Department of Psychology, Manonmaniam Sundaranar University, Tirunelveli-627 012, Tamilnadu.

PART-I
SOCIAL OCCURRENCE IN INDIA

1

Sociological Analysis about the AIDS Affected Children in Vallioor Block, Tirunelveli District, Tamilnadu, India

I. JENITTA MARY

INTRODUCTION

The first case of HIV/AIDS was reported in India in Tamil Nadu in 1986. Since then the virus has been spreading from the high-risk groups to the general population. Today, there are 5.7 million people living with HIV/AIDS in India. Women and children are increasingly becoming vulnerable to HIV/AIDS. The new findings conclude that 38% of the infected persons in India are women. This indicates the increasing feminization of HIV/AIDS in India. This alarming trend is being observed closely as more HIV positive mothers will unknowingly pass the virus on to their children. India has an estimated 220,000 children infected by HIV/AIDS. It is estimated that 55,000 to 60,000 children are born every year to mothers who are HIV positive. Without treatment, these newborns stand an estimated 30% chance of becoming infected during the mother's pregnancy, labor or through breastfeeding after six months. There is effective treatment available, but this is not reaching all women and children who need it.

Jaison M J, Xaier, mentioned in his study, "A study on the perception of parents and the problems of children infected/affected by HIV/AIDS in Chennai". It was found that 65 percent of the respondents were not attending schools. Sixty three percent were living in the rural areas. Seventy two percent of the mode of infection was from father through Commercial Sex Workers. Eighty six percent were not aware of the rehabilitative measures. Seventy four percent were not treated properly by the family members. Sixty percent of assistance was given by NGO's. Ninety percent of the respondents were not having any illness before pregnancy. Sixty four percent mentioned that the society did not accept them and their children as a normal person. Sixty eight percent get treatment from the Government Hospital, Chennai. Seventy eight percent of the respondents preferred allopathic treatment.

AIDS is rapidly becoming a major health crisis in India for which the government is only beginning to address in a limited fashion. The real extent of the disease and its impact are not known but various estimates put the number of deaths a year in the six-digit realm. The World Health Organization (WHO) publication Epidemiological Fact Sheet on HIV/AIDS and sexually transmitted infections (2000 update) estimated that a staggering 310,000 adults and children died of AIDS during 1999.

According to the latest figures released by Indian Department of Health on March 20, the number of adults believed to be HIV-positive was 3.86 million in 2000. UNAIDS estimated that 5 million people were HIV-positive in India at end of 1998 and WHO put the number at 4 million. If one expresses the WHO figure as a percentage, then 0.4 percent of the population or 0.7 percent of the adult population is HIV-positive. Although the rate is less than 1 percent, the sheer volume of HIV-infected people makes India second only to South Africa in terms of overall numbers. India is now near to 12 percent of the HIV-positive people in the world.

The number of identified cases of HIV-infection is relatively low as a result of serious underreporting due to general ignorance of the disease, cultural taboos and other factors. According to the government's National AIDS Control Organization (NACO), the number of reported cases from 1986 to February *2001* was just 19,115. NACO stopped publishing the data explaining that there was "gross under-reporting of HIV infections" and the data was therefore of limited value.

The surveillance study was done by the NACO reveal a dangerous spread of the disease. Over five years, HIV infection has grown from

1 percent to 51 percent among commercial sex workers in Bombay in Western India and from 1 percent to 55.8 percent among drug users in North-East State of Manipur. Among truck drivers in Tiruchi in the south Indian state of Tamil Nadu, the rate increased 2.7 percent to 5 percent in just two years.

Dr Rajan Gupta, a nuclear physicist at Los Alamos National Lab in the US, who is concerned at the spread of AIDS in India warned of a disaster: "Given the current conservative numbers of HIV-positive individuals (UNAIDS estimates 5 million HIV positive people in India at end of 1998) and doubling every 2-3 years means that there will be 50 million by 2007 and 100 million by 2010. This is one in 10 people, i.e. on average one in every family. Also, it is important to realize that all socio-economic levels are already affected. Thus life as we know of will cease to exist by year 2010, if not sooner.

A World Bank report published in September 1999 entitled "India's National AIDS Control Program" warned: "By early in the next century, India will have the highest number of AIDS cases in the world. Even if HIV infection reaches the' low' level of five percent seen in many other countries, more than 37 million Indians would be HIV-infected."

Poverty and inadequate health services are contributing to the spread of the disease. The same World Bank report pointed out: "HIV infection in India is concentrated among poor, marginalized groups, including commercial sex workers, truck drivers, and migrant laborers, men having sex with men, and injecting drug users."

INDIA'S AIDS PROGRAM

Even though the first HIV case was identified among prostitutes in Madras in 1986, the government's initial surveillance, screening and education programs were very limited. It was not until 1992 that it established the NACO under the ministry of Health and Family Welfare. According to a WHO report, NACO only began to seriously establish consistent HIV surveillance in each state in 1998.

The total funding for first five-year plan for NACO was just $USI00.5 million, of which only $15 million came from the government. The remainder was made up of $84 million of interest free credit from the World Bank-affiliated International Development Association and $1.5 million from the WHO. In the second phase of the program for the period up to 2005, financing has increased to $328 million, which is a pittance compared the latest defense budget of around $13 billion or the tax concessions of $1.2 billion provided for big business.

Dr Gupta commented: "The money we see for HIV/AIDS prevention in India has mostly come from international sources. The Phase II of NACO is 86 percent funded by loans, primarily from the World Bank and USAID. The 14 percent Indian contribution is of the same size as the foreign exchange incentives given to Indian business for hard currency trade. So, in spite of the rhetoric, as far as the indigenous government funding is concerned, India is treating HIV/AIDS no different than any other disease. Also, there is no sustained awareness campaign through TV or the newspapers, or any other media."

As in South Africa, access to anti-retroviral drugs to retard the onset of AIDS is developing as a major issue. In the West, a triple-drug cocktail costs was $US 10,000-15,000 a year per patient. Indian drug companies such as Cipla Ltd. have charged markedly less until recently $1,800 per year per patient. Now Cipla is offering the drug combination at $800 per patient per year to the Indian government, $600 for underdeveloped countries and $350 to Doctors without Borders.

Signiticant of the Study

Most fearful disease in the present world is AIDS. At the end of 2007, there were 2 million children living with HIV around the world. An estimated 370,000 children became newly infected with HIV in 2007.0f the 2 million people who died of AIDS during 2007, more than one in seven were children. Every hour, around 31 children die as a result of AIDS. If this state continues, there will be less population in the world in future. In the mean time, research about these children will help to reduce the incident rate and protect them from it.

Scope of the Study

This study covers the socio-economic condition of the AIDS affected children. It also analyzes the causes for the disease; examine the present problem and real condition of the affected children. Moreover, it will help the family, government, non-government and the public to know the current scenario from their perspective. It observes the whole life of the affected children.

Objectives of the Study

1. To know about their socio-economic status.
2. To find out their need and expectations
3. To explore their problems

Selection of Study Area

The researcher had selected Vallioor Block as the study area for this study. It was one among the Panchayat Union (Block) of Tirunelveli district. Many people from this region are affected by AIDS because most of them worked in Mumbai. So the investigator selected this area for this study.

Selection of Sample

The researcher had selected the respondents through census study method. It means all the children who are affected by AIDS from the Vallioor Block had interviewed for this study. So this study covers 24 children from AIDS Child Care Home and the affected children's houses.

Tools of Data Collection

Case study method was used for collecting the primary data from the respondents. It gave us the real picture of the AIDS Children. Moreover, it was an in-depth study.

Findings

The following are the major findings of this study. This study covers only 0-14 age group of AIDS affected children in Vallioor block, Tirunelveli district. One-fourth of the respondents (25%) were young child 0-5 age group. Half of the respondents (50%) were belongs to 6-12 age group and remaining of them (25%) comes under 13-14 age group. Most of the respondents (60%) were living in AIDS Child Care Homes and remaining of them (40%) was living in their houses. Over three-fifth (60%) of the respondents were males and rest of them (40%) were females. Half of them (50%) belong to Hindu religion, 40 percent of them belong to Christian religion and 10 percent of them belong to Muslim religion. Regarding the community, most of the respondents come under Backward Community (BC) and Most Backward Community (MBC). Rest of them comes under SC and ST. Very few belong to forward community. Many of the respondent's type of family were nuclear. And overall respondent's family income was below Rs.2500. Above all, Majority of the respondents lost their parents either Mother or Father.

CAUSES

All the respondents were affected by AIDS through their Mother. More than three-fourth of the respondents went to children home due to socio-economic factors. All the respondents were confident of living long through the medicine. Most of the respondents belong to remote rural area. In these areas, most of their father went to Mumbai and other places for their occupation. Unfortunately, many of the fathers were affected by AIDS in their working place. Surprisingly, rest of their mother affected by AIDS through marriage. All the respondents were suffered by biological problems and health problems. T.B, Fever, Cough and other infectious diseases often affects these respondents. Once, any illness affects them, it is very difficult to recover from it.

PROBLEMS

Beside the physical problem, the respondents face psychological and social problems in their life.

Psychological Problems

Many respondents feel inferior while comparing to the normal children. They also felt shy, fear and guilty in interacting with other children's in the initial stage. Many of them didn't tell others about their infection. Because, they fear that it might change their surroundings. All the respondents know that they are affected by the killing disease AIDS from the birth itself. They were always in a sorrowful state. And think about their final days for death. Most of them compare themselves with their friends and siblings. Rarely few of them imagine themselves as more sinner for having this disease. All felt that they were isolated and deviated from the normal functioning of the society.

Social Problems

Many of the respondents felt that their future is questionable and they had no ideas for it. Neighbours, family members and class mates also hate these types of children in this modem society. In the rural area, other family members restrict their children not to mingle with such types of children. So, many of the parents take them to Child

Care Homes. The affected children are scolded and teased by the neighbours in this area. Moreover, some of the respondents family members itself hate them and give only economic support. This kind of happenings made majority of them to live in the child care homes. We all found a good comparative finding between the affected children who live in child care homes and their houses.

In that, respondents who were living in Child Care Home were well protected than the children who were living in their houses. Even in daily events also make a difference in Child Care Home children and house children. Though child care children lose their house but they gain many things from the child care home. Importantly the educations of the affected children were very good in the home and poor in the houses. All the events from morning to night are scheduled in the Child Care Home. They are planned and worked in that scheduled manner. Mainly, they live with affected children. So they face only limited problems. Moreover, they gave counseling and guidance in a regular basis to all. They also regularly check the children's health.

In the Child Care Home, type of food, level of food were all pre-planned and for small child a worker give a medicine. But, others take medicine as prescribed by the nurse. If anybody from the family comes to the home it psychologically affects not only that children but also affect other children. So, the director of home, allow the family members to see them once in a month and communicate through in a week. Because, family matters and remembrance about family members and incidents were emotionally affect the children. Though, the affected children play together, conflict with each other but they enjoy with one another.

CASE STUDIES

In the total cases, three cases from the Child Care Homes and three cases from the house are summarized below.

Case 1

Sabitha was 10 years old, but she was affected by AIDS. She lost her mother who died 3 years before due to AIDS. Her family was small. She had one elder sister. She lives with her sister, father and grandmother. Her father was a cooley working in Mumbai. Her grandmother only takes care of herself and her elder sister. Her elder sister was 12 years old. Both of them are living in Avarakulam village and studying 5th and 7th respectively in that rural government school. Once in a year, her father will come to see them. She suffered psychologically than physically by the infection of AIDS. Because, she was teased, isolated and frustrated by the neighbours, relatives and even by her sister. She was taken to the hospital regularly by her grandmother once in a month. Her sister pinpoints her disease in every movement and for every matter in the house. Her father talks to her very well. So only she was physically and psychologically not so bad. AIDS also affect her education too. She is often affected by various health problems. In the school, the teachers and her classmates, not allowed her to participate and mingle with them and others. The people's mind was very traditional one. So they never saw her as child rather they were looking her as a sin girl. She was very inferior and in a sorrowful situation. In the hospital, some kinds of counseling only motivate her life. She also attempts for suicide two times due to the touchier from others.

Case 2

Santhiya was 7 years old. She was also AIDS affected child. She lost her parents, who died when she was 2 years old due to AIDS. She was only one child. Her parents affected by AIDS during their work in Mumbai. Now she was cared by uncle and aunty. The property and savings of her parents were under their control. They were also poor farmers. But they took special care towards her. Because they had no child. They also went to fight with the neighbours and other peoples who mistreat their child. So she was well protected in the village. She was often suffered by physically. But she was mentally well set to face anything in her life. She never felt fear about the disease. She was studying well. She was confident of living more years through the medicine. Her future aim is to help the AIDS people. She also lives happily with her friends. She lives like a normal child. Only one thing which differentiates her with other children was the disease.

Case 3

Manikandan was 9 years old. He belongs to Panakudi. His parents were living with AIDS. But they were living separately and he was living with his mother. He was studying 4th in a nursery school. Even now, his friends, neighbours and school staffs don't know about his disease. Because, at 5 years before his parents lived in Tripur. His mother was affected by AIDS through his father. That made her to live separate. Now she was working as an office-staff in a school. Both the mother and child take regular treatment without fail. But the child had fear about the disease and his survival. He also often compares him with other children in all activities. His mother only guides his life totally from birth. His mother hides the matter to their living area which reduces psychological and mental disturbness. His mother had confident to bring her child to a good position in future.

Case 4

Ramya was 9 years old child. She was studying 3rd standard, and affected by AIDS. She was the last child in her family. She belongs to poor economic family. Her parents also affected by AIDS and died before four years. She had only one sister who was studying 10th std in Chennai. she and her sister were sponsored by an international NGO. With the help of social worker, she was living now in AIDS Child Care Home. She had known about her problem. But she was a young child. So she didn't realize about the consequences of the disease. She used to take her medicine and food in a systematic manner like other children in the home. Her sister speaks to her through phone once in a week. She also met her sister atleast once in three months. Their relations didn't support them in any way. She was studying well. She was totally ignored by the family background and environment in her life.

Case 5

Abishek was-belongs to the age of 10, who was studying 5th std. He was living in the AIDS Child Care Home with his elder brother. Both of them were affected by AIDS. His father was only the cause for .this disease, because during that time he worked in Mumbai. Due to illegal relationship he was affected by HIV. Then it was hidden by him. So his wife and children were infected. Their parents died 2 years ago. Their grand parents only admitted them in this home, because of their relations compulsion and problem. But the grandparents meet them once in a month and take them to their house in holidays. They also gave economic and social support to their grand children. They also felt sorrow for the disease which affected both their children and grand children. Both the grand children were studying normally. But they often struggle due to health disorder. They also felt very happy in stay with home and village. In their school, only the teachers know about their disease. Both the children know about the disease. They had never feared about it. Because they had given regular health checkup and counseling for their betterment of life.

Case 6

Manimalla of 13 years was studying 9th std. She was living in the AIDS Child Care Home at 2 years ago. She was affected by AIDS through their parents. Now her father was alive. Her mother died before three years. She was only one child in her family. She likes to live in the home. But her relatives and neighbours irritation made her father to put her in the stay home. She was often felt inferior. In the stay home itself, she compares herself with other children and felt that her life was very sorrowful one. If anyone's parents or relatives came to the home, she used to cry. In the last 6 months only, she had changed her mind set. She also never mingles with others. She also tries to go out of the home in the initial period. Her physical condition was very worst. Due to this physical and psychological condition, she was very poor in her education. In holidays, she used to sit alone and think about the past events. In school, she had only one friend who knows about her total life. She also had less confident level about her future.

CONCLUSION

Many diseases threaten the life of man. In that, one among them is AIDS. Adults and mature people suffer by AIDS due to their own causes. Young children suffer by AIDS not by their causes but by their parent's causes. Physical problems are known by others, while psychological and social problems are unknown. The young AIDS children real life was in a miserable position. To resolve the present condition, more health advancement is required. Beside this, many research works had to be done to find their real status and create a way for the possible solution.

REFERENCES

1. Deepal Jeyasekera, 4th May 2001, www.wsws.org/articles/200 1/ may2001/aids-m04.shtml
2. International Conference on AIDS, 2002, July 7-12, 14: abstract no. G1 2607, Loyola College, Chennai.
3. www.unicef.org/india/children
4. www.gateway.nlm.nih.gov/MeetingAbstracts/1 02252206.html

□□□

2

Contemporary Religious Experience - A Contribution to the Understanding of Christian Charismatic Movements in Kerala

P. Renu Cherian

INTRODUCTION

Religion retains its presence even in the secularized post modern society by adapting itself into the changed situations. As the pace of globalization picks up, the crosscurrents of the global cultures - and reactions against broad social changes - make spiritual life interesting and diverse. (Lester R Kurts, 2007, p.211). At this juncture it is worth studying the diverse religious practices in our social milieu. Religious space fabricated by popular religious practices in our contemporary India, develops new knowledge and moulds the religious selves of the followers. Popular Indian Christianity indeed takes us to the 'messy' terrain in which religious identities, borders and authority are not concrete and absolute, but often fluid and subject to negotiation. (Selva J. Raj & Dempsey, 2002, p.2). It takes various moulds like festivals, processions, rituals, iconic miracle workers, gods, saints, religious gathering resenting to official one, worship centers etc that acts as the embodiment of peoples religious selves. Fast growing Pentecostal Christian charismatic movements are indeed popular expressions of Christianity in our contemporary social scenario. Its escalating growth and success could be attributed to diverse factors. It refers to the emerging trends within the domain of Christianity, and having a different expression from the existing traditional Christian churches in terms of practice and performance. Its globalness hides in the role played by the media (religious broadcasting), fellowship networks with overseas connections, mega churches that seem to function as international corporations, international conference programmes, and prayer links; in fact rather transnational movement (Poewe,1994,p.2).

Pentecostal Christian charismatic movement took their origin from the spreading of Pentecostal and charismatic movements from America and Britain in the 1960s. From 1980 onwards, such movements began to flourish in Kerala. Pentecostal Christian Charismatic movements (here after PCC) can be defined as the gathering or worship groups outside the institutionalized religious domain, having leaders of local origin with charismatic identity. This movement is characterized by "exuberant worship, an emphasis on subjective religious experience and spiritual gifts, claims of supernatural miracles, signs and wonders - including a language of experiential spirituality rather than of theology - and mystical 'life in the Spirit' by which they daily live out the will of God" (Burgess,2002,p.XVII).

In Kerala, Pentecostal Christian charismatic movement shows a mushrooming growth. Everywhere in the street we can observe big posters and advertisements of these groups. The structures, ideologies and practices of such movements are entirely different from traditional Christianity. People participating in these religious groups, easily become part of the knowledge system produced in that space. This spatial discourse within the religious space produces new religious experiences different from that in traditional religious space. This study problematises the process of the construction of the religious space in the contemporary social domain on the basis of the theoretical concepts put forth by Henri Lefebvre. According to him, there are three elements vital for the construction of the social space. They are 'spatial practices', 'representation of the space', and 'representational space', which are used here to analyze the religious space and the charismatic aura fabricated by PCC in the contemporary globalised social situation.

POPULAR CHRISTIAN MOVEMENT IN CONTEMPORARY INDIA

One of the Pentecostal Christian Charismatic movements in Kerala, which could be used as a representative of the PCC, is the

Heavenly Feast Global Worship Centre with its head quarters in Kottayam district of Kerala State. The Heavenly Feast Global Worship Centre (HF) was started 10 years ago by Matthew Kuruvilla and Thomas Abraham. Its main church is situated in Kottayam town. Worship is conducted on every Friday and Sunday at daytime. More than twenty thousand members and visitors assemble there for worship at a time. Men, women and children participate in the meetings. Among the worshippers, women form the majority. Although people from all classes, castes and religion come for worship, people from the lower middle class constitute the majority. Majority of the gathering are members of the movement while visitors are only a minority. Those who wish to join HF have to get baptized, even if they were baptized in their mother church before. All the visitors may not try for membership in HF. There are devotees who attend the worships regularly but avoid membership of HF in order to retain their relationships within the mother parishes and their traditional belief system. HF receives everybody irrespective of their religious identity or financial status. Most of the believers are in their search for solutions to their physical, financial or spiritual problems.

This movement is grouped under the category of Pentecostal Christian Charismatic movement because of its peculiarity in the religious and social domain. This sort of movement gives more stress on the Good News, speech along with acts like prophesying, speaking in tongues, dancing, and miraculous healing. These practices have created a new wave of religious experience among the believers, penetrating the traditional religious consciousness of individual and society. This movement projects itself as offering solutions to the complex problems of human life. They present themselves as having the power to answer the difficult questions of human life. In this way, one can say it is meant for the oppressed. The claims of possession of extraordinary qualities of the leaders and the ideologies provide the movement a charismatic image and identity.

PRODUCTION OF RELIGIOUS SPACE

Social space is different from geographical space, though it exists in a geographical environment. According to Henri Lefebvre, 'social space is a social product' (Lefebvre, Henri, 1991), and the three elements that are very much critical for the construction of the social space, are Spatial Practices, which is the lived space; Representations of Space, which is the conceptual space or the verbal or worked out signs; and the Representational Space, which is the system of non-verbal symbols and signs. These elements are employed in this study to analyze and understand the construction of religious space which is charismatic in nature. HF is analyzed accordingly. The performative worship, which is peculiar to HF, encompasses the spatial practices of the HF. Representations of the Space includes the conceptual ideas concerning the movement and the Representational Space is the encounter of the HF with the public realm through symbols. This in turn results in the construction of the religious space having charismatic identity.

Spatial Practices - *The Religious Space through Performative Worship*

The worship pattern followed in HF is entirely different from that practiced in traditional Episcopal churches. The spatial practice followed in HF is the Performative Worship practiced exclusively in that religious space. This performative worship emphasizes the importance of the Charisma of the movement through their spatial practices. The English word 'worship' is a contraction of the original Anglo-Saxon word 'worth - ship'. Thus, to give worship to any one simply meant to accord him the proper recognition of his inherent dignity and value or, to put it another way, to accord him his worth or his worthiness.' (Robert G. Rayburn, 1980, p.23). It is significant to observe the unique worship practices of HF, which makes this particular movement different from the general Christian religious and spiritual practices. Here two things are important: the presentation and performances of the spiritual/religious authority/leaders and the participation and synergic responses of the gathered devotees. The performances are accompanied by music, bodily gestures and exhorting speeches of the leaders and the cooperation and response of the stimulated devotees ideally creates the domain of the charismatic spirituality within the space of HF. The gathered devotees here become subjects of the charisma and power pertained in that space. The worship practices followed in the HF seek the mental and bodily submission of the gathered devotees. Nevertheless, it can be said that the worship and performance pattern of both the charismatic leaders and gathered devotees are significant to understand the aura of religiosity and spirituality diffused by HF.

Spatial practices of the concerned religious space include activities such as prayers, speaking in tongues, miraculous healing, prophesies, songs and Eucharist. We shall discuss these performative elements in order to understand the construction of charismatic religious space.

SPEAKING IN TONGUES

Speaking in tongues is considered as a significant aspect of the HF worship. It could be considered as a kind of religious performance. Speaking in tongues is otherwise known as 'Glossolalia'. 'Glossolalia', translated literally from Greek, means 'tongue speech'. It is a form of unintelligible vocalization which has non-semantic meaning to the speaker, and is interpreted in the Bible as a divinely inspired spiritual gift.' (Virginia H. Hine, 1969, p.211) The HF is famous for the practice of speaking in tongues. The main pastor practices this, as the symbol of the presence of Holy Spirit in him. This practice occurs throughout the worship especially at the time of healing prayers and at the time of speech. The movement insists that for a true devotee 'Glossolalia' is an essential quality symbolizing the presence of Holy Spirit in oneself. The movement conducts special prayer session for the achievement of speaking in tongues.

Thus, the act of speaking in tongues can be viewed as the essential requisite for a devotee in a charismatic religious space. For HF this element of performative worship should be practiced by every believer as it is the gift of Holy Spirit. For defining a true devotee HF considers the act of speaking in tongues as one of the essential determinants, so devotees try to get this requisite. Thus, 'tongue speaking is a personal ritual which can bring about a deepening of the spiritual dimension of human existence.' (Richard A. Hutch, 1980, p.265). Thus the practice itself changes into an essential ritual practice for a devotee to be practiced.

HEALING MINISTRY AND CHARISMA

Faith healing or miraculous healing can be defined as 'improving health in body, mind, or sprit by means of prayer or other extra normal states of consciousness, usually occurring apart from orthodox medicine and consider miraculous.' (Rondey J. Hunter ed, 1990, p.401) The believers and the followers, who are assembled for the meeting, have a great expectation of healing. Healing is achieved in the meeting by the prayer of the charismatic person, while the community of worshippers gathered there fervently prays along with the needy. The gathering believes that the leader has the power to do miracles in the name of Jesus. Healing is considered as the gift of Holy Spirit and those who have that gift can heal the sick ones. Charismatic people believe that they can obtain these spiritual gifts or powers through prayers and can use them in a variety of ways, particularly to heal or cure people of physical ailments or remove afflictions caused by evil spirits. 'Thus, the stress in the movement is on the spiritual power that charismatic obtained from the Holy Spirit and its use in Healing.' (Rowena Robinson, 1998, P-201)

The sick one is instructed to pray to God for the forgiveness of his/her sin and guilt and they believe that the miracle occurs through these prayers. The sick person is forced to believe that his/her sickness is due to their sin. As the pastor is considered as the representative of God, healing is delivered through him. Leader is supposed to have the power to do miracles as Jesus Christ has granted him the authority to do it. Thus a divine identity is bestowed on the leader, which is evident from the talk of the devotees.

HF conducts special prayer sessions for miraculous healing in all prayer meetings. Main pastor initiates the prayers for healing. In these prayers, the whole worshippers pray along with the charismatic pastor for the healing. During the prayer the pastor announces that people with certain diseases are going to be healed soon. He emphasizes that the presence of Jesus Christ is there in the meeting, and he will touch the sick ones and relieve them from their sickness and sufferings. These prayers last for half an hour. As the prayer progresses the believers enter in to a highly excited condition, a hallucinated state. It is often claimed that after the prayers that most of the diseased are healed. Healing prayers are even conducted in the houses of the sick persons.

EUCHARIST

'The Eucharist or Holy Communion or Mass or Lord's Supper is probably the ritual most participated in and most discussed in Human history.' (David F. Ford, 1999, p.137) This term, 'Eucharist' is derived from the Greek verb "eucharis tern" which means "a thanks giving". The theme of thanks giving is an important element of the breaking of the bread making this an entirely appropriate term for the service in question.' (Alister E. Mc. Grath, 1999, p.121)

HF celebrates Eucharist in all Sundays, where HF addresses it as Lord's Supper. For the practice of Lord's Supper, they won't use any written liturgy and the leader is the main celebrant of Eucharist. On the stage, Wine and Bread are placed in a tray. Then it is distributed among the entire community of devotees. Those who are baptized are only allowed to take part in the Eucharist function. Every body will be standing on this occasion. This is the entire process of Lord's Supper in HF congregation

'The Eucharistic service has meaning because it is related to the already existent idea that the Christian has about Jesus Christ. These derive both from scriptural and apocryphal traditions.' (Susan Visvanathan1993, p.161). In HF the celebration of Eucharist is based on the Biblical portion which describes the Crucifixion of Jesus Christ. They are not using any apocryphal traditions. They avoid the adoration of St. Mary or saints in the celebration of Eucharist as practices in traditional Churches. HF's teaching and perception about Eucharist is similar to that of Pentecostal doctrine. In Pentecostal background, 'the breaking of Bread is following the references of fellowship and it appears as a symbol of that fellowship.' (T.G.Abraham, 2003, p.163). In HF they also consider it as a symbol of fellowship among the members. Eucharist is also understood as the act of remembering Jesus Christ's crucifixion and resurrection. 'It is probably sufficient to state that Jesus may have expected his followers to maintain the table fellowship which they had experienced with him.' (Norman A. Beck1970, p.197). In the same way, HF presents it as a table of fellowship. That is why the congregation is pinching from same bread, and having wine together. But this is not the case in traditional Churches. There the ordained priest only could conduct the Eucharist. He follows particular liturgical texts, and he himself serves the bread and wine to those who participate in Holy Mass. In contrary, HF does not have an ordained clergyman to conduct the Mass and people have equal participation with the leader in the Eucharist service. The HF way of celebrating Mass is totally a different experience for the members of traditional Episcopal churches.

What is the use of these spatial practices? These practices provide the spiritual awakening and salvation for devotees that address the life, both, in this world and the other world simultaneously.

Representations of Space - ***The Religious Space through the Teaching and Ideologies***

Representations of space are the conceptualized space of the charismatic movement. This is the space of verbal or intellectually worked out signs. In the present condition this space imbibes the teachings and ideologies of the movement. From the above given description of the performative worship we can figure out the teachings and ideologies of HF. Teachings of Heavenly Feast, as a charismatic movement is very much different from that of the traditional Churches. Even though its teachings are very similar to that of Pentecostal Churches, it shows some differences with them. Seven doctrines of Pentecostal movement are followed by HF too. They are Confession, Baptism, spiritual awakening, separation (pure living), communion, Holy Communion and prayer.

Apart from this the main pastor adds some more points. According to the main pastor, the basic principle of Heavenly Feast is to "Focus on Christ". Since Jesus Christ is the path to God, they always pray to Jesus Christ. They negate the "Tradition and Legality" which is practiced in the conventional Churches. HF argues that they are doing every thing according to the inspiration /direction given by Holy Spirit, not by following any liturgies. They consider miraculous healing as the gift of Holy Spirit. HF criticizes the traditional churches as following the worship practices and canons without questioning or interpreting its meaning in contemporary situations. But for HF these traditional practices and canon is not according to the teachings of Bible, and therefore such practices should be changed. HF do not use any liturgy and their worships are based on the direction given by Holy Spirit. Along with this the pastor adds that they are different from Pentecostal churches in one concept. In the Pentecostal denomination they don't want to reduce their poverty and sufferings as they consider it as a part of Christian life. But HF always preaches prosperity to their followers. From the worship it is evident that they always preach prosperity to the congregation. For them worship is the means to get religious satisfaction along with physical prosperity in one's life. They insist that through the prayers and religious life one can improve his/ her social status and security.

Thus we can observe that the performative worship pattern

provides the charismatic habitus for the devotees and it acts as the signifier for the devotees' spirituality.

Representational Space - *The Encounter with the Urban Public Sphere*

Representational space is the result of the movement's encounter with the public space. This include two aspects, firstly, the symbols used by the charismatic leaders in order to communicate with the devotees at the time of prayers in a religious space, secondly, it includes symbols used by the movement for spreading the representations of the charismatic religious space, such as advertisements, electronic religious space, cyber space etc.

We can use Erving Goffman's interpretation of performance to analyze the symbols. Goffman introduced a term 'Front' to refer the expressive equipments intentionally used by the performer, which include 'settings' and 'personal front.' Setting is the physical layout, whereas, the personal front is the features associated with the performer. These concepts can be deployed to analyze the performance of HF. In the HF worship they create a setting, which enables them to be a charismatic religious movement. The stage and the entire tent like structure of the Church and the captions written on the backdrop of the stage create the physical environment. The simplistic and captive settings attract the devotees towards the movement. Performers (pastors) present themselves as the religious leaders having charismatic aura. The 'personal front' of the performer is defined in such a way that, they can sustain their identity of a charismatic person. They wore neat and tidy dresses. Their facial expressions and their speeches tend others to believe that they have a liminal identity. Their speech easily captures the attention of their followers. Their 'body' also tries to articulate their charisma. During prayer, they lift their hands upward and pray. This creates an impression among the believers that they are going to be blessed by the prayers of their leaders. The leaders, through their activities try to present themselves as acceptable in front of others. Speeches always directly deal with the human sufferings and the solutions for that suffering. They induce the observers to follow their teachings. The pastors always try to maintain this condition through their activities in order to sustain the impression of others towards them that they are performing in the desired manner.

Electronic Religious Space - *Popularization of the Charismatic Movement*

It is observed that HF uses electronic media as a means for spreading their ideologies for establishing a space in the society. HF uses media such as television channels, C.Ds, news papers and web sites for spreading their beliefs. HF is trying to generate a religious environment through these media. 'The appropriation and use of modern media technologies facilitates the dissemination of the Word to the masses. The use of the media is clearly a tool of expansion, a reflection of globalizing aspirations, but it is also part of a calculated attempt to transform and Christianize popular culture so that it is safe for consumption by "born-again' Christians. The 'modern' media are deemed an acceptable weapon for God's army in the battle against Satan.' (Rosalind I.J.Hackett, 1998, p-258) Similarly through the electronic media HF retains its identity as a charismatic movement thereby resulting in the formation of an electronic religious space. Through these media the message or ideologies of HF reach far and wide.

Religious practices and messages telecasted through media is only an image of the real situation. Even if the believers are not in direct proximity with the real situation, the words, gestures, emotional outburst etc. in the worship provides religious experience for the viewers. Media can establish religious experience only on viewers with a presupposition of religiosity and charisma. We can observe that such interactive space between the viewers and the media itself is the electronic religious space. Viewers who identify themselves as one among the real participants in the meeting telecasted on the media feels all the emotional bursts as if they are in the real situation and experiences miraculous healing even through the virtual image.

At the time of telecasting the worship there are only two entities, the viewer and the worship environment. Here media exists as a religious entity rather than an electronic instrument. Another thing to be noticed is that this 'virtual reality' can be re-played at any time. And the viewer is able to recollect those prior religious experiences and to reaffirm their belief. HF emphasizes the importance of electronic media and there by making electronic religious space as another source for the production of charisma. Apart from this, the electronic religious space can be viewed as initial process for stabilizing the charismatic authority of the movement and acquiring a global outlook.

ADVERTISEMENTS- ENCOUNTERING THE PUBLIC SPHERE

We shall discuss the role played by these advertisements in creating a religious space within the community. The primary aim of an advertisement is to catch the attention of common people towards the product. 'Advertising language is of course a loaded language. Its primary aim is to attract our attention and dispose us favorably towards the product or service.' (Gillian Dyer, 1982, p-139) Generally, advertisements are done only for those things, which are brought under the category of commodity. Now religion has come under the category of commodity that needs advertisements for its publicity and popularity. Apart from traditional churches, HF has advertisements for its publicity in order to familiarize itself in the society. The main purpose of these advertisements is to publicize the nature and specialties of the movement. Advertisements attract people towards HF by giving the testimonies and other miraculous events. These advertisements are packed with charismatic leader's message, captivating captions and testimonies of believers along with their photos. In addition, headings, statements and layout are created with an intention to attract those who are facing problems or disabilities in their lives to attend HF's meetings. They publish their advertisements in different newspapers, periodicals, leaflets, flex boards etc. HF also sells C.D's regarding their worship and testimonies. They present big cut-outs depicting the images of its main pastors around street corners and road side. They also publish notices and pamphlet giving details of their worship and ideologies.

We can note that they have given more emphasis on certain captions in their advertisements, for example, **'Are you in the shadow of curse? Come, Jesus will give you deliverance' 'Miracles are happening today. Come and receive the blessings'**. These induce a person to feel that he has some problems to be solved and it can only be solved by approaching HF. Testimonies of healed ones are the attracting segment of their advertisements. These testimonies include incidents showing redemption from sufferings. These sufferings range from financial problems to health problems. A person with the same problem while reading the testimony feels that he also can get solution to his problem through HF.

CONCLUSION

Religious space constructed by this popular Christian movement has a charismatic aura which encourages a person to be part of that charismatic religious habitus. The basic motto of the religious space such produced is based on the prosperity theology that one can improve his economic, social and health status in the society through religious life. HF guarantees prosperous life for its followers, which is the quest of people in the present age of consumer culture. Another peculiarity of the movement is that it binds both this world and the other world simultaneously. For HF salvation means a comfortable prosperous life in this world and a heaven in the other world. The religious space uses some symbols which can be read as the sign of urbanity. The pastors wear modern dresses and ties; they use English songs even though most of the followers do not follow the meaning. The movement often brings pastors from west for speeches. The religious leaders present themselves attractively in the advertisements and we can say that 'the leaders looks more like a religious entrepreneur than a local pastor' (Rosalind I.J.Hackett, 1970, p.197). The movement uses electronic media as means for circulating their ideas and for spreading the nature of the religious space, thereby, constructing an electronic religious space for the devotees. This space also enables healing and religious experience for the devotees having predispositions of the charismatic religious habitus. In a wider context it is important to remember that the fast growing Pentecostal Christian Charismatic movement emerging in contemporary India is a popular global movement challenging earlier notions of religiosity and life.

REFERENCES

1. Badone, Ellen, Religious Orthodoxy and Popular Faith in European Society, Princeton University Press, New Jersey, 1990.

2. Bayly ,Susen, Saints, Goddesses and Kings-Muslims and Christians in South Indian Society 1700-1900, Cambridge, Cambridge University Press, 1989.

3. Bourdieu, Pierre, The Logic of Practice, translated by Richard Nice, Polity Press, Cambridge, 1990.

4. Bruckner, Heidrun and Elizabeth Schombuhrer,"Performance"in

Veena Das,ed. Hand Book of Indian Sociology, New Delhi, Oxford University Press, 2004.

5. Dalmia, Vasudha, Angelika Malinar and Martin Christof, eds, Charisma and Canon-Essays on the Religious History of the Indian Subcontinent, New Delhi, Oxford University Press, 2001.
6. Dempsey ,Corinne G, Kerala Christian saint hood-Collisions of culture and world view in south India, New Delhi, Oxford University Press, 2001.
7. Dyer, Gillian, Advertising as Communication, London, Routeledge, 1982.
8. Gennep, Arnold Van, The rites of passage, translated by Monika B. Vizedom, And Gabrielle L. Caffee, London, Routledge and Kegan Paul, 1960.
9. Goffman, Erving The Presentation of Self in Everyday Life, England, Penguin Books, 1990.
10. Holm, Jean and John Boweker, ed. Sacred Place, Printer Publishers, U.K, 1994.
11. Kurtz, Lester R. Gods in the Global Village-The World Religions in Sociological Perspective, 2nd edition, California, Pine Forge Press, 2007.
12. Lefebvre, Henri, The Production of Space, translated by Donald Nicholson-Smith, U.K, Blackwell, 1991.
13. Poewe,Ken, Charismatic Christianity as a Global Culture. Columbia, University of South Carolina Press.
14. Raj., Selva J, and Dempsey, CorinneG, Popular Christianity in India-Riting Between the Lines, New York, State University of New York Press, 2002.
15. Robinson, Rowena, Christians of India, New Delhi, Sage Publications, 2003.
16. Robinson, Rowena, Conversion, Continuity and Change-Lived Christianity in Southern Goa, New Delhi, Sage Publications, 1998.
17. Turner, Brayan, The Body and Society, Second Edition, New Delhi, Sage Publications, X1996.
18. Uzukwu,E.E. Worship as Body Language-Introduction to Christian Worship, An African Orientation., Minnesota, The Liturgical Press, 1997.
19. Varrier, Maya, Hindu Selves in a Modern World: Guru Faith in the Mata Amritanadamayi Mission, Canada, Routledge Curzon, 2005.

20. Visvanathan, Susan, *The Christianity of Kerala: History, Belief and ritual among the Yakoba,* Mumbai, Oxford University Press, 1993.

21. Williams, Peter W. Popular Religion in America-Symbolic Change and Modernisation process in Historical Perspective, Chicago, University of Illionois Press, 1989.

22. Hackett, Rosalind I.J, "Charismatic/Pentecostal Appropriation of Media Technologies in Nigeria and Ghana" in Journal of Religion in Africa, vol.28, 1998, accessed from www.jstore.org

23. Hine, Virginia H., "Pentecostal Glossolalia toward a Functional Interpretation" in Journal for the Scientific Study of Religion, Vol.8, No-8, 1969, accessed from www.jstore.org

24. Hutch, Richard A, "The Personal Ritual of Glossolalia" in Journal for Scientific Study of Religion, Vol.19, No.3, 1980 accessed from www.jstore.org

25. Mohan, Sanal, "Narrativizing Oppression and Suffering: Theorizing Slavery" in South Asia Research, Vol.26, 2006.

26. Ojo, Matthews A, "The Contextual Significance of the Charismatic Movement in Independent Nigeria", Africa: Journal of the International African Institute. Vol.58, no.2, 1988 accessed from www.jstore.org

27. Ojo, Matthews. A "Deeper Christian Life Ministry: A Case Study of the Charismatic Movement in Western Nigeria", in Journal of Religion in Africa, Vol.18, 1988, accessed from www.jstore.org

28. Poloma, Margaret and Lynette F. Hoelter, "The 'Toronto Blessing': A Holistic Model of Healing" in Journal for the Scientific Study of Religion, Vol.37, No.2, 1998, accessed from www.jstore.org

29. Ruth, Ann & Dorothy Williner, "The Rise and Role of Charismatic Leaders" in Annals of the American Academy of Political and Social Science, vol.358, 1965 accessed from www.jstore.org

30. Stacey, William and Anson Shupe, "Correlates of Support for the Electronic Church" in Journal for the Scientific Study of Religion, Vol.21, No.4, 1982, accessed from www.jstore.org

31. Alastair and V.Campell, A Dictionary of Pastoral Care, Great Britain, SPCK, 1987.

32. Burgess, Stanley M., et.al. The New International Dictionary of Pentecostal and Charismatic Movements, Michigan, Grand Rapids, 2001.

❏❏❏

3

Impact of Mass Media in Indian Society

C. CHIDAMBARANATHAN AND M.V. SATHYA

INTRODUCTION

Every coin has two sides. There are both positives and negatives of one single given notion. The media, known as the fourth pillar of democracy, has a huge impact on the society. The effects are of course, positive as well as negative. It is upto the people to decide which effect they want to bask in. Media is such a powerful tool that it literally governs the direction of our society today. It is the propeller as well as the direction provider of the society. Opinions can change overnight and celebrities can become infamous with just one wave by the media. Read how media affects the society today by reading its effects.

The communication media are the different technological processes that facilitate communication between (and are in the "middle" of) the sender of a message and the receiver of that message. The mass media include newspapers, magazines, radio, and films, CDs, internet, TV, etc. The media communicate information to a large, sometimes global, audience.

PROGRESS OF MASS MEDIA

Traditional media generally, cover folk song, folk dance drama that depicts the stories of most common rural dwellers. Traditional folk media can not present what it wants to deliver, in glamorous and colourful manner equally, as compared to other organized sector of mass medium that we have. Traditional folk media cultivate the rural lifestyle and culture specifically, as to match their needs and demand, which are illiterate and backward as well. Traditional folk media go with rural masses side by side, bringing slower change in their development. Although, they provide so many messages, that contribute to the rural development significantly. Traditional folk media can command a very strong position in the rural people's mind, as it weaves almost of its messages to serve the various needs and purposes as well as entertain the numerous rural people as well.

Government efforts at using radio and TV for development communication have met with varying degrees of success. Major projects include rural radio forums for agricultural development (1967), SITE (75-76), and the Kheda project (1976-1989) and the 1995 GRAMSAT experiment using radio for training of women panchayat (local village level governance) members. These large-scale projects to meet core development needs yield valuable lessons on the software, hardware and organizational management needs of such efforts.

All India Radio and Doordarshan were state owned until 1997 under the Ministry of Information and Broadcasting; primary declared aims of promoting the social objectives of the nation such as literacy and family planning. Launch of satellite television in the form of the Hong-Kong based Star TV with its 39-nation footprint. Star TV transforms the face of Indian television, with its multiple channels and aggressive market-driven entertainment programming. Other private channels follow such as Zee TV, Sony TV, Sun, and Gemini. Doordarshan's revenues are fast depleted. After 2000, many changes had occurred in newspapers, magazines, radio, and films, CDs, internet, TV, etc. These had made major influence on various sectors in our society.

THE RELATIONSHIP BETWEEN COMMUNICATION AND CULTURE

The relationship between communication and culture is a very complex and intimate one. First, cultures are created through communication; that is, communication is the means of human interaction through which cultural characteristics— whether customs, roles, rules, rituals, laws, or other patterns—are created and shared. It is not so much that individuals set out to create a culture when they interact in relationships, groups, organizations, or societies, but rather that cultures are a natural by-product of social interaction. In a sense, cultures are the "residue" of social communication. Without communication and communication media, it would be impossible to preserve and pass along cultural characteristics from one place and time to another. One can say, therefore, that culture is created, shaped, transmitted, and learned through communication. The reverse is also the case; that is, communication practices are largely created, shaped, and transmitted by culture.

Positive Aspect of Mass Media

Information on the latest happenings reaches people in just a matter of minutes. The vision of media reaches even the remotest corners of the country and makes sure that everyone is aware of what is going on in the country. The easy and swift availability of any given information makes media one of the most reliable sources for forming public opinion. It bridges the gap between the leaders and the masses by becoming their channel of communication.

It brings into open the innumerable achievements that are going on in the country. Media gives ordinary people the power to reach out to the society as a whole. It can make heroes out of ordinary men. The media acts as a deterrent on corrupt practices and keeps a check on the working of the government. Media has significantly promoted social causes like literacy, health management, anti-dowry practices, discouraging female feticide, AIDS awareness, etc.

Negative Aspect of Mass Media

Media can adversely affect the thinking capability of individuals and instill negative or destructive thinking patterns in the society as a whole. Media can portray an ordinary thing so negatively that it may force people to think or act in quite the opposite way. Media glorifies violence and contains graphic descriptions or images. When viewed by the vulnerable portion of the society, i.e., the children, it can have grave effects on their upcoming and thinking patterns.

The media can sometimes go out of the way in advertising or glorifying certain issues. Usually, a bad or detrimental message is packaged in a glorious way and is made accessible to the public. Movies that depict filthy rich thieves who don't bat an eyelid before killing someone or extorting someone and the getting away with it, sure give entertainment to people. At the same time, it encourages them to act in a way that promises adventure and thrill in life. This way, media glorifies the bad aspects of people and encourages them to act in forbidden ways.

Today television channels and newspapers are making fast money by cashing on the news in wrong sense and wrong way. In the race to become more popular and to make money they have broken all the limits media must follow while serving to build a healthy and progressive society. They have no respect for the sentiments and ethics of the people and land whom they serve to, with their immense power to influence the masses they just make judgment like a true dictator rather than a good advice of a true friend as they previously used to do. If it will be going in the future then we people have to think about the role of media in our life.

IMPACT OF MASS MEDIA

Mass Media and Gender

Mass Media played a major role in decreasing gender discrimination and inequality in our society. It had made many women to participate in all fields equal to men. Women also had a part in all type of mass media. Though it had lifted the women in one hand, on the other side, it portrait women as bad image. It made women as a commodity in the form of glamorous pictures and sensitive reports to gain more money.

Mass Media and Children

The children gain more knowledge through the media by reading scientific news, daily happenings, participates in quiz and puzzles. They also see the natural and environmental reports in the channels. They select their role model by seeing and knowing the right person life history. But the media also spoil the children through the TV programmes (Cartoon, chutti TV and other action oriented programmes). The children imagine themselves as the cartoon or action heroes and they attempt in their life. In the mean time, media reduces their playing time and made them to sit in front of TV for longer time, this create them lazy and inactive.

Mass Media and Violence

Social violence is increasing day by day in this modern period. In all type of mass media they exaggerate the violence issues and made the people to imagine in a negative way. Especially, cinema create a wrong imagine about the violence and they show a rationality for that occurrence. But it cannot be happen in reality. The people to make heroism and to shine in the society easily follow from the cinema. Moreover, media indirectly teach the unknown people to do theft, sexual harassment, fraud and murder. The ignorant people by reading and seeing more violence reports and scenes, they also made in a critical situation. Sexual violence also increased by reading and seeing erotic and glamorous pictures from media through internet and other sources.

Mass Media and Politics

Mass Media also had a significant role in deciding the political party to rule of our country. Political participation also increased among the people with the help of mass media. Political awareness had been created through mass media. Political parties launched their own channels and printed media for their political purpose. Cinema had shown both negative as well as positive side of the politicians. People were highly brainwashed by creating a political party can only make our country glorious in the election period. This made people to select wrong persons in the election or nonparticipation in election. Finally, some people misuse their vote by media.

Mass Media and Education

Much type of educational oriented programmes and reports were spent in the media to develop the educational status of our country. The media guide the young people to select their course and colleges in an effective manner. By giving rewards and awards, they encourage the rank holders and motivate the others too. Scientific programmes, innovative games, IQ programmes and games will improve their physical and mental ability. They also create awareness from unrecognized and cheating in the name of education.

Mass Media and Religion

Starting the day with religious events may give more peace and success through out the day in every event thought by all people in our society. The media helps the people to get these religious events from their home itself, by telecasting religious programmes and reports. This made separate channels and print media for each religion in multiple ways. This had both ups and downs. Some programmes irritate other religious people and it wills religious conflict. Impure religious preachers were explored by the media to create the awareness of anti-religious practices.

CONCLUSION

Life is composed of good and bad but man only selects the right path in every aspect. Some agencies will guide to go in a right manner. In that mass media also had a special and vital place in driving our life. It is like an ocean consists of peace and disaster, the people had to select the wanted and unwanted things in it. Finally, mass media had emerged as a powerful determining in all aspects of our life in our country.

REFERENCES

1. The Asian Communication Handbook, 1998: Published by the Asian Media Information and Communication Center (AMIC) and the School of Communication Studies, Nanyang Technological University.
2. Seminar, October 1997, New Delhi.
3. Through the Magic Window: Television and Change in India, by Sevanti Ninan. 1995. Sage Publications.
4. Annual Report, Indian Newspaper Society, New Delhi.
5. Annual Report, 1997-98 GOI, Ministry of Telecommunications, Department of Telecommunications.
6. Annual Report, Ministry of Information and Broadcasting, GOI.

4

Information and Good Governance – Is That Right to Information Act 2005 as a Practical Tool for India's Good Governance?

V. N. VISWANATHAN

"The root of the all problems is lack of democratic practices done by the people of India. Now, at this stage, we Indians need a complete transformation from representative democracy to participatory democracy. People should take interest and should have the right in the decision-making process. Every single Indian should be empowered. The Right to Information (RTI) Act is like an important tool for empowering the poorest of the poor." "It is the foundation of Good Governance in modern times" **—Viswanathan V.N**

(During in an RTI Campaign in Tamilnadu)

INTRODUCTION

India is a possible fertile ground for the decay of democracy and governments plagued by corruption, authoritative leadership and ruthless bureaucracy. While the West Minister system stood the challenges of Indian democracy in the first two decades of post-independent India, it failed to cope up with new challenges posed by the new actors in the Indian politics. Therefore, the appendages of rule of law have been tinkered to cope up with new political situations. Incidents of powerlessness have been a great factor for the rising frustration among the younger generation and ultimately they take recourse to radical movement and try to destabilize the government.

Democracy in modern times requires three important elements to fulfill the basic objective of 'Welfare State'. They are as follows

- Application of Rule of Law in spirit and in practice.
- Wider participation of excluded groups in politics.
- Dissemination of information for taking rational decisions.

Early in Greek city States, the information regarding governance can easily be transferred because the limitation democracy in terms of numbers and rulers. Besides, many people were divided as subjects and citizens and the slavery was considered as a legitimized institution that must be protected by the State. However, modern democracies have evolved many facets unknown to our past experiences with democracy. I am trying emphasis that, today; democratic government must necessarily reach the unreachable people. Communication plays a vital role for mass participation of people in the political life. India's experimentation with democracy spill out a variety of experiences and to some extend it has been successful, at least, in sustaining the democratic principles. Much legislation which was brought under the instigation of the Union Government has fulfilled the basic aspiration of the people and thus provided an opportunity for 'inclusive democracy.'

In the analysis of Indian democracy, our fellow scholars from America and British hardly realized one important characteristic feature of India's experiences with democracy, i.e. to frame a thin line of force that unites the people to sustain democracy. It is only in this context, the Right to Information Act can be looked into. Let me also explain that there are external forces which also accelerated the phase of Indian democracy like the World Bank, IMP and the WTO regimes. The Right to Information Act 2005 mandates a timely response to citizen requests for government information. It is an initiative taken by Department of Personnel and Training, Ministry of Personnel, Public Grievances and Pensions to provide much need information to the public by the officials.

SETTINGS

My argument is that RTI 2005 was vehemently supported by the Government for to face three important challenges faced by the people of India. These challenges were mostly claimed for share in political power by hitherto groups without powers. Secondly, the RTI Act 2005 was indented to reorient the 'governance' aspect than the 'Government' aspect. RTI was evolved not to reform institutions but the mindset of people involved in governance. It paves way for a result oriented government which is based on the following premises:

- Open Government
- Transparency
- Accountability and responsibility.
- Corrupt-free government.

The RTI Act 2005 has successfully replaced the Official Secret Act 1923 which more suitable for colonial government than the democracy we were experimenting with since 1947. As an Act, the RTI has one important feature i.e., it was evolved as a bottom up movement than top-down approach to the problems of the people. My experience with RTI as an activist in Tamil Nadu and as a NDTV volunteer for creating awareness among vulnerable groups exposed much needed headway for its implementation. I have toured many parts of Southern States in propagating the idea of RTI for the common man and I was surprised to know that many ordinary people were really interested in making RTI as a workable concept. Interestingly many national and international NGOs readily took RTI as a right tool for correcting the mistakes of the governing process. From a common man perspective RTI stood for:

- As tool to question the government
- As tool for an effective participation and
- As a tool for empowerment.
- To built an inclusive democracy.

Before going for the explanation of how RTI was used as an empowering tool, I would like to present the bureaucratic views of the RTI which can be listed as such:

- It slows down the work of bureaucracy which is already caught in the web of red tapism.
- It is designed to curb the traditional powers of the bureaucracy.
- Considered as a political strategy to build up the support base from the excluded groups.

Based on these general percepts one can develop a hypothetical question which goes like this.

GENERAL HYPOTHESIS

The perspective of common man and the bureaucracy are in fact at loggerheads and every possible effort will be made by people in power to threat the very existence of RTI in near future. Though I very much pessimistic about the RTI in future, I have strong impulses that many civil society organizations will keep a vigil over these developments and make a dent in making the RTI to sustain itself in the long run. It is better to treat RTI as a human right issue than a political one. Denial information may amount to denial freedom expression and to take decision affecting one's own life. The constitutional backing of RTI can read in Article 19- the freedom of expression as a fundamental right.

Today, we live in Knowledge Society and all citizens must be informed of all the activities of the government and the governance aspects. Perhaps, it is only for that main reason the Government of India established the Knowledge Commission. The necessities of RTI as become so vital to empower people as well to make them to live in a knowledge society. Informed citizens are assets to a nation. India, in its true spirits represents a knowledge society and citizens having access to information is more empowered in all dimensions. Information is power today. In course my paper I will demonstrate how through having information people are empowered. Network information is necessary for to have access to Government welfare measures.

Freedom of information is a fundamental human right and the touchstone of all freedoms to which the United Nations is consecrated .The right falls under freedom of expression (defined as the right to seek, receive and impart information). There can be no enjoyment of the right to freedom of expression if people do not have access to information.

This right imposes a duty on the government to facilitate public access to information. Freedom of information involves access to information held by public officials and by private bodies that carry out activities that affect the public in general.

The right to freedom of information is encapsulated in International Instruments. It is enshrined in Article 19 of the Universal Declaration of Human Rights and protected in international human rights treaties including the International Covenant on Civil and Political Rights (ICCPR) and the African Charter on Human and Peoples' Rights. Article 19 of the ICCPR provides that everyone shall have the right to hold opinions without interference, everyone shall have the right to freedom of expression; this includes freedom to seek, receive and impart information and ideas of all kinds, regardless of frontiers, either orally, in writing or in print, in the form of art, or through any other media of choice.

The UN Special Rapporteur on Freedom of Opinion and Expression has also stressed the overriding importance of freedom of information. In his 1995 report to the UN Commission on Human Rights he stated that freedom will be bereft of all effectiveness if the people have no access to information. Access to information is basic to the democratic way of life. The tendency to withhold information from the people at large is therefore to be strongly checked.

Freedom of information and freedom of expression may however be restricted in limited cases. These are cases where enjoyment of such rights threatens national security or privacy. Article 19(3) of the ICCPR states that the exercise of the rights may be restricted in cases provided for by law and that are necessary. These are: For respect of the rights and reputations of others; and for the protection of national security or of public order or of public health or morals.

Freedom of information promotes good governance, democracy, trust and accountability in government. Public Information is collected using tax payers money and should therefore be easily accessible. Governments often hold this information secret and attempts by the public to gain access it are often frustrated by government officials. Records should be made available and provided to members of the public when needed, with the government acting as a custodian of information.

Access to information eases government's decision-making process as a result of the participation of an already informed citizenry. Citizens can only exercise their rights or influence decision making if they have access to reliable and adequate information. Democracy is achieved when people engage with their leaders and influence decision making process. Leaders are often elected based on mere political slogans but essentially, the public needs information to properly exercise their democratic rights. They will be better placed to choose their leaders based on information giving their record rather than mere political talk. Citizens can then hold their leaders accountable for policies and decisions made while in government.

With access to information, citizens will then be empowered to demand action against the corrupt and recovery of diverted development expenditure. Lack of free flow of information impairs and slows down economic and social development. For most African countries, economic development is often undertaken in participation with private contractors and /or international donors. It is important that all those involved in such economic deals are held accountable to the public. This can only be realized if information on development deals is shared with the public. Members of the public through access to information will increase their economic opportunities. Members of the public are aware of government funds available and make use of them in improving their lifestyles, business persons can find out about licensing requirements, taxation and trade regulations, workers access information about labour regulations and their entitlements. Provision of such information increases economic opportunities for the less powerful as well as for big players.

Freedom of information is a vital tool to fighting corruption which best thrives in an uninformed society. Citizen's right to seek information from the state on any issue promotes transparency and accountability in government. Freedom of information also promotes transparency and openness in public and private decision making process. Statistics reveal that in countries where freedom of information has been enforced, positive results have been realized in terms of reduction in corruption, inefficiency and mismanagement.

Statistics show that in 2005, of the ten countries scoring best in transparency International's annual corruption perceptions index, no fewer than nine had effective legislation enabling the public to peruse government files and of the ten counties that were perceived to be worst in corruption, only two had freedom of information legislation. Freedom of information reduces corruption and promotes transparency in governments, since citizens are empowered through information. Demystification of rules and procedures, proactive dissemination of relevant information touching on matters of public policy and regular consultation with the public is a strong safeguard against corruption.

Freedom of information is important for the achievement of meaningful democracy. With access to information citizens are better placed to choose their representatives on the basis of strength of their record, hence they can hold their governments accountable for the policies and decisions it promulgates. Democracy is further enhanced when people meaningfully engage with their institutions of governance and forms their judgments on the basis of facts and evidence, rather than just empty promises and mere political talk.

Freedom of information reduces electoral fraud and promotes proper public participation in elections. Documents such as the voters' register should be available to the public long before elections to avoid cases of rigging and inconsistency in voter turn out. Democracy is further enhanced when the public engage with public institutions and form their judgment on the basis of facts and evidence rather than just empty promises and meaningless political slogans. With freedom of information, the government is more sensitive, accountable and responsive to the needs of its citizens.

INFORMATION AND DEMOCRACY

More rarely recognized and analyzed than assumptions concerning models of democracy are those associated with information and democracy. The most straightforward are based on the generally held view that information equals knowledge and knowledge equals power. As noted above, telematics – the convergence of information-processing and communication technologies – is fundamental to electronic democracy. Consequently, ICTs with their vastly expanded (and expanding) power to collect, store, process and transmit information are seen as the keys to unlocking access to information and therefore knowledge and power. Acceptance of this straightforward view of the value and role of information has led many exponents of electronic democracy to assume that because ICTs can influence the distribution and flow of information throughout society they are inherently democratic. A more clearly argued correlation between information, ICTs and democracy was presented by Manor. He argued that '... there are three main sources of distrust and skepticism concerning democracy:

- The complete loss of control over the leaders by those led,

- The inability of democracy to provide public services efficiently,
- The impractability of participatory democracy because of the deficiencies and inabilities of citizens.'

Manor concluded that all these could be considered in some way problems of information. Therefore as computers deal with information, its communication and use then 'Computers can, in fact, be used to improve representative democracy; they can even be utilized to establish participatory democracy.' Information democracy deals with empowerment, with ensuring that people have the tools they need.

The figure- I below illustrates the various stages of the empowerment process of individual and communities within the knowledge societies. The empowerment process is unprecedented because it often happens on its own, can occur anywhere, and could be a silent empowerment revolution that can radically transform the existing governance processes. The transformation however, happens in partially unpredictable ways due to rapid increase in information levels among the society and differences in how people absorb and act upon the information.

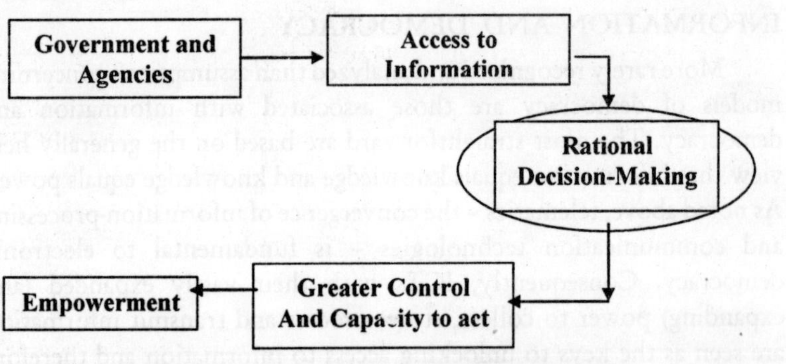

Fig. 1 : Information and Empowerment

Empowerment Process within Knowledge Societies -Knowledge Networks and Governance

Governance in broader terms may be defined as the way the society works and is organized. The definition encompasses the manner in which power is exercised in respect of the management of economic and social resource. This definition of governance is applicable at all levels from local governance to national and international governance. Information architecture therefore becomes one of the key building blocks to creation of governance regimes.

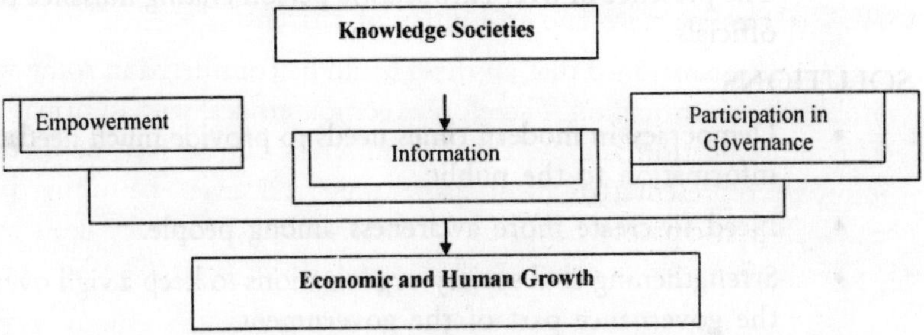

Fig. 2 : Knowledge and Net working

Attributes such as access to information and dispersion of information in the society are critical to shaping of governance structures. They define the basic nature of governance mechanisms, the people who control them, and the openness and objectivity of the Knowledge networks function on the underlying principle that access to information is empowering and strategic use of information by the citizens could become the key to popular and meaningful governance. A unique feature of the networks is its ability to matching information with its users. They perform the role of locating strategic information for active recipients to and targeting information of significance to its potential users.

FUTURE AGENDA

India marching towards an inclusive democracy and there is need to empower people who were kept out of power for a long time. As an empowering tool for ordinary citizens it has been as a blocker of powers by certain vested elements within the government as well as the bureaucracy. To prove my argument I can list certain lapses in the implementation of RTI 2005.

- Problems raised by the bureaucratic elements regarding 'file notes'
- Many exceptional clauses within the Act itself.
- Many State Information Commissions failed to provide the Annual report which mandatory.

- Bureaucracy is ill equipped to handle the demand for raising request for information.
- The presence of over enthusiastic person crating nuisance to officials.

SOLUTIONS

- Democracy in modern times needs to provide much needed information to the public.
- Need to create more awareness among people.
- Strengthening civil society organizations to keep a vigil over the governance part of the government.
- Government sponsored publicity campaign to reach the remote corners of India.
- Inducting student force to create more awareness across India.

We learn only from experiences and the RTI experiences has shown that the RTI is indeed a right tool for empowering people but not to forget that there is also momentum taking place within the government circle considering RTI as menace to their traditional role and as power wielders. Good governance, in fact, is in need of supplying the right information in the right time so that every citizen can take decision which will provide them maximum benefits. Democracy also foresees that individual is the best judge of his requirements than ant others. I have clearly demarked the line of division of interest between the public and the bureaucracy in relation to the implementation of RTI Act. However, the conflicts of interests among bureaucracy and the public is considered as a great challenge for the good governance. The social and political implications of RTI will enhance the values much needed for good governance. Institutional morbidity and bureaucratic arrogance can be effectively checked by mass awakening the poorest of poor in India.

REFERENCES

1. D. Elgin, 'Revitalising Democracy through Electronic Town Meetings', Spectrum, 66/2, 1993.
2. Y.Manor, 'The Contribution of Computers to Participatory Democracy', in E.Mumford & H.Sackman (eds),Human Choice and Computers, North-Holland Publishing Co, 1975.

3. R.Doctor, 'Social Equity and Information Technologies: moving towards information democracy', ARIST, 27, 1992.
4. Digital Governance website, http://www.digitalgovernance.org
5. ECOSOC 2000. Report of the Secretary General on the theme of Role of Information Technology in the context of a knowledge based global economy.
6. InfoDev. 2000. The Networking Revolution: Opportunities and Challenges for Developing Countries. The World Bank Group, Washington DC.
7. McConnell International, 2000. Risk E-business: seizing the opportunity of Global E-Readiness. McConnell International, LLC http://www.mcconnellinternational.com/ereadiness/EreadinessReport.htm
8. Narayan, Deepa. 2000. Voices of the Poor. Oxford University Press for the World Bank.
9. Nath, V. "ICT enabled Knowledge Societies for Human Development", Information Technology in Developing Countries. Volume 10, No. 2, August 2000.
10. UNDP 1999. Human Development Report 1999. New York.
11. World Bank's E-governance Site http://www1.worldbank.org/publicsector/egov/

❑❑❑

5

Human Rights of Diabled Persons

B. SENTHIL

INTRODUCTION

Every Tenth Person in the World is supposed to be affected with one or the other kind of physical disability. It may be congenital or acquired through infections, traumatic causes or metabolical causes. At least in the coming millennium, we should strive to minimize the problems of the physically disabled, through the concerted effort of all – may we be Psychologists, Sociologists, Medicos, Technologists, Administrators, Public opinion makers, or even the Commoners.

CONCEPTS OF IMPAIRMENT, DISABILITY AND HANDICAP

Terms that were acceptable in the past, such as 'Cripple' 'wheel chair bound' are now in disrepute. Most writers sum to agree that making use of the disability as a noun, 'the disabled, 'the blind' is tantamount to equating the person with the disability, terms, such as limited or amputee , sufferer or victim, which evoke pity and imply tragedy (La Forge, 1991; Zola, 1993).

World Health Organization (1980) defined impairment as, "the loss of functioning in the body organ or system" (for example – muscular weakness). Disability is defined as "restriction in the ability to perform a normal activity" (for example – unable to walk). Handicap refers to the disadvantage resulting from the impairment or disability and prevents the individual a social role" (for example - inability to work).

'In 1997, WHO defined the dimensions of disablement, providing a clear distinction between impairment, an abnormality of structure or function, disability, a limitation resulting from that impairment and handicap, a resultant disadvantage to the individual.

Type of Handicap

The Penguin Medical Dictionary describes the word 'handicap' as a circumstances or event that places a person a disadvantage. The Handicapped category includes the (1) Visually Impaired (2) Hearing Impaired (3) Mild - Mentally Retarded (4) Negative Lepers (5) Orthopaedically Handicapped.

1. *Visual Impaired*: Person whose degree of vision false within the range of 20/200 or 6/60 (Snellen) in the better eye with correcting lenses fall in the category of blind. In practice, the word 'blind' means total absence of vision and visually impaired persons fall in this category. Persons with limitation of the field of vision subtending an angle of 20 degree or worse also fall in the category of Visually Impaired.

2. *Hearing Impaired*: are those in whom the sense of hearing is nonfunctional for ordinary purpose of life. The deaf - mute are those who are deaf or who having been deaf are also mute. The loss of hearing is measured by means of tone audio meter and is expressed in decibels. Persons with over 60 decibels are generally regarded as Hearing Impaired.

3. *Mild – Mentally Retarded*: People belonging to this group have IQ varying from 51 to 70. They can develop social and communication skills. They can also learn academic skills up to approximately 6th grade level and can achieve social and vocation skills adequate to minimum self - support and need assistance under usual social or economic stress.

4. *Negative Lepers*: is a patient who has been cured of leprosy or is suffering from non infectious leprosy.

5. *Orthopaedically Handicapped*: Persons disabled because of defeats in bones, joints, muscles, tendons, ligaments of spine and the limbs fall in the category of orthopaedically handicapped.

Definition of Physically Handicapped

The term physically Handicapped has been defined differently in terms of Medical, Psycho - social, Education and Vocational areas. A few approaches are given below,

As per the *Medical Experts*, Physical disability would lead to a limitation of physical function whether loco meter, sensory of effecting vital organ.

According to the *Amelia Harris Survey* (1971) the physically handicapped may be defined as "a disadvantage or restriction of activity caused by disability or short – term and temporary disability or long-term and chronic condition".

According to *Bio-Medical model*, disability is defined as "an observable deviation from biomedical norms of structure or function that directly results from a disease, trauma or other health condition" (Boorse, 1975 & 1977).

The *Sociologists view* a handicapped person as 'possessing a physical defeat which reduces one's efficiency in performing one's personal obligations according to a socially determined standard'.

The term 'Physically handicapped' to a long term impairment of bodily function or other physical defeat that places the individual at a disadvantage in one or more important spheres of normal life activities such us getting education, earning a living and to fulfill their social relationships. The physically handicapped are those who have some physical defeats or disabilities to restrict such movements that place them at a disadvantageous position in our society.

From the *Education point of view*, if person's physical conditions prevent him from participating in social activities like recreational, educational and vocational nature, he may be considered physically handicapped.

The *Rehabilitation Act of 1973*, as implemented by the regulations of the Department of Health, Education and Welfare, defines a handicapped person as "One who has physical or mental disability which limits his functional Capacities (mobility, communication, Self-care, Self – direction work therapy or skills) in terms of employability (Rehabilitation Literature, 1978).

From the *Psychological point of view* Handicap is the cumulative result or obstacles which interposes between the individual and his maximum functional level.

Rights of Disabled People

Disability Act

The person with *disabilities (Equal opportunities, Protection of Rights and Full participation) Act* was passed by both the houses of our Parliament in a Single day in December 1995. There was much hope, even euphoria, amongst disabled people and their parents, families and friends. The law was a notified on 7th February 1996.

The *Disability Act of 1995* defines in the areas of:

- Blindness
- Low vision
- Leprosy - cured
- Hearing impairment
- Loco motor disability
- Mental retardation; and
- Mental illness.

Disability Discrimination Act (DDA)

According to the *Disability Discriminated Act* (DDA), describes a disabled person as 'anyone with a physical or mental impairment' which has a substantial and long-term adverse effect upon their ability to carry out normal day - to - day activities'. This is meant to be a fairly wide definition and includes:

Physical impairment - This includes week ending or adverse change of a part of the body caused through illness, by accident, or from birth. For example amongst many other situations,

- Blindness
- Deafness
- Heart disease,
- The paralysis of a limb or severe disfigurement

Mental impairment - this can include learning disabilities and all recognized mental illnesses.

Substantial - This does not have to be severe, but is more them minor or trivial

Long - term adverse effect – that has lasted or is likely to last more than 12 months.

A normal day - to - day activity – that is one that affects one of the following;

Our mobility, manual dexterity, physical co-ordination, continence, ability to lift, carry or otherwise move every day objects, speech, hearing or eye sight. Memory or ability to concentrate, learn or understand, or perception of the risk of physical danger. It does not the ability to work because no particular form of work is normal for most people.

Declaration on the Rights of Disabled persons proclaimed by General Assembly resolution 3447 (xxx) of 9 December 1975 (UN)

1. The term "disabled person" means any person unable to ensure by himself or herself, wholly or partly, the necessities of a normal individual and/or social life as a result of deficiency, either congenital or not, in his or her physical or mental capabilities.
2. Disabled persons shall enjoy all the rights set forth in this Declaration. These rights shall be granted to all disabled persons without any exception whatsoever and without distinction or discrimination on the basis of race, colour, sex, language, religion, political or other onions, national or social origin, state of wealth, birth or any other situation applying either to the disabled person himself or herself or to his or her family.
3. Disabled persons have the inherent *Right to Respect for Their Human Dignity*. Disabled persons, Whatever the origin, nature and seriousness of their handicaps and disabilities, have the same fundamental rights as their fellow - citizens of the same age, which implies first and foremost the right to enjoy a decent life, as normal and full as possible.
4. Disabled persons have the same Civil and Political Rights as other human beings
5. Disabled persons are entitled to The Measures Designed to Enable Them TO Become as Self-Reliant as Possible.
6. Disabled persons have the right to *Medical, Psychological* and

Functional Treatment, including *Prosthetic* and *Orthetic Appliances*, to *Medical* and *Social Rehabilitation*, education *Vocation Training and Rehabilitation Aid, Counselling, Placement Services* and other services which sill enable them to develop their capabilities and skills to the maximum and will hasten the process of their social integration or reintegration.

7. Disabled persons have the Right to 'Economic and Social Security' and to a decent level of living. They have the right, according to their capabilities, to secure and retain employment or to engage in a useful, productive and remunerative occupation and to join trade unions.

8. Disabled persons are entitled to have their *Special Needs* taken into consideration at all stage of economic and social planning.

9. Disabled persons have the *Right to Live Their Families or With Foster Parents and to Participate in all Social, Creative or Recreational Activities.* No disabled person shall be subjected, as far as his or her residence is concerned, to different treatment other than that required by his or her condition or by the improvement which he or she may derive there from. If the stay of a disabled person in a specialized establishment is indispensable, the environment and living conditions therein shall be as close as possible to those of the normal life of a person of his or her age.

10. Disabled persons shall be protected against all Exploitation, all regulations and all treatment of a discriminatory, abusive or degrading nature.

11. Disabled persons shall be able to avail themselves of qualified legal aid when such aid proves indispensable for the protection of their persons and property. If judicial proceedings are instituted against them, the legal procedure applied shall take their physical and mental condition fully into account.

12. Organizations of disabled persons may be usefully consulted in all matters regarding the rights of disabled persons.

13. Disabled persons, their families and communities shall be fully informed, by all appropriate means, of the rights contained in this Declaration.

NATIONAL POINT OF VIEW

Country Reports on Human Rights Practices (2006)

The persons with Disabilities Act provide equal rights to all persons with disabilities; Government buildings, introduced a 3 percent reservation for persons with disabilities in education and employment, and government buildings have made mental for wheelchair access. However, human rights activists complained that available facilities where not sufficient.

Mental health care was a problem. Hospitals were overcrowded and served primarily as dumping grounds for persons with disabilities. Patients generally were ill-fed, denied adequate medical attention, and kept in poorly ventilated halls with inadequate sanitary conditions. In July the NHRC determined that insufficient attention was paid to issues of the mental illness and called for better enforcement of national laws. At year's end, no action was taken on the 2001 NHRC recommendation to remove all persons with mental illness from jails. In March the NHRC issued guidelines to jails lodging mentally challenged persons stipulating the need for open lawns, daily physical and mental activities, and strict rules limiting the used of force to self-defense and attempted escape.

The Government provided special arrangements for voters with disabilities during the April-May parliamentary elections, but it was not able to meet their needs on a countrywide basis. Pursuant to a Supreme Court directive, the election department attempted to make all polling places accessible by providing wooden ramps. However activists criticized the Election Commission's lack of compliance and delay and were physically prevented from protesting outside of the commission's office in April. The government provided access to most polling stations in larger cities like New Delhi, but access rural areas were uneven.

The disability division of the Ministry of Social Justice and Empowerment delivered rehabilitation services to the rural population through 16 district centers. A national rehabilitation plan committed the government to provide rehabilitation centers to more that 400 districts, but services were concentrated in urban areas. Moreover, the impact of government programs was limited. Significant funding was provided to few government organizations such as the Artificial Limbs Manufacturing Corporation of India, The National Handicapped

Finance and Development Corporation, and the Rehabilitation Council of India. With the adoption of the Persons with Disability Act, nascent disabled rights movements slowly raised public awareness of the rights of persons with disabilities.

The National Commission for Persons Disabilities (NCPD) had the responsibility to recommend to the government specific programs to eliminate inequalities in status, facilities, and opportunities for disabled persons, to review the status and condition of institutions delivering services, and to submit annual reports with recommendations. In February the government constituted a new NCPD headed be a former governor, Sunder Singh Bhandari. In April the Rajasthan High Court directed the State government to promote the establishment of special schools for disabled children in both the public and private sectors; however, few teachers were trained to meet the special needs of disabled children. Also, the National Center for the Promotion of Employment for Disabled People stated. In September that there was shortage of educational institutions for the disabled and that the admissions process as marked by harassment.

In February the country's civil services introduced a quota for the employment of 20 persons with disabilities per year.

In June the central board for secondary education issued guidelines to schools requiring barrier free education in schools, colleges, libraries and hostel. It also took steps to provide Braille books to educational institutions.

In July rights NGOs reported that persons with disabilities were not able to obtain duty free imports of artificial limbs, crutches, wheelchairs, walking frames, and other medical needs. The also claimed that no effort was made to make railway compartments, platforms, and railways accessible to the disabled, and noted that less than 1 percent of the disabled were employed.

In August the government began the first disabled friendly train service between Bhopal and Nizamuddin (Delhi) station. The trained had an exclusive coach for persons with disabilities and Braille tags for seat and berth numbers in all coaches.

The Equal Opportunities, Protection of Rights and Full Participation Act of 1995 stipulate a 3 percent reservation in all educational institutions for persons with disabilities; however, statistics showed that only about 1 percent of the students had disabilities. The Times Insight Group reported in September that most colleges and universities did not know about the law.

The government provided special railway fares, education allowances, scholarships customs exemptions, rehabilitation training and budgetary funds from the Ministry of Rural Development to assist the disabled; however, implementation of these entitlements was not comprehensive. Parents of children with development disabilities lobbied the government for a special security fund, but, no action was taken on this request at year's end.

INTERNATIONAL POINT OF VIEW

What is the International Day of Disabled People about?

On the 3rd December 1982, the UN General Assembly decided on the World Programme of Action for Disabled People. The United Nations committed itself and its members to promote the full participation of disabled people in social life and development as well as prevention and rehabilitation measures.

Twelve years on, many problems are still unresolved. Disabled people are not yet fully considered within international development issues. They are still excluded from society in many countries of the world. Even where effective disability legislation is in place, the implementation lacks ideas and is hindered by negative attitudes towards disabled people.

Facts and Figures

The World Health Organization estimates that there are 600 million disabled people world wide 10% of the world population. It is also estimated that about 80% of all disabled people worldwide live in developing countries.

More and more, disability is seen as a social issue which is not only based on medical reasons. The organization "Disabled People' International" defines disability as the interaction between the person with impairment and environment and attitudinal barriers he or she may face. There for the reasons disability is always complex and can only be understood within the context societies and cultures.

Role of Handicap International

In its 20 years of existence, Handicap International has changed from being an emergency organization with a rather medical focus on disabled people, to an organization which promotes the human rights of disabled people.

Our organization is working in partnership with Disabled Peoples' Organizations at local, national and international levels to empower disabled people worldwide and encourage their inclusion into society. Our function as a facilitator can be best seen in our involvement in the process of the development of the UN Convention. Handicap International helps organizations in developing countries and Europe to implement the convention and other legal tools in every day life.

MAJOR ISSUES: HUMAN RIGHTS AND INCLUSION

The disability movement identified human rights and inclusion as major issues in the fight for equal rights and participation of disabled people. International human rights treaties are needed to set a global framework and direction for the equal rights of disabled people worldwide. Governments will then have to implement these treaties in national legislation. National and local organizations will be able to build upon these legal frameworks to develop truly inclusive movements and services for all.

What does Inclusion Mean?

Inclusion is applied to a variety of fields such as education, employment, society in general or international development. Inclusion means the acceptance of all people and is not limited to disabled people or people with HIV/AIDS.

In the disability field the concept is best known through inclusive development promoting the consideration of disabled people in all aspects of school or international development.

Human Rights

"Disability is a human rights issue". This statement made by the former UN Special Rapporteur or Disability characterizers the activities pursued by many international and national organizations and governments. In 1992 the UN publicized the "Standard Rules on the Equalization of Opportunities for People with Disabilities" Which were not mandatory, but were taken by a number of governments to shape their national disability policies. NGOs made use of the Standard Rules to define their fields of activities.

In a unique international effort, the UN is now working on a comprehensive convention for the Rights of Disabled People. This convention is planned to be ready or debate in the General Assembly in September 2005, and will make the year 2005 an important year for disabled people worldwide.

Despite all the activities in the field of human rights, there are still many unanswered questions. Although there is an international agreement about the need for an international convention for the rights of disabled people, It is not yet clear how this convention will be implanted and how governments and organizations can bring the convention to life. The magnitude and complexity of the UN convention for the rights of disabled people makes it difficult to find a starting point and to develop tools monitor the convention.

CONCLUSION & SUGGESTION

In future, professionals can play a key role in helping people with disabilities to find meaningful jobs; will provide more opportunities for the Handicapped to prove their potentials. We will try to create awareness of the needs and talents of people with disabilities and take action to provide training in fulfilling their livelihoods that will give them the dignity, they deserve.

Business and professional leaders must take the lead with the help of our many professionals especially psychologists, so that ancient prejudices official road blocks and absence of easy help can be prevented. We must assist people with disabilities in identifying potential employers and preparing for job interviews. Voluntary organizations should aim at eliminating barriers to employment for people with disabilities and created meaningful jobs.

Research input are essential to develop better, light weight and cosmetically acceptable aids and appliances suiting Indian condition and exhibitions should be held to make the public understand the potentially of the disabled and generate a confidence in the common man in the abilities of physically challenged and promote adequate manpower, in the areas of disability prevention and rehabilitation and like the national health programmes.

It is necessary that the disabled people should adequately involved in the decision making stage whenever any policy programme is drawn up for their upliftment. The handicapped should also be representing at a committees, commissions of the disabled. Vocational training for the disabled is very necessary for their gainful employment. It has to be given to priority. Vocationalization should start early enough when it is realized that the particular individual cannot benefit from any further academic education. There is no sufficient number of vocational training Institution like that of IIT's and the various National Institutes set up by the government, considering the number of disabled persons. The existing training programmes later largely to the needs of the organized sector of urban areas. It should expand at level to cover the rural area also. Three percent of the vacancies in Group-C and Group-D posts under the central Government are being reserved for the disabled persons – one percent of them is meant of the orthopedically disabled. But even this meager quota of reserved vacancies does not get filled up urgent action should be taken to fill the vacancies reserved for disabled and also clear the backlog refilled vacancies. The reservation should be extended to Group A and Group B posts also.

The private sector neglect employment of the disabled. Measures must be initiated to effect progressive employment of the disabled in the private sector too, ensuing at least 5 percent of the workforce from the disabled population, and skill training suitable for self-employment particularly in rural sector, should be developed for the benefit of unemployment disabled youth.

In most of the public places buildings, ramps and sloes do not exist, hindering the mobility of the disabled, who have to use wheel chairs. Thus the concerned authorities should take steps to provide ramps and slopes in such places, to reduce their interiority. The family members of the disabled should also take to the architectural modifications to reduce the physical and psychological trauma.

REFERENCES

1. "Enforcement of Rights of the Disables", *Journal of Indian Law Institute, vol. 38, no.4.*
2. Falk, Richard A, (1982), *Human Rights and State Sovereignty* New York: Holmes and Meier.
3. GOVT. OF INDIA. National Plan of Action: International Year of the Disabled Persons 1992. Govt. of India.
4. International Conference on Human Resource Development in the Area of Disability Rehabilitation. 25th and 26th April 2005. Ministry of Social Justice & Empowerment Government of India and

Rehabilitation Council of India. Kanishka Publishers, Distributors. p. 249.

5. Karna, G.N. (2000), Disability Rights Movement: Conceptual Framework and its Implications for India, Disabilities *and Impairments, Vol. 14, NO.1*
6. Karna, G. and K. Gaharana, (1994), *Rights* of, *Disabled Persons*, In K.P., Saksena, ed. *Human Rights: Perspective and Challenges*, New Delhi.
7. Karna, G.N. (2001), *Disability Studiers in India: Retrospect and Prospect*,: Gyan Publishing House, New Delhi.
8. Lauterpacht, Hersch, (1973), *Human Rights and International Law*, Carland, New York.
9. Macfarlane, L.J., (1985), The Theory and Practice of Human Rights: Maurice Temple Smith, London.
10. Mani, V.S., "Human Rights and the United Nations: A Survey", *Journal of Indian Law Institute, vol.40, nos.1-4*, 1998, pp.38-66.
11. A.N. Sen, Human Rights, 1st Edn. 2002, Sri Sai Law Publication.
12. Duncan , Barbara Ed. (1982), Information Services on Technical Aids for people with Disabilities: An International Perspective. Rehabilitation International, New York.
13. Mani, D. Rama. The Physically Handicapped in India: Policy and Programme. Ashish Publishing House, New Delhi.
14. Mirchandani, Vasanti. 1995. Role of NGOs in Rehabilitating the Disabled. Health for the Millions. Vol: 21. No. 6. VHAI, New Delhi.
15. Pandey, R.S. Advani. 1995. Perspectives in Disable and Rehabilitation.Vikas Publishing House Pvt. Ltd, New Delhi.
16. Sayeed Akhtar(2005) Human Rights of the Mentally Ill India Indian Journal of Social Psychiatry 103-108
17. *The Essentials of Human Rights(2005)* , Smith, Rohna K.M & Christien van den Anker.
18. UN, (1993), *Human Rights and Disabled persons*, Geneva: World Campaign for Human Rights.
19. World Health Organization (2001) World Health Report.
20. www.gujhealth.gov.in/Medi_servi/mental_health_program.htm accessed on 30/09/07
21. www.who.ch/icf
22. www.disabilityindia.com/html/news.html

❒❒❒

6

The Role of Government in the Welfare of Elderly People in India - A Sociological Appraisal

P. SETHURAJAKUMAR AND I. SINGARAM

Today Indian elderly population is the second largest in the world. One out of every ten senior citizen of the word lives in India. The elderly population is one the rise and will soon be of considerable size of the total population. Senior citizens should therefore exert their rights for their due place in the society. The elderly population in India which was 7.7 crores, as per census 2001, is projected to be around 9.5 crore in 2011. The proportion of elderly in the total population has been increasing in all the countries. In India, it is projected to further go up to 17.3 crore in 2026.

On the one hand, the population of the aged 60 years plus population has increased over the successive decades, on the other hand, the traditional family system and community based support systems for the aged have not only weakened but showing signs of complete collapse. This has seriously affected the situation of the senior citizens in society. Neither they have the earlier position of importance in the family and community, nor are they looked after the way it was done earlier. This is because of the rapid modernization and industrialization the roles and status of old people are on the decrease level. In the past, the aged were accorded a place of honour and respect in society. Providing moral and material support to the older persons was regarded as the highest virtue. These traditional practices enabled the elderly to remain integrated in their family and community, and also provided them the privilege of being head of the household, clan, village, tribe, etc

TABLE 1

Number and Percentage of persons aged 60 years and above with life expectancy rate in India, 1961-2001

Census Year	No (in million)	Life Expectancy Rate
1961	24.712	41.5
1971	32.700	46.3
1981	44.348	53.4
1991	57.554	61.2
2001	76.622	62.9

Increase in expectation of life at birth due to fall in mortality rate, particularly in the earlier stages of the life cycle, has led to an increase in number of persons aged 60 years and above. Old age is characterized by diminished physical and psychic activity and a plethora of problems. The common health problems are blood pressure, pulmonary disorders, diabetes, orthopedic and cardiovascular problems, mental problems like depression, anxiety, etc. Some of the socio-psychological problems faced by aged persons are isolation, alienation, loneliness, powerlessness, dependence, feeling of boredom, lack of emotional response from family members etc.

Except few aged, who retire from organized sectors and get some retirement benefits, the plight of the aged in the unorganized sectors is worse, because they practically do not get anything to fall back. Mishra (1996) recommends that some comprehensive programmes should be formulated to strengthen family's capacity to look after its aged members and placing destitute and disable aged in the institution. The relatively faster increase in the elderly population will contribute to a higher dependency ratio of the population in the non-productive age group. The old age dependency ratio, which was 10.6 in 1961, is likely to increase to 12.6 in 2001. Therefore, responsibility for caring for the elderly will fall either on young wage earners or on the Government.

At present due to the physical weakness, surviving with various diseases, disintegration of family system, unearned capacity in old age and increase in life expectancy leads to the aged people is in the pathetic condition without non-care taker. In our country, the senior citizens were facing such types of problems in both rural and urban.

To eradicate the crisis of elderly, different programmes have been introduced by the government for the well-being of older people to become in the category of societal responses.

CONSTITUTIONAL PROVISIONS

Indian constitution has an article for the well-being of older persons under the Directive Principles of State Policy having particular relevance for old age social security.

According to this *Article 41*, 'The state shall within the limits of its economic capacity and development, make effective provision for securing the right to work, to education and to public assistance in case of unemployment, old age, sickness and disablement and in other cases of underserved want'.

The constitutional obligation is reinforced by the Section *125(I) (d)* of the code of criminal procedure of 1973 (Cr.P.C). This section of the Cr.P.C underlines the responsibility of children with sufficient means to support their parents having no means of assistance.

Even, the *Section 20(3)* of the Hindu Adoption and Maintenance Act, 1956, makes it obligatory on the part of the person to maintain his aged and infirm parents. Besides these, it is the right of older persons that they should be treated with dignity and equality without any discrimination.

SOME IMPORTANT PROGRAMMES FOR THE WELFARE OF THE ELDERLY

(1) Integrated Programme For Older Persons (Revised Scheme effective from 01.04.2008)

The main objective of the Scheme is to improve the quality of life of the Older Persons by providing basic amenities like shelter, food, medical care and entertainment opportunities and by encouraging productive and active ageing through providing support for capacity building of Government / Non-Governmental Organizations / Panchayat Raj Institutions / local bodies and the Community at large. Assistance under the scheme will be given to the Panchayat Raj

Institutions / local bodies and eligible Non-Governmental Voluntary Organizations for the following purposes:-

i. Programmes catering to the basic needs of Older Persons particularly food, shelter and health care to the destitute elderly;

ii. Programmes to build and strengthen intergenerational relationships particularly between children / youth and Older Persons;

iii. Programmes for encouraging Active and Productive Ageing;

iv. Programmes for proving Institutional as well as Non Institutional Care / Services to Older Persons;

v. Research, Advocacy and Awareness building programmes in the field of Ageing; and

vi. Any other programmes in the best interests of Older Persons.

Programmes Admissible for Assistance under the Scheme

i. Maintenance of Old Age homes to provide food, care and shelter for a minimum number of 25 destitute older persons.

ii. Maintenance of Respite Care Homes and Continuous Care Homes for a minimum of 25 Older Persons who live in old age homes but are seriously ill requiring continuous nursing care and respite.

iii. Running of Multi Service Centres for Older Persons to provide daycare, educational and entertainment opportunities, healthcare, companionship to a minimum number of 50 older persons.

iv. Maintenance of Mobile Medicare Units to provide medical care to the older persons living in rural and isolated and backward areas.

v. Running of Day Care Centres for Alzheimer's Disease / Dementia Patients to provide specialized day-care to the Alzheimer's disease patients.

vi. Physiotherapy clinics for older persons

vii. Disability and hearing aids for older persons

viii. Mental health care and Specialized care for the Older Persons to provide Mental Health Care Intervention Programmes to the elderly. This scheme is also open to organizations / hospitals, which are already into mental health care. The scheme would help such organizations to integrate the component for older persons, which is hitherto neglected.

ix. Help-lines and Counselling Centres for older persons

x. Sensitizing programmes for children particularly in Schools and Colleges

xi. Regional Resource and Training Centres

xii. Training of Caregivers to the older persons

xiii. Awareness Generation Programmes for Older Persons and Care Givers like Self-care, preventive health care, disease management, preparation for old age / healthy and productive ageing; intergenerational bonding.

xiv. Multi facility care centres for destitute older widow women to provide shelter, educational, occupational and entertainment opportunities, healthcare, companionship to the widowed older women Volunteers Bureaus for older persons

xv. Formation of Vridha Sanghas / Senior Citizen Associations.

xvi. Any other activity, which is considered suitable to meet the objective of the scheme.

(2) National Policy on Older Persons (NPOP)

Government of India announced the National Policy on Older Persons in 1999 to reaffirm its commitment to ensure the well-being of the older persons in a holistic manner. The NPOP while promising to safeguard their interest in terms of financial security, health, legal, social and psychological security, also envisages a productive partnership with them in the process of development by creating opportunities for their gainful engagement and employment. The Policy also appreciates special needs of older persons and therefore lays emphasis on empowerment of community as well as individuals to adequately meet the challenges of the process of ageing. To fulfill these objectives the NPOP broadly provides for the following:

- *Financial security* through coverage under Old Age Pension Scheme for poor and destitute older persons, better returns on earnings/savings of Government/Quasi
- *Health Security:* The NPOP recognizes special health needs of the older persons to be met through strengthening and reorienting the public health services at Primary Health Care level, creation of health facilities and implementing health insurance.
- *Recognizing Shelter as a basic human need,* the NPOP provides for earmarking 10% of the houses/housing sites in urban as well as rural areas for older persons belonging to the lower income groups.
- *Education/information needs of older persons* the NPOP provides for proactive role in ensuring the same by disseminating knowledge about preparation of Old Age. It is also emphasizes the need for schools to have programme on inter-generational bonding.
- *Welfare and Institutional Care:* Institutional Care has been provided for in the NPOP as the last resort. The State should also create infrastructure in partnership with voluntary organizations to provide for poor, destitute and neglected older persons whose care cannot be ensured within the family.
- *Protection of Life and Property of Older Persons*: Maintenance of elderly within family, resorting to the provisions of law whenever needed is required to be ensured.
- *Training of Human Resource to care for Older Persons:* The Policy lays emphasis on need for trained personnel/care givers.

(3) The Maintenance and Welfare of Parents and Senior Citizens Bill, 2007

The enactment of " The maintenance and welfare of parents and senior citizens Act, 2007" has been a major milestone to provide for maintenance, shelter, health and security of senior citizens in the country. This bill enables the senior citizens to obtain maintenance from their children to meet their basic requirements and lead a life with dignity. The most important provision of the Act is to make the maintenance of parents by their family a legal right. The object/ purpose of the Act is,

- To provide an effective mechanism for senior citizens to claim need based maintenance from their children including foster children, adopted children, step children, grandchildren and also from such relatives to whom they have provided financial support
- To make provisions for maintenance to be provided or steps to be taken by the government for the benefit of such senior citizens, who do not have children grandchildren or relatives from whom they can claim maintenance.
- Set up appropriate mechanism to provide need-based maintenance to the parents and senior citizens
- Providing better medical facilities to senior citizens
- Institutionalization of a mechanism for protection of life and property of older persons
- Setting up of old age homes in every district

Highlights of the Bill

- Senior citizens who are unable to maintain themselves shall have `he right to apply to a maintenance tribunal seeking a monthly allowance from their children or heirs.
- State governments may set up maintenance tribunals in every sub-division to decide the level of maintenance. Appellate tribunals may be established at the district level.
- State governments shall set the maximum monthly maintenance allowance. The Bill caps the maximum monthly allowance at Rs.10, 000 per month.
- Punishment for not paying the required monthly allowance shall be Rs.5, 000 or up to three months imprisonment or both.

Offences and Penalties

- On failure to comply with the maintenance fee, the tribunal may issue a warrant for collection within three months of the due date. Should the fee remain unpaid, the accused may be imprisoned for up to one month or until payment, whichever is earlier.

- Punishment for abandoning a senior citizen shall include an imprisonment of up to three months or fine of up to Rs.5, 000, or both.
- The tribunal can declare a transfer of property (as gift or otherwise) from a senior citizen to a transferee as void if the transfer was made under the condition of maintenance, and the transferee neglects the agreement. A registered voluntary organization may take action on behalf of the senior citizen if he or she is unable to enforce these rights.

(4) National Old-Age Pension Scheme (NOAPS)

Under National Old Age Pension Scheme, Central Assistance is available on fulfillment of the following criteria.

- The age of the applicant (male or female) should be 65 years or more.
- The applicant must be a destitute in the sense that he/she has no regular means of subsistence from his/her own source of income or through financial support from family members or other sources.
- The amount of old age pension is Rs. 200 per month from the Central Government. This scheme is implemented in the State and Union Territories through Panchayats and Municipalities. The State's contribution varies from State to State and is as under:

Appraisal about the programmes of elderly

- The National Policy for Older Persons approved in 1999 falls short in several respects and even its limited provisions have not been adequately implemented. There are no signs of a pension fund for ensuring security for unorganized sector workers. There are too few old age homes and day-care centers and legislation for ensuring compulsory geriatric care in public hospitals is still awaited.
- The quality of medical care in India varies considerably. Medical care is available in the major population centers that approaches and occasionally meets Western standards, but

adequate medical care is usually very limited or unavailable in rural areas.

- Though India having the second place for having high level of bed's in the hospitals, for thousand Indians we have the hospital bed level of 0.9. It shows we have to implement the basic infrastructural facilities in the hospital (HOSMAC, 2010).
- In India only 60 doctors are available for the population of one hundred thousand people. At present India has more 4.40 lakhs doctors, but due to the ever-increasing population, the number of doctors in India are quite below the global standards.
- It is a response in a nation where experts say at least 600,000 more doctors and a million nurses are needed to achieve the 1:1000 doctor-patient ratio recommended by the World Health Organization.

Under the Maintenance of Welfare of Parents and Senior Citizens Act, 2007 in Tamilnadu there are four persons arrested.

- Saminathan has become the first person in the State to be detained under the newly introduced Maintenance of Welfare of Parents and Senior Citizens Act, 2007 at April 22 in 2010. Victim Manickam (77) Namakkal district, pointed out that it was he, by dint of hard work, who had set up 15 power looms of which 10 had been given to his son after a family division of properties. His son had forcibly grabbed the remaining five looms, which helped provide Manickam a livelihood and had abandoned him. While throwing him out, Manickam alleged that there was an attempt to strangulate him with a towel.
- J. Muthukrishnan (83) of alleged that his eldest son Kumar was not taking care of him. While the old man was living with his two other sons, the accused had refused to contribute any money for basic maintenance. Police arrested Kumar, produced him in a city court and lodged him in the Puzhal Central Prison in Chennai at June 25th 2010.
- Kanniyappan (104) in Chennai, a meat seller resides with

his son Thangaraj and family. He lodged a complaint with Deputy Commissioner of Police stating that Thangaraj was neglecting him and not providing him money or food. Police registered cases against Thangaraj, including under Maintenance and Welfare of Parents and Senior Citizens Act, 2007 and arrested him.

- Recently a complaint has been made by Alocious (72) from Trichy, alleged his son who refused to provide the basic need of food to his father in the past 3 months. Eventually he made a complaint against his son to police and police made enquiry and arrested his son under the parent's maintenance bill act 2007 on October 18th 2010 in Trichy.
- This shows most of the victims belong urban surroundings, though they are more elderly suffering by their family members, the above persons only made complaint against their family. While elderly in the position of severe crisis, they are not ready to come forward to charge their own family members. Due to lack of awareness about the act of parent's maintenance bill, more number of elderly facing livelihood problems in the rural areas by their own children's.
- Compare with northern states versus southern states the literacy level, education attainment; standard of living and income is better in south states. But here, the level of utilization of parents maintenance act is very low level in Tamilnadu. It shows the application of 2007 act will be the minimum level in the northern states for the reason of lack of propaganda facilities non available in the government mechanism among the elderly people.
- Kapil U; Saxena N; Nayar D; Umesh Kapil (1996) have conducted a study was with the objective to evaluate national programme for prevention of nutritional blindness (NPPNB) and national nutritional anemia prophylaxis programme (NNAPP) in the states of Maharashtra, Tamilnadu, Orissa and Uttar Pradesh. The findings of the present study revealed that both of these national programmes were given a low priority at all levels in terms of procurement and distribution of drugs, implementation and monitoring

of the programme activities. The allocation of budget at the central level was found to be inadequate in comparison to the number of eligible beneficiaries to be covered. It shows lack of basic infrastructure facilities leads to a great failure of a particular programme. Like this in India, some programmes are in the level of existing, but there is no yield achieved by that programmes because of basic needs of that programmes are not fulfilled by authorities, such as personnel, building, finance, and non enactment of the scheme.

- National Old Age Pension Scheme (NOAPS) provides up to a maximum amount of Rs.400/- per month but only covers the BPL population. NOAPS does not reach the huge number of aged destitute and poor. Artificial capping of OAP allocations has meant that only a small proportion of the aged are reached every year. The money provided (up to Rs.400 per month, depending on the state) is by no means sufficient considering the cost of medical expenses. Consequently, pensioners remain either dependent on their children or must continue to work. The limit for old age pension is differ from state to state in India. In Tamilnadu 60 years eligible for receive the old age pension at the same time in Rajasthan the eligible age is 58 for males and 55 for females to receive the old age pension. In Andhra state govt provide Rs.75 per month at the same time Rajasthan provide the share of Rupees up to 300 per month for older persons for its share with the central govt share of Rs.200.
- In whole India, under old age pension scheme the age and pension amount should be the same age and the amount should be equal in all states.

CONCLUSION

As described above the Indian government has promoted several policies and programmes, some integrated, for care of the elderly. However, the policy makers have never deemed it fit to involve the elderly or even consult them in the process of formulation of the same. In the absence of information on the level of awareness among the potential beneficiaries and effective implementation of these programmes, it is difficult to say whether the programmes do address the true concerns of the elderly. Hence the government should consult with the representatives or experts in the field of aged before establish a programme to avoid the future negative result of the particular programmes which involves millions of life in our country.

REFERENCES

1. Nasreen, Asiya (2009) Urban Elderly – Coping strategies and Societal responses, New Delhi, Concept Publishing Company.
2. Bose, A.B. (2006) Social Security for the Old – Myth and Reality New Delhi, Concept Publishing Company.
3. Joshi K. Arvind (2005) Older Persons in India, New Delhi, Serials Publications.
4. HOSMAC (2010) Research Report.
5. UNDP Human development Reports 2002 and 2007.
6. http://www.oldagesolutions.org/Facilities/Noaps.aspx
7. Kapil U; Saxena N; Nayar D; Umesh Kapil (1996)Health Population: Perspectives & Issues.

❑❑❑

7

India in the Modern Era – A Socio-Psychological Perspective

T. YUVARAJ

India is a country with diversity everywhere; in terms of culture, language, caste, food, economy and many more. In spite of these many differences, India stands adorable, because of the united strength that it has from the citizens of India. Beyond all these diversities, Indians are surely bonded by the human values amongst them, much stronger than one can see elsewhere. Indians are brought up by the most essential human values through Indian traditions, for over thousand years.

At the same time, it is in India, and it is the reality in India, that, we find huge exploitation of human race in the form of crime and social evils, as in many other countries. There are worldwide reports to substantiate this. In India, women and children are always treated the weakest and so, they are abused often at home, workplace, school and even in public. There are many laws for children and women, protecting their rights, which are still to reach them. Crime against children in India has increased by 3.8% nationally. In 2005, 14,975 cases were registered, from 14,423 cases in 2004. According to a UNICEF report (2010), 12.6 million children are engaged in hazardous occupations in India. Child rape has increased by 13.7%. Around 1,400 children were reported murdered in 2005, from 1,304 in 2004. Nearly 45,000 children go missing every year in India; of them, more than 11,000 are never traced. 3,518 children were kidnapped in 2005.

Inter-state migration has been increasing in the last 10 years, mainly due to the growing up of India, especially, in terms of infrastructure development. People, mostly from states like Bihar and Jharkand, have been migrated for employment in building of IT industries and roadways development. While migrant do get employment, there is no safety net for their children; they get neither education nor healthcare (UNICEF report, 2010). Children, especially those of single migrant workers, are often not counted anywhere in the census or included in any government schemes.

India has the largest number of street children in the world (Khan, 2010). It is still not clearly known, as what do they do, where do they go, what will be their future? Most of such children fall in the hands of traffickers, who trade them for begging, prostitution, theft, or at the worst, for their organs. There are reports showing evidence, that such children are traded by such traffickers for army of the terrorists.

According to the 2008 report of National Crimes Record Bureau, nearly 2 Lakhs cases of crimes were registered, every year, against women in India. Of them, 7000 cases were registered in Tamilnadu. Andhra Pradesh ranks first state with highest crime records against women and Tamilnadu, the 24th. There were 32,000 murders of women in 2008, 22,000 kidnapping & abduction, 21,000 rapes, 8,000 deaths related to dowry, 12,000 women are sexually harassed and 39,000 being molested. Nearly 67 cases were registered for girl importation.

In India, as many as 18 women are assaulted in some form or the other every hour across the country. Nearly 200 women are killed every year in the country after being tagged as witches. In the past 15 years, more than 2,500 women were killed in such incidents. There are approximately 15 million prostitutes in India. 50% OF RAPES OCCUR IN GIRLS UNDER 18 YEARS. In almost 90% of them the rapist is known to the victim, making it a heavily underreported crime. According to the recent statistics of the Crime in India, 2008, 33 million girls are missing from India's population. Still, in many rural parts of the country, female infanticides are being practiced. Among illiterates, women are more in numbers. Girls and women were more likely to be poor, hungry, illiterate or sick than boys and men (Source: National Crime Records Bureau, Times of India, 2008).

Poverty in India is another devastating factor. 40% of children in India are malnourished and this is mainly due to the poor health status of the mothers. Recently, The Times of India (2010) reported that 7 of the Indian states, Bihar, Chattisgarh, West Bengal, Jharkand, Madhya Pradesh, Orissa and Rajasthan were declared to have more poor people than 26 poorest African countries, by the new method of Multidimensional Poverty Index. Thus, a relatively larger section of India is deprived of their essential needs, such as food, shelter, health care and education. Dropout rates in schools are increasing every year.

Being the second most populated country in the world, today, in India, almost 70% of the population are the youth, those in the ages of 15 to 34 years (youth portal, 2010). This means that within the next 15 years, India is going to be governed by these many Indians. Hence, the nation is focusing more on this particular segment of India, towards their empowerment and their welfare.

However, looking at the real scenario, in India, those under 25 years account for the 50% of HIV infections. Every 14 seconds, a youth is infected with HIV. Nearly 3 per 1000 pregnant women in India are HIV positive and around 100,000 HIV positive Indian women become pregnant every year. Changing lifestyle, insufficient education and threatening socio economic conditions seem to deteriorate the foundation of our nation from emerging into a developed country or super power.

Nearly 30% of girls in India, have their first child before 19 years. Pregnancy before 18 years, the teenage, carries many health risks among women. And teenagers are more likely to die in pregnancy period or during child birth. Every year, 14% of abortions are done for adolescents. Statistics even prove that rising the mother's age, most importantly, the age of a woman at marriage from 18 years to 23 years will reduce the country's population momentum by as much as 40%.

In India, today, and so in many other countries, the leading causes of death in a year are due to chronic illnesses, such as cancer, stroke, AIDS and cardiac diseases. Other leading causes, such as suicides and accidents, are preventable.

Statistics show that 3 out of 10 students live in homes where others smoke in their presence and almost 50% of students in India are exposed to smoke in public places. Today, there is a law prohibiting smoking in public places. But, to what extent this law has protected children and non - smokers is questionable.

Every year, over 6 Lakh men in the age group of 25 to 69 years die due to the ill effects of smoking. This indicates an alarming rate of mortality. Reports show that the expenses spent towards health care for smokers is much higher than what was gained as income from tobacco products for the country (WHO, 2010).

Today, the average age in which a person may suffer a heart attack has come down from 40 years to 30 years and this is mainly a result of today's changing lifestyle. Death due to chronic illness is increasing every year due to the increasing demands of every family and that has lead to continuous working without rest pause and also a shift in human personality where people do not attain satisfaction. Distress becomes a major indirect factor.

There are much more to list in the form of statistics. These are not for threatening the readers of this article, but to realise the fact that it is the right time for every Indian citizens to be responsible and bring about a healthy society. When I mean healthy, it means a holistic development in terms of physical, cultural, psychosocial, economic and spiritual uplift (David et al, 2000).

Every discipline of knowledge, today, has to work on achieving this goal of bringing about a positive change in the world. Being a psychologist, I list here, the 5 steps for fostering this positive change in the social psychological perspective.

1. Practice Good Lifestyle: Lifestyle refers to the way of life a person or group follows; someone's way of living. The things that a person or particular group of people usually do (Cambridge Advanced Learner's Dictionary). A lifestyle is a characteristic bundle of behaviors that makes sense to both others and oneself in a given time and place. It includes social relations, consumption, entertainment, and dress. The behaviors and practices within lifestyles are a mixture of habits, conventional ways of doing things, and reasoned actions. Lifestyle typically also reflects an individual's attitudes, values or worldview and hence, in many ways our lifestyle determines our joy as well as our sorrows. By simply following a proper lifestyle, one can be free from diseases, live long and healthy and most importantly, in continuance of a healthy generation.

A good lifestyle means having a positive attitude, and practicing positive health behaviours – behaviours undertaken by people to enhance or maintain their health. These include: Sleeping 7 to 8 hours a night, Not smoking, Eating breakfast each day, to be free from alcohol, Regular Exercises, Not eating between meals, Being no more than 10% overweight, Clean drinking water and Eating Fresh Vegetables and Fruits every day.

What affects this lifestyle are stress, socio economic conditions, social pressures and occupational hazards. One should be aware of these factors and try to live a life that is free from any of these or such factors so as to lead a happy life.

2. Counselling for effective living: Gone are those days, where there were slogans of NO VACANCY everywhere. But today, with the emergence of IT era, many MNCs have entered India, paving the way for enormous job opportunities. Indian companies too have started competing with these MNCs, which has led to industrial growth and diversification and thereby, a need for human resources at large. People throng towards IT and ITES sectors for the huge monetary benefits, sophistications and pride that they gain. This is clearly evidenced from the significant rise in rich men in India within the past decade (NDTV, 2010).

At the same time, the negative side of this growth must also be considered. Attrition rate today in IT sectors is painstaking on one side. On the other, more and more of patients admitted in cardiac centres, kidney care hospitals, for back bone ailments and even worse, in psychiatric wards. Rate of impotence is also increasing these days (Indian health statistics, 2010). There seems to be major imbalance in human placements. People take up careers that do not suit their personality as such. They simply take up jobs for its monetary gains. Thus, they fail to identify their real potentials.

It is high time that every school needs a counsellor who must counsel every child at their primary level; identify their inner potentials and create an environment at schools where they can realise their abilities and fulfil their developmental tasks with complete freedom to live as they are. Children have to be given proper career counselling and guidance.

With the rapid changes happening everywhere, the importance of joint family is perishing gradually. Today, people work at places far away from home. As a result of these, family bonding is becoming weaker day by day. People today, find it difficult in making decisions at various phases of their life; in choosing a right career, choosing the right partner for life, deciding to have a child, and many more. One thing that was misunderstood is that conflicts occur at every point of life and it is important that we must consult someone who can give the right help. At least, we need someone to share, failing which, frustrations occur, leading to a disturbed life. Today, professional counsellors are available nearby us, to whom we can consult for our conflicts. There is no point in still believing the myth that counsellors are basically professionals who treat the mentally ill. The myth has perished years before.

3. Life skills education for children and adolescents: *Life skills education is a unified and developmental approach to help children and adolescents learn how to deal with difficulties of daily life, growing up and risk situations* (WHO, 2001). It was believed that life skills greatly help children handle their problems of life effectively and in health promotion among them as well. Life skills help in development of a healthy personality, respect for human rights and to be a responsible citizen of the society.

The World Health Organisation (WHO) categorizes life skills into the following three components (Module 7: Life Skills, 2001):

(a) **Critical thinking skills/Decision-making skills** - include decision making/problem solving skills and information gathering skills. These skills help children at evaluating the future consequences of their present actions and the actions of others. They will be able to determine alternative solutions and to analyze the influence of their own values and the values of those around them.

(b) **Interpersonal/Communication skills** - include verbal and non-verbal communication, active listening, and ability to express feelings and give feedback, negotiation/refusal skills and assertiveness skills. These skills influence ones' ability to manage conflict, ability to empathize with others, be able to work together as Teams and the ability to respect and cooperate with those around us. Development of this skill set enables the adolescent to be accepted in society. These skills result in the acceptance of social norms that provide the foundation for adult social behaviour.

(c) **Coping and self-management skills** refer to skills to increase the internal locus of control, so that the individual believes that they can make a difference in the world and affect change. These include self esteem, self-awareness, self-evaluation skills and the ability to set goals. These skills help the individual learn to enhance positive thinking about oneself and about his/her surrounding and also to cope with loss or trauma.

4. Education: History has been created in the field of Education. Thanks to the present government, for making education, a fundamental right (The Gazette of India, 2009). To educate means to enlighten someone's way of life. By offering the right education to children, we actually provide them their rights, protecting them from all the social evils. An educated child understands what is right and what is not. Education is the best means by which we can provide a child the best care and also make them self sufficient.

5. Values for life: I remember even now, those value based stories taught to me in my school days; those that still inspire me in my life and those that I would never want to give up in my life. But this was up till a point; thereafter, when I went to higher grades in school, these moral education classes turned to be special classes for unfinished portions and at times, we were even made to simply sit in the class, without disturbing other classes. But, it was misfortune for those children wherein, these moral education classes were totally removed away from the curriculum or in some cases, children were made to sleep during these classes. Then, later on, in my profession, when I happen to work with juvenile delinquents, did I realise, how important it is, to teach values for children. Values mould a child into a disciplined adult, who respects self and others' independence, never tries to cause destruction of it and is able to understand and accept the consequences of every action. Values motivate an individual to love every creature in the world and for being born as a human being.

Human values are many, and to follow them is a hard task in today's world. But it's the same world, where, it is most essential to follow these values. Mahatma Gandhi framed out 5 basic and most essential values for human life, which I believe is enough for an effective living. They are:

- Being Truthful
- Right Conduct
- Lover of peace
- Unconditional love amongst everyone
- Non- violence

All of these values stated above, are self explanatory. Gandhi, once had an argument with his grandson, Arun, a few weeks before he was assassinated. He replied to his grandson, the seven blunders out of which, grows violence. They are:

- *Wealth without work*
- *Pleasure without Conscience*
- *Knowledge without character*
- *Science without Humanity*
- *Worship without Sacrifice*
- *Politics without principles*

(Source: Nature, 2005)

This article is presented as a short illustration for an effective living from a social psychological perspective. Statistics shown in this article indicate more on crime and negative health practices followed in India. There are also positive signs of developing India, in terms of an increase in literacy rates, improved recognition for Women rights, decrease in child labour, emergence of so many entrepreneurs, especially women entrepreneurs and much more. It was the theme, Issues and Challenges for India, under which this article has been presented, that made the author to present some of the debilitating facts about India. The steps included here, are only stated as the most essential elements for effective living. There are much more to describe, taking up from other fields of knowledge. The ultimate goal is to bring about a developed India by 2020, where there must be controlled crime rates and tremendous potentials identified and enriched.

REFERENCES

1. Child Protection, UNICEF Report.
2. Crime In India – 2008 Statistics. National Crime Records Bureau, New Delhi.
3. Forbes Rich List: India's Wealthiest People. NDTV Correspondent & Agencies, March 11, 2010.
4. Khan, I. (2010). Child Trafficking In India: A Concern. New Delhi.
5. Regional Framework For Introducing Lifeskills Education To Promote The Health Of Adolescents. World Health Organisation, New Delhi, April 2001.
6. The Gazette Of India. The Right Of Children To Free And Compulsory Education Act, 2009. Ministry Of Law And Justice.
7. The Seven Blunders. Nature, 2005.
8. 8 Indian States Have More Poor Than 26 Poorest African Nations. The Times of India, July 12, 2010.
9. Indian Health Statistics. http://www.Indiahealthstat.Com/Default.Aspx, 2010.
10. Indian Youth on the Peak of a New Era. http://www.Youthportal.Gov.In, 2010.
11. Tobacco. http://www.who.int/topics/tobacco/en, 2010.
12. http://www.unicef.org/india/child_protection.html, August 17, 2010.

❏❏❏

PART-II
SOCIAL EVILS AND ITS COLLISIONS

8

Child Sexual Abuse : Issues and Challenges

M.D. Allen Selvakumar

INTRODUCTION

Child sexual abuse has been defined as "the involvement of dependent, developmentally immature children in sexual activities they do not fully comprehend, to which they are unable to give informed consent" (Henry Kempe 1984). Sexual abuse includes any contacts or interactions between a child (under the age of 18 both boys and girls) and an adult (who is significantly older than the victim and is in a position of power or control over the child, or may even be an acquaintance or an unknown person) in which the child is being used for the sexual stimulation of the perpetrator or another person. The activities involved in child sexual abuse include, besides actual sex action, inappropriate touching, exposures to indecency, and forcing to participate in sexually stimulating acts.

INDICATORS OF SEXUAL ABUSE

Sexual abuse is not often identified through physical indicators alone. Frequently, a child confides in a trusted person (mother, friend, neighbour, kin...) that she or he has been sexually assaulted or molested by a family member or the employer or the caretaker or a family acquaintance. There are however, some physical signs of 'sexual' abuse. These are: difficultly in walking or sitting, torn, stained or bloody underclothes, complaints of pain or itching, bruises or bleeding, venereal disease, and pregnancy (in early adolescence) (Sloan Irving:1983;6).

There are some behavioral indicators too of sexual abuse. The sexually abused may appear withdrawn or retarded, may have poor peer relationships, may be unwilling to participate in activities, may indulge in delinquent behavior, may run away, or may display bizarre or unusual sexual knowledge.

CHARACTERISTICS OF SEXUAL ABUSE

The characteristics which child sex offenders often share in common are: isolation or alienation from others, dysfunctional interpersonal relationships, poor self-concept, and lack of impulse control. Most adults, who commit sexual offences against children, suffer from a personality disorder but are not considered mentally ill or psychotic.

First there is also a lack of knowledge in our society of the true prevalence of the phenomenon of child sexual abuse and the characteristics of the persons involved. This has remained an under-researched problem. Sexual molestation of children, both outside the family and in the family, does not readily lend itself to study by standard survey techniques.

Second we were handicapped by the extreme difficulty of separating out the antecedent conditions, correlates and effects of sexual abuse. This problem was because of the secret, shameful nature of the act and the fact that it goes undisclosed for long periods, and the strength and complexity of the emotion that accompany it.

Third interviewing perpetrators of abuse were not possible in all reported cases. Though we did interview a few attackers, such respondents are known to bias their response in the direction of social desirability or sensitive topics and child sexual abuse is surely a very sensitive issue.

Finally, we were not trained in analyzing personality characteristics of individuals. We only assumed the role of personality maladjustment and concentrated on environments in family and work-place in sexual abuse.

Socio-ecological Factors

The number of intra-family sexual abuse cases may not be very large in the total number of child sexual abuse cases but the family environment and the work situation of the job are definitely related to the occurrence of child molestation because they either reduce normative constraints or increase the opportunities for illicit sexual contact. Surprisingly congestion in the family was not found related to sexual abuse. Chronic conflict between parents and weakening of inhibitions leading to neglecting the children, absence of affectionate parent-child relationship within the family unit that failed to give support and protection to the child, alcoholism of earning male member and lack of adequate control on the children and the alcoholic parents feeling that he is not accountable to anybody in the role of parent/ protector, illicit relations of mother with some man and paramours hold on his mistress, dominance of step-father, and social networks or community activities.

A word about relationship between alcoholism and child sexual abuse, Lewis Herman (1981:40) describes alcohol abuse in the sexually abusive family as a "common but not a distinguishing factor".

Family Isolation

A little clarification about isolation too, isolation contributes to sexual abuse in many ways. The isolation may be social or physical. The loneliness of the victim in the house with her male employer when his wife and children away, or with the employer when other employees have gone to their homes, or with the teacher when there are no other students present, make her more susceptible to the overtures of the perpetrator. Thus, isolated within the house or within the work-place predicts danger. Justice and Justice (1976) have also referred to this type of isolation in child sexual abuse in the family.

Social Isolation: social isolation in which the family withdraws from the world around. This isolation limits the degrees of scrutiny the family is subjected to and exempts parents from evaluation by kins, neighbor's caste members and friends. Social isolation in which the parent lives with a sole child (daughter or daughter-in- law) and the loneliness and the exaggerated importance of the elderly male member or the dominant paternal figure ruling with an iron hand in the family build together. Isolated from each other by fear, but dependent upon the relationships in the family as the sole source of human contact these adults males may turn to the female children to reduce their sense of personal isolation. Increase in intra-familial intensity offers the opportunity to the male member for lapse in judgment. Henderson (1972:299-313) too has referred to this type of social isolation in incest analysis.

Individual Predispositions

It is difficult to diagnose psychological disorders in child sex abusers, but it is true that the maladaptive personality characteristics o both individual adults as perpetrators and children as victims do contribute to sexual abuse. For example, we found in our study sexual per activity (as revealed by family members), social inadequacy and immaturity to be at the heart of the problem. Seven abusers were found sexually hyperactive or pedophilic (the tendency to engage in multiple sexual aberrations) has also confirmed the strong possibility of this type of maladaptive personality type in sexual abuse. Five abusers came from "socially deprived" backgrounds, that is, they felt deprived of affection, attention, and intimacy. Four were emotionally dependent. Bauman also has described the presence of dependence problems in sexual offenders. The offenders were dependent upon his wife as though se were his mother. The response of his male is passive behaviour and occasional sexual dominance, over the weaker members-the children. Control and anger play a crucial role in this child molester's behaviour. In seeking out a child, he discovers an individual he can control. This also demonstrates to his wife that he does not need her.

Three respondents in our study were immature and suffered from feelings of inadequacy and helplessness. They lacked influence within the family and feel incapable of providing protection to their family members. Groth (1982:136) has also identified recurrent feelings of adequacy, immaturity, helplessness and isolation in adult sexuality. One widower and one deserted employer felt sexually estranged. Two were prone to alcohol abuse. Ferraculti too, has described the sex offenders as being prone to alcohol abuse. The individual predispositions of the perpetrators of child sexual abuse may be described as: sexual hyperactivity (pedophilia), social inadequacy, emotional dependence, immaturity, sexual estrangement and proneness to alcohol abuse.

Consequences of Sexual Abuse

The victims interviewed for this study indicated that they felt embarrassed, disgusting, unhappy, depressed, tormented, guilty and sometimes suicidal. What is that some male victims in our study themselves became the abusers of sex.

The re-victimization in the male victims is directed towards other children-both males and females. But this also does not mean that all males so victimized will become child molesters; only that it may increase the risk. Yet this is a bilateral risk, for the male once-victim-now-perpetrator not only victimizes a child but continues his own victimization in this way.

Finkelhor has maintained tat the subsequent assaults of the molesters are to be seen as a result of the male victim's efforts to control the pain and anger by moving against another. This stands in contrast to the female's internalization of pain and acceptance of responsibility for the victimization. The 16 female victims of sex abuse in our study became aggressive and hostile. However, it appeared that sexual assault had diminished self-esteem in all cases of female victims. Kilpatrick and Amick (1984:2), Stone, Tyler and Mead (1984: 75-82), and Tsai and Wagner (1984) have also referred to similar experience in sex victim.

James and Nesjleti have pointed out how a victim of sexual abuse develops a negative feeling against herself or himself. Two female respondents in our study said that they felt to be less worthy than other girls. Three respondents had even developed self-hatred for themselves. But nobody had attempted to commit suicide because of the feeling of self-blame or self-hatred.

STRATEGIES AND SOCIAL RESPONSES TO CHILD SEXUAL ABUSE

Although child abuse, or at least public attention to it, is considered by some to be a relatively new phew phenomenon, that is not the case. Historical review of the circumstances under which parents have lost their children or their autonomy over them indicates that since colonial times, such circumstances always have occurred and some form of community sanctions employed. Present day arrangements for dealing with child mistreatment-both legal and social services responses-have roots in the nineteenth century. Impingement on parents' rights has called for legal responses, while removal of children from mistreating parents has called for social service responses to substitute for the parents care.

The legal apparatus empowering states and localities to remove children from their parents' custody first arose in situations where the children's own behavior brought them into conflict with the community. Children, formally accused of no crime, could be removed to the reformatory and their parents held legally responsible. The doctrine of parent's practice- the state is the ultimate parents of children-means that was the State's rights supersede those of individual parents; this doctrine was invoked as the legal base on which such intrusion into family life could be justified. In time these statutes were amended to include parental failure that did not necessarily manifest itself in children's delinquent behavior.

At first the preoccupation was with the moral failures of parents and with physical abuse. Physical neglect of children was gradually incorporated into the law toward the end of the nineteenth century, while only in recent decades has their emotional mistreatment been considered. Children adjudicated under these laws could be sent to orphanages or to foster homes, rather than to reformatories. At the turn of the century, juvenile court was established in countries across the nation as the legal institution for handling child abuse and neglect as well as juvenile delinquency. Previously, children's cases were handled either in criminal or probate courts. It should be noted that throughout this time a parallel legal system, the poor laws, which regulated the dispersal of public relief parents as a means of and as a condition of grading relief from economic destitution. The philosophy underlying this practice changed early in the twentieth century, but it was not until the initiation of federal involvement in poor relief, through the AFDC program, that the actual practice has slowly eroded. Although less directly, poverty continues to be a major cause of family dissolution.

Along with the evolution of legal response to the problems of child mistreatment, the social service response has developed gradually. Child Welfare, as it relates to abuse and neglect, has generally consisted of two parallel and often poorly integrated systems, one concerned with child protection and the other with the provision of substitute care. Until very recently, the functions of practice in child protection were to investigate and validate complaints of child mistreatment and when so validated to see that the situations were adjudicated and, if necessary, the children protected through removal from their parents.

A return of those children to their parents was not considered an integral function of child protection. Rather, once children passed into the substitute parental care system, management of their lives, including return to their parents, was delegated to the foster care system. Although the provision of social services to forestall or eliminate the nee for removal of children has for many decades been an ideology of child protection, the actual provision of such services has been ambiguous and haphazard.

Rehabilitation measures for Exploited and Abused Children

- The most distressing consequences of child abuse included physical problems, developmental problems and profound psychological and emotional disturbances. Physical problems such as bruises, bite marks, backaches, unwanted pregnancies and liaisons, infections in the vagina or anal sections of the body were common. Illegal abortions were another common problem, particularly abortions performed by unqualified health practitioners, resulting in vaginal bleeding and even infertility. Various skin infections such as scabies were also found. Most victims had frequent fits of cough, cold, fever, headache and nasal tract infections. Some had tuberculosis, while others complained of intestinal problems, worms and lice. There were also signs of stress and physical trauma caused by sexual abuse.
- Many victims suffered from Sexually Transmitted Diseases (STDs) such as syphilis, gornorrhoea and HIV. Some also suffered from uterine prolapses, and while pus and white discharge was observed in girls, boys had infected and passages and penis.
- Children suffered from problems of psychological distraction, often reflected in falling grades, string into space and difficulties in communication. They also exhibited other behavioural problems such as temper tantrums, aggression, anxiety, guilt feelings, and depression.

Health and Social Services

- The provision of health and social services to the victims of sexual abuse and exploitation were very limited in all the countries in the sub-region. Though all the countries hade health services, these did not cater to the psychological needs of the victims of sexual abuse and exploitation. Their focus was more on dealing with the immediate physical needs of the patients and prevents the spread of sexually transmitted diseases (STDs) such as HIV and AIDS. Other State institutions in the sub-regions that catered to children focused on remanding them to custody on the orders of a court and provide them with formal or informal education. Few of these institutions addressed the psychological needs of these children that would help them recover from their trauma and reintegrate them into society.

- NGOs and private practioners were the only organizations that provided recovery and reintegration services to victims of child sexual abuse and exploitation. But even in these agencies, the quality of services provided varied greatly from one organization to the next.
- The main issue involved in providing medical services to victims was that the victims were not in a position to avail of expensive medical assistance. Consequently, many victims ended up seeking the help of unqualified practitioners, which only aggravated their problems.
- Victims tend not to seek medial assistance until the symptoms of their problem were acute. This was linked to their fears that their abuse or exploitation would be known to others and also because of their fear of the law.
- In Sri Lanka, There are only a few institutions in the NGO sector that provided institutional/residential rehabilitative care for victims of sexual exploitation. But these, too, do not have sufficiently qualified counselors and infrastructure.

In Nepal, the majority of NGOs and reintegration centers observed had their own health clinic that preceded general services to children through health assistants and nurses. They also provided recreation facilities like indoor games, music, dance, etc. In India, the services available were more of a curative nature, which succeeded in meeting there needs of medical care, counseling, education, vocational guidance, etc. Some of the organizations doing commendable work depended largely for their quality of work on the presence and skills of key workers. It is therefore, difficult to sustain this quality of services in the event of the workers leaving the organizations. In Pakistan, there were few organizations that provide services for recovery and reintegration to victims of sexual abuse and exploitation. There was great need to build the capacity of agencies to respond to the growing needs of the victims. The Bangladesh report highlighted the lack of knowledge about sexual abuse, particularly of public services providers. There was need for training and building of human resources to help address the issue.

SUGGESTIONS

- Existing national policies and programmes should be thoroughly reviewed and a comprehensive plan and policy formulated and implemented to needs of child victims of sexual abuse and sexual exploitation and their families, based on a vision founded on children's rights and social justice.
- The government and the political parties of each country should be committed to follow the new policies for them to be successful.
- More resources should be allocated to prevent further child sexual abuse and exploitation and help in recovery and reintegration of victims.
- Reintegration strategies should be developed that involve the national network of hospitals and various health centers in addition to NGOs.
- All services and interventions should adopt participatory strategies and respond to the child, the family and the community.
- Facilities for formal and effective counseling should be set up for helping victims.
- Training programs targeting medical staff, law enforcement officials, lawyers, judges and others involved in providing services to victims of sexual abuse or exploitation should be organized.
- National awareness raising campaigns about the issue of child commercial sexual exploitation should be developed and launched I collaboration with key members of civil

society. Such campaigns should aim at removing taboos that prevent people from talking about these issues. Campaigns should work towards their eventual reintegration in society and raise awareness about HIV and AIDS.

- Compulsory education for all children, including girls, should be enforced everywhere. The curriculum should include children's basic rights and reproductive health education to develop a healthy attitude towards sex, sex-related issues (such as safe sex) and diseases such as HIV. Such programmes should also target parents, teachers, and social workers.
- Tourism marketing and promotion policies of national tourist boards should be reviewed and re-aligned in order to encourage responsible tourism and discourage child sexual exploitation.
- Income generation schemes should target the high risk sections of society to reduce the poverty levels and avoid the commercial sexual exploitation as a means of survival. Skill training should form an important part of the income-generating process.
- More research should be undertaken to understand the phenomena of sexual abuse and exploitation of children and provide effective remedies.
- Laws dealing with sexual abuse and sexual exploitation should be strengthened and strictly enforced by law enforcers.
- Extra-territorial legislation should be enacted that would allow or the prosecution of nationals who violate the rights of children abroad.
- Rescue operations aimed at removing children in prostitution should seek coordination of all relevant agencies; ensure that rescued children are taken care of by an appropriate infrastructure and agency.
- Networking and coordination between services providers as well as relevant Government and Law Enforcement Agencies should be made operational and for an integral part of any action plan.

- Programmes implemented should be monitored to determine their effectiveness and modified as required.
- Income generation schemes should be coordinated with poverty alleviation programmes and micro credit schemes of the government. These should target victims and the perspective victim's family at the grass roots level.

REFERENCES

1. Sexually Exploited and Abused Children: A Qualitative Assessment and their health Needs and services Available to them in the South Asian Sub region –United Nations Economic and Social Commission for Asia and The Pacific.
2. Kumar, A., *Social problems*. New Delhi: Anmol Publications Pvt.Ltd, 2002.
3. Qadri, S.M.A, *Criminology*. Lucknow: Eastern Book Company, 2005.

❑❑❑

9

Human Trafficking in India (Sources, Destination and Transit) – A Contemporary Overview

SYED UMARHATHAB

INTRODUCTION

Human trafficking is growing regional, national, and global problems. This complex, webbed system of global crime violate fundamental human rights (Kofi Annan, 2007); threaten the security and welfare of national and international civil societies; and undermine the authority and capacity of national governments to protect their populations. This illicit activity damage and destroy millions of lives. Most vulnerable victims are women and children. Trafficking is more widespread than most people realize or recognized. Efforts to eradicate this blight appear to be losing ground to criminal elements. Statistics show that current trafficking efforts have increased steadily over the last 15 years, but the incidence of trafficked persons has also continued to increase, so that the traffickers have prevented counter-trafficking workers from bringing a decrease in human trafficking related statistics. Hence, author argues the continued increase results from the non-comprehensive strategy that has been employed by the international community have failed to reduce the quantum of human trafficked especially the in-country. The following are some statistics, which portrays the results which has not changed significantly in the last 8 years, even in United States.

600,000- 800,000 people are bought and sold across international borders each year; 50% are children, most are female. The majority of these victims are forced into the commercial sex trade (U.S. Department of State, 2007, p 10)

An estimated 14,500 to 17,500 foreign nationals are trafficked into the United States each year. The number of U.S. citizens trafficked within the country is even higher, with an estimated 200,000 American children at risk for trafficking into the sex industry (U.S Department of Justice, 2006, p 35).

In case of India, the regional or internal trafficking is immeasurable as there is no research statistics available, compliant and actions taken against these crimes are very minimal. Although, India is considered a vulnerable country for this offence in particular, it has done a lot for curtailing the offence. Human Trafficking is one form of organized crimes and also called modern-day slavery is considered the third largest criminal industry in the world and it is the fastest growing.

DEFINITION-HUMAN TRAFFICKING

According to the protocol to prevent, suppress and punish trafficking in persons, especially women and children, which is supplemented by the United Nations convention against transnational organized crime, trafficking in persons is defined as follows (UNGIFT, 2007, p 7), "Trafficking in persons" *shall mean the recruitment, transportation, transfer, harboring or receipt of persons, by means of the threat or use of force or other forms of coercion, of abduction, of fraud, of deception, of the abuse of power or of a position of vulnerability or of the giving or receiving of payments or benefits to achieve the consent of a person having control over another person, for the purpose of exploitation. Exploitation shall include, at a minimum, the exploitation of the prostitution of others or other forms of sexual exploitation, forced labor or services, slavery or practices similar to slavery, servitude or the removal of organs.*

Who are Victims of Human Trafficking?

According to the U.S. State Dept Trafficking in Persons Report (2009) victims in India are about 300,000 their entry and exit in to the Indian Territory is made easy through land border. Victims are mostly from SAARC Countries. One quarter of the victims trafficked in to India are children; victims are probably about equally women and men. Within the India, both citizens and non-citizens fall prey to traffickers. According to the United Nations office of drugs and control following is the situation in SAARC Countries, India is high in origin and destination as well medium in transit countries (Trafficking in persons, 2006, p 18)

Origin countries:

High — Bangladesh, **India**, Nepal, Pakistan
Medium — SriLanka
Low — Bhutan, Maldives

Transit countries:

High — Maldives
Medium — **India**, SriLanka
Very Low — Nepal, Pakistan, Bangladesh

Destination countries:

High — **India**, Pakistan
Medium — SriLanka
Low — Bangladesh
Very Low — Bhutan, Maldives

How are Victims Trafficked?

Basically, when we take any case were a human is trafficked they are likely to have experienced one of the following force, fraud and coercion are methods used by traffickers to press victims into lives of servitude or abused.

Force: Rape, kidnapping and abduction, beatings and confinement.

Fraud: Includes false and deceptive offers/ promise of employment, marriage and better life.

Coercion: Threats of serious harm to, or physical restraint of, any person; any scheme, plan or pattern intended to cause victims to believe that failure to perform an act would result in restraint against them; or the abuse or threatened abuse of the legal process.

Human Trafficking as a Criminal Process

- The process of human trafficking begins with the abduction or recruitment of a person (***Origin***).

- It continues with the transportation from the place of origin to the place of destination. In case of transnational trafficking in persons, the process includes the entry of the individual into another country (***Transit***).
- This is followed by the exploitation phase during which the victim is forced into sexual or labor servitude. This often includes violence against the victims (***Destination***).
- The criminal (***organization***) may find it necessary to profit launder the criminal proceeds. There may be further links to other criminal offences such as the smuggling of migrants, weapons or drugs (***Market of Exploitation***).

India is world largest democracy, second most populous country and fourth largest economy of the world. Indian's after independence believed in "Unity in Diversity", there is no country as India, with poly-cultured people, polyglot, and more than anything multi-ethnic and multi-caste people living in parts of India. With this background it is very odd to understand the victimization or identify the victims of human trafficking. Hence, through readings and personal experience author recommends the following clues for identifying the victims.

Identifying Crime of Human Trafficking

Non-verbal crime scene clues to link to human trafficking: Check if any individual have the one in each or more clues in one of the following heads.

Section I: Living conditions of the potential victims

- Symptoms of physical abuse and silence
- Bad working conditions and no sense of complaining the issues
- Restriction of movement as an indicators
- Behavior indicators of severe dependency
- Possession of other's documents or no legal documents/ work permit/ living permit
- Insistence on providing information to local or police officer
- Possession of false or fraudulent documentation

Section II: Evidence of control and lack of ability to move freely or leave job

- Bruises or other signs of physical abuse
- Sense of insecurity
- Intense fear or depression
- Untold fear of others
- Strange look at the people around the neighborhoods
- Not able to speak local language
- Unable to interact with locales and cope up with culture

Section III: Recent arrival from neighboring and other countries/ region

- Local law enforcers most likely first to come upon crimes of human trafficking
- Check seasonal arrivals and genuinely of the travelers
- Check the money carried with them
- Check each arrived for document and illegal or duplicated items/documents

Immediate concerns for law enforcement

- Insist on the no extension of the visit permit during the immigrations clearance
- Exact the visit of odd members to place and shadow them until the return
- Identify when crimes of trafficking taking place and seriously change them
- Identify and distinguish between victims and perpetrators
- Taking steps to stop/control crime of trafficking
- Manage victims of trafficking as witnesses
- Secure evidence of trafficking for prosecution(s) and trial(s)

Victims of Human Trafficking and their Potential Field of Employment

Traffickers have targeted specific people or groups who are vulnerable to such manipulation such as women and children, stateless individual or group (s), and individual or group(s) in under developing/ developing nations. Human trafficking or the illicit transnational movement of people through organized criminal networks may take several forms. These include a) the trafficking of migrants in search for work, b) the trafficking of asylum seekers in search for a safe refuge, c) the trafficking of women and children for the purpose of prostitution, d) the trafficking of human materials for medical purposes.

Sex trafficking:

Commercial sex act induced by force, fraud or coercion, or in which most of the person performing the act is under 18 years. Victims are mostly women and children can be found working in brothels, massage parlors, strip clubs and escort services.

Labor trafficking:

Traffickers employ a person for labor, services or involuntary servitude, such as peonage, debt bondage or slavery. Victims can be found in domestic situations as nannies or maids, brick making, mining industries, agricultural field, sweatshop factories, janitorial jobs, laborers in construction sites, farm work, restaurants, fire works, pan handling, beggars and camel jockey. Crime of trafficking occurs with the exploitation of the victim. The physical movement of the victim is not a requisite. Traffickers employ men, women, or a child for domestic help in households as servitude, or as slave. Victims can be found in domestic situations as nannies or maids, servant, gardeners, cleaners, gatekeepers, and helpers in domestic situation.

Asylum seeker:

They can be found in the refuge camp after arrival from the homeland, doing illegal jobs outside, then and there, most of the time they are from refuge or asylum camp.

By employing the victims in the industries traffickers most often break state laws such as: Fraud, cheating, criminal breach of trust, kidnapping and abduction, domestic abuse, assault, sexual battery, pornography, prostitution rings, illegal entry in to country, murder, child laboring, illegal massage parlors, strip clubs, beggary and under waging.

RECOMMENDATIONS

- *Rise awareness*- informs the world of this crime and mobilizes people to stop it.

- *Strengthen prevention*- warn and educate vulnerable groups and alleviate the factors that make people vulnerable to trafficking, such as poverty, underdevelopment and lack of opportunity.
- *Reduce demand*- attack the problem at its source by lowering incentives to trade and decreasing demand for the products and services of exploited people.
- *Support and protect victims*- ensure housing, counseling, medical, psychological and material assistance, keeping in mind the special needs of women and children and people at risk, such as those in refugee camps and conflict zones.
- *Improve law enforcement*- strengthen information exchange between law enforcement agencies on international trafficking routes and traffickers profiles in order to dismantle criminal groups, leading to the conviction of traffickers.
- *Implement international commitments*- ensure that international agreements are turned into national laws and practice by assisting countries in need and improving the monitoring of compliance.
- *Enrich knowledge*- deepen world understanding of the scope and nature of human trafficking through more data collection and analysis, joint research initiatives and the creation of an evidence-based report on global trafficking trends.
- *Strengthen partnerships*- build up regional and thematic networks involving civil society, inter-governmental organizations and the private sector.
- *Create a special purpose fund*- to attract and leverage resources into funding projects around the world committed to ending human trafficking.
- *Create an informal contact group*- to give like-minded member states ownership of the process and create long-term momentum.
- Formation of *Anti-trafficking squads in every district* headed by Deputy Superintendent of Police, comprising and supported by academician, women police officials, juvenile welfare officials and NGO's.

- The *family should ensure* that their children's are safe and aware of the facts about traffickers and methods to keep away them from victimization.
- The *school syllabus* shall include the information on trafficking and methods to identify the traffickers.

CONCLUSION

Although an important step in the fight against trafficking, and anti-trafficking legislations have failed to make sufficient strides in addressing the problem of human trafficking. Some researchers called for loosening the requirements that victims must meet in order to receive protection and benefits; author suggest the government to dedicate greater funding to NGO's civil rights lawyers working on behalf of trafficked victims, and some believed that expanding investigative efforts, and educating more state and local officials will help recognize and rescue victims. All of these suggestions are good, and have a potential to help more exploited people. However, all of them are still working within the existing framework.

Among the four major players involved are,

1. Immigration control/border security in case of land border crossing
2. Criminal justice agencies
3. Anti-trafficking agencies and
4. NGO's

India requires continues assessment of the entire problem as well control and counter measures are to be charted. As far as this crime is concerned early identification of trafficked persons is a prerequisite for their recognition as victims and consequently, their access to justice, assistance and protection. According to the United Nation report on trafficking in person 2004, India was placed on Tier 2 Watch list country. According to CIA, 2008 India is still placed on Tier 2 Watch list country. Asian victims are reported to be trafficked from Asia to Asian and other countries, in particular to Bangladesh, Sri Lanka, Maldives, Thailand, Japan, India, Taiwan and Pakistan (UNODC Trafficking in Persons: Global Patterns, April 2006). There are few ways to encounter this problem in particular they are as follows; ***Author suggest the following in the view of Indian scenario and*** *further of his experience as data collection supervisor in a UNDP and TANSAC funded project on "Mapping the human trafficking in TamilNadu, India".*

3 R's – Return (Recover), Reintegration and Rehabilitation

3 P's – Protection, Prosecution and Prevention

3 C's – Coordination, Cooperation and Commitment Public Awareness and Education

PUBLIC AWARENESS AND EDUCATION

India with her multi cultural, linguistic, ethical and religious make herself difficult in identifying the crime of human trafficking but now it is time for India to check both the international and the interstate and inter-district trafficking or else the situation is expected to be more unpredictable and go worsen. To better assist the victims of human trafficking, we need to first carefully study the situation and understand it. Moralistic languages and illusions of blameless innocent victims would not help to solve the problem. We would also need to examine our own values, under our humanistic claims, what are our hidden values that we do not want to admit? Then, we need to evaluate different strategies, which ones are more effective and have less harm? Only then, can we find a new and more effective way to address the problem. Closing remark of the author in order to protect people from in-country and followed by the transitional human trafficking is ***"Think globally, act locally and achieve rationally"***

REFERENCES

1. CIA (2010). "The world factbook" Retrieved from https://www.cia.gov/library/publications/the-world-factbook/fields/2196.html on 19 July, 2010.
2. Contemporary Forms of Slavery, (2000). U.N. High Commission for Human Rights fact sheet regarding contemporary forms of slavery, including trafficking, forced labor, debt bondage, and the sale of children, p 15.
3. Global Programme against the Trafficking in Human Beings, (1999). An outline for action from the UN Center for International Crime Prevention, [PDF].
4. Kofi Annan, H.E. (2007), Address both Houses of Parliament, UK, London. Retrieved on 25 June, 2010 from http://www.unodc.org/unodc/en/about unodc/speeches/speech2007_05_08.html.

5. United States Department of State publication, (2006). Trafficking in Persons Report– The Global Patterns, p 18.

6. U.S Department of Justice, (2006). Report to Congress from Attorney General John Ashcroft on U.S. Government Efforts to Combat Trafficking in Person (2008 NCVRW Resource Guide, p 35).

7. U.S. Department of State, (2007). Trafficking in persons report, Washington, D.C.(p. 10).

8. U.S. State Dept Trafficking in Persons Report, (2009). Retrieved on 25 June, 2010 from http://gvnet.com/humantrafficking/India-2.htm.

9. UN-GIFT, (United Nation -the global initiative to fight human trafficking) (2007). Think Globally, Act Locally (UNODC, 2007, pp 7).

10. UN-GIFT, (United Nation -the global initiative to fight human trafficking) (2007). Retrieved on 18 June, 2010 from http://www.ungift.org/ungift/en/humantrafficking/index.html.

□□□

10

Tech-Addiction – Causes, Symptoms and Consequences

S. Gayathridevi, Syed Umarhathab and K. Paramasivan

INTRODUCTION

It is an understatement to say that the electronic devices and the internet have changed the way we live and communicate. We turn to our computers in search of information, e-mail friends rather than pick up the phone or write a letter. Many of us have more faceless online friends, customers, and people we communicate with than those whom we have seen and know. Some of us shop over the internet, while others spend hours reading and replying to email, playing games, or even look for romance and/or matrimonial alliances. Many of us play with electronic gadgets rather than human, it increases the chance to develop addiction, this anonymity continues till the old age, later human search for individual's concerned and to care about them. However, unlike socially established addiction, which many are aware of, addiction to drugs, alcohol, tobacco and gambling, many are unaware of electronic forms. Addiction is one of the most costly public health problems in the world. It is a progressive syndrome, which means that it increases in severity over time unless it is treated. The term addiction has variety of components in it. It is classified in to two major types: substance addictions (for example, alcoholism, drug abuse, and smoking); and process addictions (for example, gambling, spending, shopping, eating, and sexual activity). There is a growing recognition that many addicts, such as poly-drug abusers, are addicted to more than one substance or process (Peele, S., 2007, p. 13). While considering process addiction psychologists continue to debate the very existence of this disease (can one be addicted to the electronics or internet, itself, or does the network merely serve as a means of feeding a more basic compulsion?) popular culture seems to have readily accepted its existence. As quickly as this new affliction has spread, so too have services offering diagnoses and treatment. Since there is no commonly accepted definition for addiction especially tech-addiction author define tech-addiction as follows.

DEFINITION OF TECHNOLOGY ADDICTION

The word *Technology Addiction* may be defined as excessive indulgence or use of technology as a behaviour for which a person has a passion and live for and live with psychic compulsion to involve in such as web browsing (including electronic mail, cyber sexual behaviour, including watch prone sites, cyber-relation, net compulsions, internet gaming including net-gambling, net-lottery, excessive shopping and information overload), electronic gadgets (invariably using playing electronic games, play station, listening to radio, walkman, MP3 players, i- pods and watching television), mobile communication (Sending SMS, MMS, making group and talking to them unnecessarily), reading e-books and running blocks in public site (such as orkut, facebook, twitter, tubely, zorpan and etc.). It may be considered as one form of process addiction.

Other Related Definitions

According to *Encyclopedia of Mental disorder* (2010), *Internet addiction disorder* refers to the problematic use of the internet, including the various aspects of its technology, such as electronic mail (e-mail) and the World Wide Web. The reader should note that internet addiction disorder is not listed in the mental health professional's handbook, the *Diagnostic and Statistical Manual of Mental Disorders*, fourth edition, text revision (2000), which is also called the *DSM*. Internet addiction has, however, been formally recognized as a disorder by the American Psychological Association.

Stedman's Medical Dictionary (2010), defines addiction as "habitual psychological and physiological dependence on a substance or practice beyond one's voluntary control."

Types of Internet Addiction

"The term 'Internet addiction' actually refers to a broad range of behaviors. Researchers in the field have identified five different types of internet addiction. According to Jeri S., and Beth K., (2006) who run the 'not my kid' website for internet addicts, they are as follows:

- Net-Gaming
- Cyber-Relational Addiction
- Information Overload
- Computer Addiction
- Cyber sexual Addiction

According to Kimberly Y. (1996), center for online addiction, founded in 1995, purports five subtypes of addictions: cyber sexual addiction, cyber-relational addiction, net compulsions, information overload, and computer addiction. Perhaps ironically, the center is an internet-based organization, offering treatment via chat-room.

Some Causes and Symptoms

Causes

No one knows what causes a person to be addicted to the technology, but there are several factors that have been proposed as contributing to technology addiction. One theory concerns the mood-altering potential of behaviors related to process addictions. Just as a person addicted to shopping may *feel a "rush" or pleasurable change in mood* from the series of actions related to a spending spree- checking one's credit cards, driving to the mall, going into one's favorite store, etc. - the person with an internet addiction may feel a similar "rush" from booting up their computer and going to their favorite web sites. In other words, *some researchers think that there are chemical changes that occur in the body when someone is engaging in an addictive behavior.* Furthermore, from a biological standpoint, there may be a combination of genes that make a person more susceptible to addictive behaviors, just as researchers have located genes that affect a person's susceptibility to alcohol.

In addition to having features of a process addiction, use of electronic devices might be *reinforced by pleasurable thoughts and feelings* that occur while the person is using such devices. Although researchers in the field of addiction studies question the concept of an "addictive personality" as such, it is possible that someone who has one addiction may be prone to become addicted to other substances or activities, including technology. People with such other mental disorders or symptoms as depression, feelings of isolation, stress, or anxiety, may "self-medicate" by using the technology in the same way that some people use alcohol or drug abuse to self-medicate the symptoms of their mental disorder.

From a social or interpersonal standpoint, there may be *familial factors* prompting use of the technology or electronic gadgets. People, who develop problems with technology or the electronic gadgets, should have used it on a casual basis and then progress to using the technology in dysfunctional ways. Use of the technology or electronic gadgets may interfere with the person's social life, school work, or job-related tasks at work. Many of the treatments that have been used for internet addiction have been modeled after other addiction treatment programs and support groups.

Illustrative example, a person might "surf the Web" to escape family conflict. Another possibility is that social or peer dynamics might prompt excessive internet use. Some affected persons may lack the social skills that would enable them to meet people in-person rather than online.

Peer behavior might also encourage technology use if one's friends are using it. For instances the interactive aspects of the internet, such as chat rooms, e-mail, and interactive games like Multi-User Dungeons and Dragons (MUDS), seem to be more likely to lead to internet addiction than purely solitary web surfing.

Modeling may play a role-users can witness and experience, how others engage in play station use and then replicate that behavior. One question that has not yet been answered concerning technology addiction is whether it is a distinctive type of addiction or simply an instance of a new technology being used to support other addictions. For example, there are gambling casinos on the internet that could reinforce a person's pre-existing gambling addiction. Similarly, someone addicted to shopping could *transfer their addiction* from the local mall to online stores. Persons addicted to certain forms of sexual behavior can visit pornography sites on the internet or use chat rooms as a way to meet others who might be willing to participate in those forms of behavior. Researchers may need to determine whether there is such a disorder as "pure" technology addiction. The important symptoms of tech-addiction are give below, one or more applicable to a person. It means that he/she need to check the mental and physical health.

Craving, Impaired Control, Physical Dependence, and Tolerance

Are the four major reasons why most of people are addicted and when these symptoms are recognized on matter it has to be handled cautiously and effectively controlled? It is start of the disease called addiction. In some respects, addictive use of the internet resembles other so-called "process" addictions, in which a person is addicted to an activity or behavior (including gambling, shopping, or certain sexual behaviors) rather than a substance (mood-altering drugs, tobacco, food, etc.). Many people believe that spending large amounts of time on the internet is a core feature of the disorder. The amount of time by itself, however, is not as important factor as the ways in which the person's technology gadgets use is interfering with their daily functioning. Use of the technology may interfere with the person's social life, school work, or job-related tasks at work. In addition, for example some cases have been reported of persons entering internet chat rooms for people with serious illnesses or disorders, and pretending to be a patient with that disorder in order to get attention or sympathy. Treatment options often mirror those for other addictions. Although only a limited amount of research has been conduct on this disorder, the treatments that have been used appear to be effective.

Symptoms

Psychological symptoms

- Unable to talk peer group
- Neglecting the appointment or commitment
- Having a sense of well-being or euphoria, while at the computer or play station
- Inability to stop the activity / such shopping or cyber sexual behaviour
- Craving for more and more time at the electronic games or public sites
- Neglecting family and friends, loving chat friends

- Feeling empty, depressed, and irritable when not with the electronic gadgets
- Lying to family and friends about activities
- Problems with school or work progress
- Dilemma in continuing any work

Physical symptoms

- Elbow pain
- Carpal tunnel syndrome
- Dry eyes
- Migraine headaches
- Backaches
- Eating irregularities, such as skipping meals
- Neglecting personal hygiene
- Sleep disturbances and changes in sleep patterns
- Over weight
- Changes in eyes power / spectacles
- Tiredness

Social symptoms

- Excessive time to deal with electronic gadgets
- An individual might have difficulty cutting down on his or her time on electronic gadgets when they are threatened with poor grades or loss of a job
- Decreased interest of life is one of the social symptoms
- Irritable when not alright with electronic gadgets
- Angry over family member
- Instant irritation when wanted move

Other symptoms of addiction may include lack of sleep, fatigue, declining grades or poor job performance, apathy, and racing thoughts. A person may lie about how much time was spent online or deny that they have a problem.

DIAGNOSIS

As previously noted technology addiction has not yet been added as an official diagnosis to the *DSM*. The following, however, is a set of criteria for internet addiction that can be appropriate to technology addiction is being proposed by authors. The criteria are based on the diagnostic standards for pathological gambling.

The patient must meet all of the following criteria:

- He or she is preoccupied with the Internet (thinks about previous online activity or is anticipating the next online session).
- He or she needs to spend longer and longer periods of time online or using electronic devices in order to feel satisfied.
- He or she has made unsuccessful efforts to control, cut back, or stop internet use or time spend an caring, cleaning and updating the electronic devices
- He or she is restless, moody, depressed, or irritable when attempting to cut down or stop internet or electronic devices use.
- He or she repeatedly stays online or with electronic devices longer than he or she originally intended.

The person must meet at least one of the following criteria:

- He or she has jeopardized or risked the loss of a significant relationship, job, educational or career opportunity because of the technology addiction
- He or she has lied to family members, a therapist, or others to conceal the extent of involvement with the electronic devices.
- He or she uses the electronic devices as a way of escaping from problems or of relieving an unpleasant mood (such as feelings of helplessness, guilt, anxiety, or depression).
- "The Internet is unlike anything we've seen before," says David G. (2000), The Center for Internet and Technology Addiction, "It's a socially connecting device that's socially isolating at the same time."

Who are Vulnerable?

David Greenfield has conducted one of the largest surveys on the topic to date: a 1998 study of 18,000 internet users who logged onto the ABC News Web site, www.abcnews.com. He found that 5.7 percent of his sample met the criteria for compulsive internet use. Those findings square with figures from smaller studies done by others, which range from 6 percent to 14 percent. Study participants who met Greenfield's criteria (adapted from criteria for compulsive gambling) were particularly hooked on chat rooms, pornography, online shopping and e-mail, he found. About a third said they use the internet as a form of escape or to alter their mood on a regular basis. In addition, the "addicted" people were far more likely to admit feelings of losing control in their dealings on the net than "non addicts." Greenfield believes that the loss of control is just one indication of the potency of the psychoactive nature of the internet. Other signs include time distortion, accelerated intimacy and decreased inhibition. For instance, 83 percent of those who fit the addiction criteria reported a loss of boundaries when they used the net, compared to 37 percent who didn't meet the criteria. Meanwhile, 75 percent of "addicts" said they had gained "feelings of intimacy" for someone they'd met online, compared to 38 percent of "non addicts." Of those who met Greenfield's criteria for internet addiction, 62 percent said they regularly logged on to pornography sites, spending an average of four hours a week viewing the material. And 37.5 percent of that group masturbated while online, they said. "Regardless of the technical definition of internet addiction, there is clearly something unique and powerful going on here," Greenfield says. "The most widely affected areas seem to be marriages and relationships due to compulsive pornography, cyber sex and cyber affairs."

CONCLUSION

The addiction is loved by many youngsters. Then, why should technology addiction is taken seriously? There is a very wide range of behavior that might be considered addictive, and not all of it is necessarily harmful. In the past, people reported to have an internet addiction disorder were stereotyped as young, introverted, socially awkward, computer-oriented males. While this stereotype may have been true in the past, the availability of computers and the increased ease of access to the technology are quickly challenging this notion. As a result, problematic technology use can be found in any age group, social class, racial or ethnic group, level of education and income, and gender. The positive benefits derived from the pleasure of the addiction need to be weighed against the negative effects it may have on the rest of a person's life. It is clearly negative if internet use becomes obsessive, causing financial, emotional, social, health or marital problems. When asked Alan A., psychology expert, Canada, if this addiction can cause emotional disorders, he replied, "As with all addictions, it's hard to state a straight-line connection. Someone obsessed with making money, for instance, might be happy and productive only when doing so, whereas someone equally obsessed with a movie star might feel distress and seek treatment when others deem this to be inappropriate and wasteful. Moreover, how do we separate the addiction from the secondary effects? For instance, one gambling addict becomes suicidal when all the money is gone, whereas another, who gambles only 'on paper,' writes books on probability theory. A common concern with computer addiction is that it's anti-social." Electronic devices have become essential to our daily lives and it is up to us, to determine, if we wish to be addicts or not. However, if you or you know someone who is a technology addict, remember they need to stop living in denial and seek help. You can find help online or with help of family and 'real' friends, and make a conscious choice to change. The technology makes our planet a small world, but just makes sure that this wonderful tool, which binds us, does not become bondage. Hence, tech-addiction should dealt very serious, the lode out on the issue is very sensible but very little is researched on the area. Only future research will answer the question which promotes this type of addiction. In future, while making research it is necessary to separately conduct, with indicator of problems of symptoms, causes and remedial measure advocated by the researcher's experience. These researches would solve the problem of tech-addiction and help the next generation in using the technology in appropriate way in order to enhance the technology growth and application.

REFERENCES

1. Answers_com - Description of addiction retrieved from www.answer.com /topic/ addiction on 15 August, 2010, p 1.
2. David Greenfield (1998). Is Internet addiction real? Retrieved on 29 July, 2010 from http://www.apa.org/monitor/apr00/addiction.aspx.
3. David Greenfield (2000). The Center for Internet and Technology Addiction. Retrieved on 19 August, 2010 from www.virtual-addiction.com.

4. Encyclopedia of Mental disorder, Retrieved on August, 2010 from http://www.minddisorders.com/flu-inv/internet-addiction-disorder.html, p 1.

5. Jeri, S & Beth, K. (2006). Internet Addiction - The Effects on Children and Facts and Strategies for Parents. Retrieved on 17 June, 2010 from www.notmykid.com.

6. Kimberly Y. (1996). In Suler, J. (2004). Computer and cyberspace addiction. International Journal of Applied Psychoanalytic Studies, 1, p. 359-362.

7. Peele, S. (2007). Addiction-Proof Your Child. New York: Three Rivers Press. p. 11-25.

8. Why there is no such thing as internet addiction http://mindhacks.com/2007/08/20/why-there-is-no-such-thing-as-internet-addiction/

9. Stedman's Medical Dictionary. Retrieved on 19 August, 2010 from http://medical-dictionary.thefreedictionary.com/

10. The Center for Online Addiction http://www.netaddiction.com

11. http://www.computeraddiction.com

❑❑❑

11

Struggle Against Child Trafficking Within the Perspective of Child Rights

M.D. ALLEN SELVAKUMAR

INTRODUCTION

India has the dubious distinction of being the source, transit, and destination country-all in one. There are various forms of trafficking within the Indian context, even though trafficking has most often been linked to prostitution. The issues of forced marriage for labor and other forms of forced labor in agriculture as well as industry, domestic service, begging, camel jockeying, organ transplant, etc., cannot be ignored. Entry and consolidation of major crime syndicates in the sphere of trafficking makes it difficult to probe and intervene into specific cases. Evidence of trafficking for forced begging marriage, and labor in informal work ghettoes are on the rise within the Indian context.

CHILD TRAFFICKING

Another gross violation of child rights takes place when innocent young children are trafficked for the sex industry for begging and soliciting, for manual labor and as domestic workers. Trafficking in human beings and the abuses associated with it are explicitly prohibited under a wide range of India's domestic laws, including the Indian constitution, specific anti-trafficking acts, the Indian penal code, and in state and local ordinances. Studies, Boded Child Labour in India, hand-rolling beedi and cigarette. The Indian constitution specifically prohibits trafficking in persons. Article 23, in the fundamental rights section of the constitution, states "traffic in human beings...and other similar forms of forced labor are prohibited." Article 39 guarantees equal treatment of men and women and obligate the state to ensure that the health and strength of workers men and women... and children are not abused... and that children and youth are protected against exploitation... article 42 provides protection against inhumane working conditions.

TRADITION PRACTICES

In India, traditional systems of children in prostitution varied as the *devadasi* or the *jogini* and the trafficking system that moves young girls across South Asia and into urban centers reveal the active exploitation and the socio-economic realities that make such exploitation possible. In the last few years, increasing number if instances of commercial sexual exploitation of children have also come to light in popular tourist destinations like Goa.

INCIDENCE

A survey sponsored by the Central Social Welfare Board (CSWB) in 1991 in six metropolitan cities if India indicated that the population of women and child victims of commercial sexual exploitation would be between 70,000 to 100,000. It also revealed that about 30% of them are below 18 years of age. The major contributory factors for the commercial sexual exploitation of women and children are poverty and unemployment or lack of appropriate rehabilitation. Seventy percent of them are illiterates; 43% of them desire to be rescued. Most of those who want to leave have given the reasons like desire to save their children from commercial sexual exploitation, protection of the future of their children, fear of diseases, etc. The others continue to be exploited due to absence of alternative sources of income, social non-acceptability, family customs, poverty, ill health, and their despondence.

LEGAL MEASURES

Trafficking was first dealt with by The Suppression of Immoral Traffic in Women and Girls Act 1956 (SITA), which was passed on 31 December 1956. The legislation was enacted in pursuance of the UN Convention of 1950. This Act had several loopholes. Some of the drawbacks were:

- The Act did not conform fully to the international convention on the subject.
- The definition of prostitution was unsatisfactory.
- No provision for dealing with policing and punishment of criminals who have set up interstate and international networks to procure children.
- No specific provisions to deal with prostitution of children.
- No provision for dealing with sexual exploitation of boys.
- Lesser sentence compared to that in the Indian penal code to offenders who induct children and women into prostitution.
- Customer not made accountable.
- Protective homes set up under the Act were mainly custody homes and not properly staffed.
- No provision for the children of prostitutes.
- No accountability placed on the superintendent of the protective homes.

The Immoral Trafficking (prevention) Act 1956 (ITPA OR PITA)

By the use of presumptions, the burden of the prosecution is lightened by the ITPA 1986. There are certain presumptions under the Act in favor of the child victims. These are:

- If a child is found in a brothel or under suspicious circumstance in the custody of a person, other than the parent of lawful guardian who is unable to explain satisfactory the presence of such a child, that person shall be presumed to have procured the child for the purposes of prostitution.
- A report in a newspaper on the use of certain premises as a brothel is deemed to be sufficient proof of the landlord, occupier, or tenant knowingly allowing such use.
- If a child is found accompanying, in suspicious circumstances, a person who is neither its parent nor lawful guardian and who is leaving the country, that person is committing the offence of immoral trafficking.

Rescue and Rehabilitation of Children and Minors under the ITPA, 1986

A minor or a child rescued under this Act it's treated as a neglected child (section 2 (1)) under the juvenile justice Act1986 now the Juvenile Justice (Care and Protection) Act, 2000, and has to be produced before the Juvenile Welfare Board (section 4 (1)), now the Child Welfare Committee for reception and rehabilitation, and placing in safe custody. There is a provision for providing for intermediate custody in a shelter home or corrective institution (section 2 (b)) after rescue pending detailed inquiry.

Judgment on Trafficking

This was a public interest litigation wherein the Supreme Court issued directions that all State Governments must direct their law-enforcing authorities to take appropriate speedy steps against the evil and directed to set up advisory committees with experts from all fields to make suggestions regarding measures for eradicating child prostitution, for care and rehabilitation of rescued girls, for setting up of rehabilitative homes, and for a survey of the devadasi and join traditions.

Law Reform

The enforcement of law in India has been weak in dealing with abusers, exploiters, and traffickers of children. There have been several gaps in implementation. Some fo them are:

- Under the Immoral Traffic Prevention Act 1986, 75% of those arrested are females. It is evident that the spirit of the Act has not been followed as the victims are being harassed.
- There have been several instances of occurrences of sexual abuse and exploitation of children within families and homes. The law generally presumes that guardians of the child are innocent and it takes a lot of professional commitment to establish such an offence against such guardians.
- Law relating to pedophiles inadequate. Therefore, the police is generally ineffective when it comes to registering the crimes, especially when it actually comes to registering the cases against foreign tourists where passport officers and international links are involved. The judiciary and the police are not aware of the laws and rights of the children.

- The laws governing prostitution are biased against the prostitute. Under the prevention of Immoral Traffic Act 1986, the customer is not an offender. For a fixed sum of money, a man is able to obtain women or girls to satisfy his sexual needs, with or without her consent. In other words, what constitutes rape outside the brothel is converted to prostitution inside the brothel and both children and women are deprived of their rights.
- To prevent secondary victimization during interrogation/ examination by investigating agencies as well as during court procedure, where a child is made to recall minute details of the sexual acts and experience, and is grilled proof, a model code of conduct should be evolved, there should be a standardized questionnaire for examination of the prosecutor, indicting the parameters for supervision.
- Examination of the victim/ witness should be in the presence of social workers/ women police/ parents or others who have the trust or confidence of the child. Examinations should also be done in a familiar atmosphere and not in police stations.
- Age and other tests of the rescued victim should also be done in the presence of child supporting individuals and preferably in the homes where the children are lodged after rescued. The homes should therefore, be provided with these facilities.
- Questioning should be done mostly by women police officers.
- The mental health aspects of the children have to be kept in mind. There should not be too much pressure on the child to speak all the details of the traumatic incident.
- Adopting a multidisciplinary approach to the crime should be attempt by co-opting additional members into the investigating team so as to include doctors, social workers; co-opting mental heath exerts counselors, or anyone who would be useful in the overall rehabilitation of the child.
- Investigation should necessarily be conducted into the trafficking angle in all cases of missing persons, procurement

of minor girls, buying and selling, child marriages, and all cases of kidnapping and abduction.

- Police officers should not be in uniform while examining the child and specially trained child-friendly police officers should examine the child.
- The venue of the trial should be a safe place other than the usual court buildings.
- Law and order and 'VIP' duties of high priority for police, whereas child sexual abuse cases are low priority crimes. This should be rectified.
- Criminal Compensation Injuries Board should be set up.
- Special Courts, within a certain time frame, should handle all cases involving sexual abuse of children.

The Prevention of Immoral Traffic Act 1986, to be more effective, needs the following measures:

- Notification of public place
- Closure of brothels keeping minors
- Setting up of special courts for speedy trials
- Rescue operations to be more humanely and sensitively carried out along with a rehabilitation plan protecting the human rights of the prostitutes.
- Age verification of the rescued children to be immediately carried out. Infact, it should be linked to the rescue operations.

The Convention for the Suppression of Trafficking in Persons and of the Exploitation of the Prostitution of Others 1949: The preamble to the Convention states that prostitution and the accompanying evil of the traffic in person for the purpose of prostitution are incompatible with the dignity and worth of the human person and endanger the welfare of the individual, the family and the community.

The SAARC Regional Convention on Combating the Crime of Trafficking in Women and Children for Prostitution: The male Declaration adopted by SARRC member states at the close of the Ninth SAARC Submit called for a regional Convention on Combating the Crime of Trafficking. Some of the significant features of this Convention agreed to by the parties are as follows:

- Trafficking in women and children for prostitution is a crime against human dignity and as such effective measures, including legal, socio-economic, and administrative, to be taken to effectively prevent trafficking in women and children.
- To specify in their national legislation, the procurement, enticing, or taking away of another person for the purposes of prostitution and exploitation even with consent as a serious offence.
- To provide in their national legislations, punishments for any person who keeps or manages or knowingly finances or takes part in the financing of a brothel or rents out a building or a place or any part thereof for the purposes of prostitution.
- In a spirit of cooperation among themselves, the parties agree to assist and coordinate the various aspects of trafficking in women and children inside and outside their countries.

Action against Trafficking and Sexual Exploitation of Children (ATSEC)

This is a network that deals with cross-border activities between West Bengal and Bangladesh to facilitate advocacy, research, social mobilization, technical assistance, and programme support at the national and regional levels. It also aims to develop capacity of the government and non-government organizations to plan and implement advocacy programmes.

The Network against Child Sexual Exploitation and Trafficking (NACSET)

This is a network against commercial sexual exploitation and trafficking. As the prevention of trafficking and CSE is a major orientation and thrust of NACSET, it has given adequate importance to approaching organizations which can play a crucial role on this front. For example, village-based-organizations engaged in water conservation, drought relief, soil conservation world in the perennially drought-prone areas along with women's organizations and youth organizations are encouraged to join the network. NACSET believes effective prevention can be achieved primarily by expanding in this manner to all the relevant organization and social forces. Action aid is working to curb the trafficking of women and children. The Action Aid India campaign, aimed at promoting coordinated action against trafficking, looks closely at interventions at the grass roots and links it to policies and action at state, national and international levels. Prevention at source is attempted by using strong systems and a community-based approach through exact mapping and tracking of the vulnerable areas from where trafficking takes place.

A comprehensive analysis of the situation on the ground with respect to trafficking has been carried out. In the course of conducting sensitization and training exercises, a training manual has been developed for use by those doing prevention work. An assessment tool has been designed to go with the tanning manual. Rehabilitation and reintegration of trafficked persons is attempted through interventions which are sensitive to the situation of the trafficked persons and in keeping with their aspirations. Support has been given to create an organization of trafficked persons themselves to have self-regulatory boards to prevent children from being trafficked into prostitution.

Campaign against Child Trafficking (CACT)

The CACT has been initiated by Terre des Homes aiming at developing a national strategy for combating child trafficking using three broad dimensions for addressing the problem: awareness generation, legal interventions, and projects at the grass roots creating and strengthening a region-specific intervention through database and building local strategies; and building partnership with the appropriate groups like decision-makers, media, and citizens to ensure implementation on international conventions, initiating national legislative processes, and aiding its conversion into enforceable law as an obvious outcome a major focus of Sanlaap's activities is centered in and on the re-light areas of Kolkata and its suburbs. Sanlaap is particularly engaged in lobbying with the government, judiciary and police to get access to the rescued children commercially abused in prostitution, who are in custody, and the children of the prostitutes, to support them with necessary counseling and care. An effort is also made to rehabilitate the young girls trafficked from suburban and rural areas of West Bengal, Nepal, and Bangladesh.

The two principal laws that address trafficking and prostitution are the suppression on Immoral Traffic in Women and Girls Act of

1956 (SITA), and the immoral Traffic in Persons Prevention Act of 1986 (ITPA), COLLOQUIALLY CALLED PITA, an amendment to SITA. ITPA recognizes that children can also be sexually exploited for commercial purposes. Unlike SITA, ITPA was concerned about prostitution of minors and children, and introduced stiff penal measures against those who profited with punishment of not less than seven years and not more than ten years. ITPA's additional clause addressing the offences of procuring carried rigorous imprisonment of seven to fourteen years in the case of a minor, and seven years to life in the case of a child. Similarly, prostitution of a minor or child in a public place was punishable with seven years to life, or up to ten years along with a fine. However these measures were effectively weakened by the discretionary powers given by ITPA to the court to reduce the term of imprisonment to below the seven years minimum for offences such as detaining a person for prostitution or seduction of a person in custody.

Other existing legislation including the Bonded Labor System (Abolition) Act and article 376 of the Indian Penal Code (IPC), explicitly forbids the purchase and sale of human beings, forced labor and all forms of bonded labor. The IPC also prohibits the trafficking and sale of minors. In addition, since many brothel inmates are under eighteen and most report the systematic use of threats and physical assaults to force new girls to serve customers, existing rape, assault, and abduction laws can be used to address the systematic abuse of women and girls in brothels. Article 375 of the IPC defines rape as the act of engaging in sexual intercourse with a women when the act is against her will; with out her consent; with her consent, when her consent has been obtained by putting her or any person in whom she is interested in fear of death or injury; with her consent when she is incapable of understanding the consequence of her consent; or when she is under sixteen years of age. Under the IPC minimum term of seven years of imprisonment may be imposed for rape. Rape laws are applicable to both brothel staff and customers. At least hundreds of thousands and probably more than a million young girls are employed in Indian brothels. Many are victims of the increasingly widespread practice of trafficking in persons across international borders. In India, a large percentage of the victims are women and girls from India who are trafficked to various big cities.

CONSEQUENCES

In concrete terms this means:- we are talking about children until 14 years of age. Often they already start to work with six or seven years. The work may be characterized by long working hours sometimes up to 12 to 16 hours without sufficient breaks-physically or psychologically hazards working conditions in quarries, for production/ in factories or on the street-very low payment and no social security in case of illness or accidents-insufficient or missing access to schools or missing opportunities to visit one-ill-treatment by the employer through malnutrition, punishment, intimidation or sexual abuse forms of bonded labor.

Child will be given to a money lender as a pawn in order to receive a credit. With his or her work he or she is supposed to pay off the debt. However, the wage will be insufficient to cover the interest, so that the child will in fact remain in bonded labor forever. This definition obviously does not include all kinds of work done by children, but only those characterized by exploitation, health hazards and conditions restraining the development of the child. How many child labors does India have? In the year 2000 the national census of the Indian government counted 8.4 million child laborers. The ministry of labor speaks about 17 million, which would be twice as much.

The United Nations (UN) assumes that there are even 100 million child laborers. According to the statistical data of the National Sample Survey Organization (NSSO) which delivers detailed reports every five years since 1972, the number is at 84 million. Another estimate is based on the number of children of school age not attending any school. It assumes that these children work and therefore counts 62 million child laborers. How can we explain these differences? The official statistics exclude huge numbers of children (about 75 million), especially those who work on the frame of their parents or in the agriculture in general those who are employed in the informal sector which means small enterprises, in family run enterprises or at home girls who work in the so called domestic service as maids. However, these children have to be included as this sector represents the most problematic and core area of child labor. It is my impression that the current situation is better portrayed by the statistical reports of the

NSSO which means that more than 80 million child labors are employed throughout India.

Most child laborers are to be found in agriculture about 85%. Most of them are children who work on the frame of their parents. They take care of the cattle, collect wood. Carry water, cook in the household, clean, or guard their sisters and brothers. Some of them go to a government or a non-formal school. Roundabout half of all rural child laborers belong to this category. Another large group (about 40%) is formed by those child laborers who are employed as daily wage laborers on medium size farms or by wealthy landowners. They are exploited on a high level, have to work for very long hours, do not possess any social security, only receive minimal wages and do not get any school education. Within this group you still find extreme forms of exploitation like bonded labor. (1992 ILO estimated the number of bonded labor at least 15 million).

CONCLUSION

India is a wonderful country. However, India does not only have nice faces, but in spite of all progress very ugly ones, too. Ones of these are the shocking degree of work done by children. The international Labor Organization (ILO) describes child labor in a very illustrative way in their World Labor Report 1992: "Work had done by children robbing them of their childhood and dignity, denying them access to education and the acquisition of professional skills and taking place under conditions which are damaging to their health and development".

REFERENCES

1. Nanjunda D.C. (2009). Encyclopedia of Child Labor Myth or Reality. New Delhi: Anmol Publications Pvt. Ltd.
2. Purushottam Sharma, (2000). Organized Transnational Crimes. Delhi: Classical Publishing Company.
3. Asha Bajpai, (2003). Child Rights in India : law, policy, and practice. Delhi: Oxford University Press.

12

Drug Abuse and Youth

K. PARAMASIVAN, SYED UMARHATHAB AND S. GAYATHRIDEVI

INTRODUCTION

The problem of drug abuse has set its evil foot on every inch of the growing global scenario, which no country could escape from it. Drug abuse among the youth is high and has created unending debate both nationally and internationally. The picture is grim if the world statistics on the drugs scenario is taken into account. With a turnover of around $500 billions, it is the third largest business in the world, next to petroleum and arms trade. About 190 million people all over the world consume or come in contact with one drug or the other. Drug addiction causes immense human distress and the illegal production and distribution of drugs have spawned crime and violence worldwide. Today, there is no part of the world that is free from the curse of drug trafficking and drug addiction. Millions of drug addicts, all over the world, are India too caught in this vicious circle of drug abuse, and the numbers of drug addicts are increasing day by day (The Times of India, 2010). Only by using tobacco in various forms one billion people will die in 21st century compares to 100 million deaths in 20th century (Narayanan, 2010). This novel epidemic of drug abuse is spreading at such an alarming speed all over the world and it badly needs immediate attention and stern societal action in order to stop it further occurrence any delay in judicial or legal vanity will take this society to destruction. The problem has been more acute with the development and use of powerful drugs which have harmful effects on the mental and physical health of the individuals and have often proved to be fatal (Benegal, Velayudhan, Jain, 2000). Maurer and Vogel (1973) in their work explained drugs which are consider being a major problem was used merely for medication by the venerable father of medicine, Hippocrates in the 4th century B.C.; he prescribed juice of the opium poppy for his obviously contented patients. Sumerian clay tablet dating out to 7000 B.C. contains instruction of preparing opium. The Greeks, Syrians, Egyptians, and Persians were familiar with opium. The spread and entrenchment of drug abuse needs to be prevented, as the cost to the people, environment and economy will be colossal. The unseemly spectacle of unkempt drug abusers dotting lanes and by lanes, cinema halls and other public places should be enough to goad the authorities to act fast to remove the scourge of this social evil. Moreover, the spread of such reprehensible habits among the relatively young segment of society ought to be arrested at all cost. There is a need for the government enforcement agencies, the non-governmental philanthropic agencies, and others to collaborate and supplement each other's efforts for a solution to the problem of drug addiction through education and legal actions.

DEFINITION OF DRUG ABUSE

According to the World Health Organization (2010) substance abuse (Substance abuse and drug abuse are words interchangeable) refers to the harmful or hazardous use of psychoactive substances, including alcohol and illicit drugs. Psychoactive substance use can lead to dependence syndrome- a cluster of behavioural, cognitive, and physiological phenomena that develop after repeated substance use and that typically include a strong desire to take the drug, difficulties in controlling its use, persisting in its use despite harmful consequences, a higher priority given to drug use than to other activities and obligations, increased tolerance, and sometimes a physical withdrawal state. Policies which influence the levels and patterns of substance use and related harm can significantly reduce the public health problems attributable to substance use, and interventions at the health care system level can work towards the restoration of health in affected individuals. The Expert Committee recommends substitution of the term 'drug dependence' for the terms 'drug abuse' and 'drug habituation' (Eddy, Halbach, Isbell, Seevers, 1965).

INDIAN SCENARIO

The country of tradition and tactfulness is India so far, but India is greatly affected by the problem of drug abuse. It is considered immoral behaviour and unethical (Bouquet, 1954; Leech, 1969). While there is no exact figures are available about the extent of drug addiction in India. The continued stream of stories that appear in the dailies, weeklies, monthlies and journals, stories of drug addiction by student, professional and sport person, smuggling rings of crime with narcotic and psychotropic drugs as concomitant, have brought to in sharp focus of the interrelated aspects of the problem. Menace of the problem in India is basically of the strategically placement of India geographically between the two of the most important routes of drugs trafficking namely golden triangle (Myanmar, Thailand and Laos) and crescent (Iran, Afghanistan and Pakistan). Experts in the field of drugs comment that various observation and surveys indicate that in India, drug abuse and drug dependent is more widespread today than it was decades ago. According to the Times of India (2010a), UN reported, one million heroin addicts are registered in India, and unofficially there are as many as five million. What started off as casual use among a minuscule population of high-income group of youth in the metro has permeated to all sections of society? Inhalation of heroin alone has given way to intravenous drug use, that too in combination with other sedatives and painkillers. This has increased the intensity of the effect, hastened the process of addiction and complicated the process of recovery. Cannabis, heroin, and Indian-produced pharmaceutical drugs are the most frequently abused drugs in India.

Though Indian youth use less hard drugs compared to youth in any other country (Khan, 1985 p 19). This is because in India, most of drug abuser start with tobacco (available in many forms), followed by drinking (alcohol) and later step in to hard drug but many cases they don't try more harder drugs, because using tobacco and drinking is labeled or considered a immoral behaviour by the Indian societies. Most of the drug addicts in India learn the habit when they are young and continue till their life. Why the problem is considered so serious with all the developments in medicine and treatment techniques. It is because of *youth diversion* which is a serious social problem and shall result in damaging the image and production capacity of the Indian youth.

In India, one million people die every years of tobacco abuse, which is more than the number of deaths in motor accidents, AIDS, alcohol and other drug abuse put together (Narayanan, 2010a p 20). At first, Indian researchers thought it was only the problem of the west. But by mid–way through the 1980's Indian society received the rude shock that an alarming proportion of the Indian youth had experimental with drugs in one form or the other, and worse still several had continued to use drugs, regularly ultimately leading to addiction. Today the picture is even gloomier, despite various anti drug abuse drives and campaigns. Drug addiction among college students persists, hostels particularly have become one of the favorite "dumping grounds for peddlers" more than anything; drug abuse among youth is a tragedy (Khan, 1985a p 21). It begins innocently as a result of curiosity or peer pressure. Then it leads to a move sustained use of drugs, subsequent dependence on it and finally makes the individual a drug addict. Apart from the evident ill- effect of the addict's health is a great financial pressure on the family and states. For example excise is the second largest source of revenue for state government after value added tax (VAT) in India, according to an estimation made in 2007-08, the state government earned Rs. 26000 crores as revenue from tax on alcohol (Aarti, 2010 p 11), medical expenditure on the issue should have exceeded the revenue in many states. For an addict a credit from the peddlers lasts till he/she get hooked. Consequently, he/she would have to lie at home to get money. Worse still, he may have to resort to stealing or involve in some illegal act and then guilt adds to his present stress otherwise to substantiate youth look for a part-time jobs. But he cannot do anything to reduce his drug use. He has taken a one way ticket to his doom, and will never return unless he is willing to change, swallows his pride and turns for help to the right people (Chesney, and Pasko, 2004 p 118).

URBAN SCENARIO

The association of drugs addicts who celebrates in the rock music and cinema fields have not helped the situation in the metropolitan and big cities of India. It is well–known fact that particularly in the west, several rock stars come on stage for concerts "stoned". Beatles started it off in the 1950's and 1960's and the trend continues. Whereas in India, it started in late 80's but still it was stead growth, which is evident from recent statistics in few states, especially in eastern and western including metro and all capital cities in India. In urban part of India, almost every illegal drug available is abused and is typically the demand- supply issue. The expansion is high as the urban population is unaware of neighbours is one of the evidence and migrant tide and pressure on urban settlement aid in increasing (Preetha, 2010, p 10) the number of drug abuse.

RURAL SCENARIO

The situation is just opposite to that of urban as not too many drugs are available for use by the rural addict's except for those citizens living in the parts of the eastern India. The most available drugs for use are tobacco, alcohol and ganja in most rural parts of India. Unlike in urban the people living around are aware of the neighbours, near and dears also, closely associated henceforth, it is difficult to continue any deviant practices.

SPORT SCENARIO

However and fortunately rehabilitated and ex-drug addicts like Paul Mc Cartney and Marodona now urge today's youth to *"say no to drugs"*. Drugs in sports have been a common occurrence, and if presently scandals are cropping up, it is only because previously, testing was absent. It is a boon that concerned athletic federations have taken up to matter exceedingly seriously. Otherwise if one time addict like Ben Johnson had been allowed to thrive on drugs, the effect on youth would have been devastating. But later, Carl Lewis with head high can assure you that you don't need drugs to win or to be cool and many more instances. In addition genuine efforts being made by various individuals and organizations through media (both Television and Radio), concerts and other forms are definitely bringing home a vital message.

Many young people continuously use drugs for a pleasurable change which may range from a mild 'lift' to an intense *'Psycho-Active effect'*. School and college going students start experimenting with drugs out of curiosity for a thrill or an expression of rebellion or to identify themselves as trendsetters and establish a higher ego. Others turn to drugs to escape depression or other personal problems (Quadri, and Nightara, 2003 p 37). There is list of widely used drugs in India, given below with examples, slang terms, effects, identification, method of use, and dangers. The effects of the drugs are given, initially from malnutrition until insanity; it varies according to the drugs and its frequency, the dangers of the habits are also given. There are several reasons behind the habits in which most important is the *'Youth culture'* both in urban and rural India. The past is gloomy and the future is uncertain so anything that given insight and pleasure to the present is welcome. The availability of drugs is yet another important factor in the high incidence of drug- abuse. Free access to drugs makes suggestible and vulnerable individuals take to drugs. According Mrs. Jacqueline, Clinical Psychologist, TTK Hospital Rehabilitation and De-addiction centre, Chennai mere *"demand reduction"* will not reduce the incidence of drug use on the other hand it is *"Supply Reduction"* and preventive education.

Common Available Drugs in India and Details

1. Stimulant

Examples: Amphetamines, Cocaine-Crack and Nicotine

Slang terms: Speed, Pep pills, Bennies, Dexies, Snow, Coke and Dahum

Identification: Tablet, capsules, crystals, injection and chewable

Method of Use / administration: Oral or intravenous injection, sniffed or snorted and smoked or chewed

Effects: Increases heart beat rate, breathing, dilated pupils and blood pressure,

Dangers: Malnutrition, kidney damage, psychological dependence, cardiac arrest, and cancer

2. Depressants (Downers)

Examples: Barbiturates, Tranquillizers and Alcohol

Slang Terms: Barbs, Blues, and Bullets

Identification: Tablets, injection, and consumable liquids

Method of Use / administration: Mostly oral consumed otherwise injected

Effects: Clams down nervous system, drowsiness and slurred speech

Dangers: Breathing problems, illusion, delusion and vehicle accident

3. Hallucinogens

Examples: Phencyclidine and Lysergic acid diethyl amide (LSD)

Slang Terms: PCP and Magic Mushroom

Identification: Liquid, powder and tablets

Method of Use / administration: Oral or injected

Effects: Dilated pupils, delusion such as hear color and see sound

Dangers: Bad trips, terrifying flash backs, organic brain damage, in female deformed children and still birth

4. Hypnotics (Cannabis)

Examples: Charas, Bhang, Ganja and Hashish

Slang Terms: Pot, Hash and Grass

Identification: Solid rolled brown cakes and leaf

Method of Use / administration: Pipes, cigarettes and swallowed

Effects: Fast heart beat, heightens, emotions and impaired Judgement

Dangers: Psychological dependence, impaired thinking and reflexes loss fertility

5. Narcotics (Opiates)

Examples: Opium, Morphine, Heroin, Brown Sugar and Junk

Slang Terms: Apneem and Smack

Identification: Smooth balls, and liquid

Method of Use / administration: Inhaled, injected (Intravenous on main lines) and chased

Effects: Relaxed brain activity, flushed face and going on the nod

Dangers: Physical dependence, psychosis and insanity

Some International Effort to Fight Drug Abuse

According to WHO (2010a),

- 76.3 million Persons with alcohol use disorders worldwide.
- At least 15.3 million persons who have drug use disorders.
- Injecting drug use reported in 136 countries, of which 93 report HIV infection among this population.
- For every dollar invested in drug treatment, 7 dollars are saved in health and social costs.

- Drug abuse among the youth shall reduce only through societal vigilance, parental care and preventive education. Since, it just norm or practice the United Nations has come with international instruments to fights the menace of drug abuse, India is a signatory of the following treaties and conventions:
- 1961 U.N. Convention on Narcotic Drugs
- 1971 U.N. Convention on Psychotropic Substances
- 1988 U.N. Convention Against Illicit Traffic in Narcotic Drugs and Psychotropic Substances
- 2000 Transnational Crime Convention

CONCLUSION

Drug abuse is a complex phenomenon, which has various social, cultural, biological, geographical, historical and economic aspects. With reference to India the factors encouraging the drug abuse are disintegration of the old joint family system, absence of parental love and care in modern families where both parents are working, decline of old religious and moral values etc. lead to a rise in the number of drug addicts who take drugs to escape hard realities of life. Drug use, misuse or abuse is also primarily due to the nature of the drug abused, the personality of the individual and the addict's immediate environment. India is one of the fastest growing country in the world, on the other hand, a study by the National Institute of Mental Health and Neuro Sciences for WHO estimated that while the gains in terms of revenue from alcohol sales are Rs. 216 billion every year, losses from adverse effects of alcohol sales are Rs. 244 billion, apart from immeasurable losses due to multiple effects of alcohol use (Aarthi, 2010a). The processes of industrialization, urbanization and migration have led to loosening of the traditional methods of social control rendering an individual is vulnerable to the stresses and strains of modern life. The fast changing social milieu, among other factors, is mainly contributing to the proliferation of drug abuse, both of traditional and of new psychoactive substances. The introduction of synthetic drugs and intravenous drug use leading to HIV/AIDS has added a new dimension to the problem, especially in the Northeast states of the country. The phenomenon of drug abuse or drug dependence brings to the fore, essentially, a contradictory form of human behavior. Since long, it is well- established that few drugs are endowed with the bio-chemical properties; they are popularly supposed to have. But, rarely has their popularity declined, and they have continued to attract enthusiasts. Although, there have been great steps taken by both governmental and non-governmental agency to fight the problem it is very important that family members, friends and neighbors has to help the addicts in coping with matters at all level. The other governmental agencies concerned with drug abuse and its issues are police, Ministries of social justice and empowerment, health and family welfare, labour and employment, food processing, information and broadcasting, youth affairs and sports, human resources development, and the department of industrial policy and promotion, legal affairs, and the national aids control organization. Hence, the entire agency shall use the advancement in media and spread message relating to symptoms of early behavioral changes and action to be taken such condition. In most of the case of drug abuse, family gets to know the matter late because most of the time family member thinks that symptoms or early behavioral changes are due to adolescence. Also, parent should have watch on the friends and behavior of the youth (son/daughter).

PREVENTIVE EDUCATION AS SUGGESTIONS

People around the world are becoming increasingly concerned about the escalating drug- related problems that we face today. The goal of prevention is to keep people healthy, drug – free and to bolster the resistance of those at risk.

The suggestions are:-

- To increase knowledge of drug abuse and its effects among the common public.
- Positive health education and to encourage responsible behavior among the youth.
- To control the availability of drugs in the community through legislation and other means, because the less available the drug is, the fewer are the problems.
- To devise ways of getting people to recognize, in themselves and help addicts.
- Give information on early signs of drug abuse problems in all the local media.

- To educate drug addicts to know what action to take and where to go for help and support.
- Conduct exhibition or cultural program focusing the impact of the drug use.

REFERENCES

1. Aarti D. (23 February, 2010). Health department should coordinate alcohol issues: centre, The Hindu, p 11.
2. Bang A.T. and Bang R.A. (1991). "Community Participation in research and Action against Alcoholism" World Health Forum.
3. Benegal V., Velayudhan A., Jain S. (2000). Social Costs of Alcoholism: A Karnataka Perspective. NIMHANS Journal, 18 (1and2) p 67.
4. Bouquet, J. (1954). Cannabis, Bulletin on Narcotics, 3 p 22-45.
5. Chesney M. and Pasko L.L. (2004). The female offender- Girls, women and crime (2nd edition), Sage publication, USA. P 118.
6. Eddy, N.B., Halbach, H., Isbell, H., Seevers, M.H. (1965). Drug dependence: its significance and characteristics. Bulletin of the World Health Organization, 23: p 721–722.
7. Khan M.Z. (1985). Drug use among the college youth, Somaiya Publication Pvt. Ltd., New Delhi, India p 19 and 21.
8. Leech, K. (1969). The drug subculture: A Christian analysis, Church information office, London.
9. Maurer D.W. and Vogel V.H. (1973). Narcotics and narcotic addiction. 4th ed. Charles C Thomas, United States, p 313.
10. Narayanan K.K. (September 14, 2010). "Documentary to aid anti-tobacco campaign ready" The Hindu, p 20.
11. Preetha M.S. (19 September, 2010). The Hindu- The property plus, p 10.
12. Quadri Afzal S.M. and Nightara. (Jan and July, 2003). Solvent Abuse in adolescent; Assessment and Treatment, Indian Journal of Society of Criminology, 31 (1and 2) p 37.
13. The Times of India (June, 2010). Family useful in alcohol de-addiction. Retrieved on 15 August, 2010 from http://timesofindia.indiatimes.com/life-style/health-fitness/health/family-useful-in-alcohol-de-addiction/articleshow/6431041.
14. WHO. Retrieved on 15 August, 2010 from http://www.who.int/substance_abuse/facts/en/

□□□

PART-III
IMPACT OF EDUCATION IN INDIA

- The law [illegible] are biased against the prostitute [illegible] of Immoral Traffic Act 1956 [illegible] offender. [illegible] women [illegible] her [illegible] words, whatever [illegible] inside the brothel [illegible] to prostitution [illegible] and both children and women are denied [illegible] rights.
- To prevent [illegible], during interrogation/examination [illegible] as well as during court procedure, [illegible] to recall minute details of the [illegible] is guilty [illegible] of a model code of [illegible] evolved, there should be a standardised [illegible] examination of the prosecutrix [illegible] supervision.
- Examination [illegible] witness should be in the presence of [illegible] women police/ parents or others [illegible] of the [illegible] examinations should also be [illegible] atmosphere and not in police station.
- Age and other tests of the rescued victim should also be done in the presence of child supporting individuals and preferably in the homes where the children are lodged after rescued. The homes should therefore be provided with these facilities.
- Questioning should be done mostly by women police officers.
- The mental health aspects of the children have to be kept in mind. There should not be too much pressure on the child to speak all the details of the traumatic incident.
- Adopting a multidisciplinary approach to the crime should be attempt by co-opting additional members into the investigating team so as to include doctors, social workers; co-opting mental heath and counselors, or anyone who would be useful in the overall rehabilitation of the child.
- Investigation should necessarily be conducted into the trafficking angle in all cases of missing persons, procurement

13

Reforms in Higher Education Sector in India

P. ARUNACHALAM

INTRODUCTION

The 21st century is marked by a paradigm shift in education that has resulted both in threats and opportunities. It has brought new challenges and an opportunity for higher education. Higher education in India is undergoing rapid changes. The challenges ahead are multifaceted and multidimensional. Though the data show a massive growth in the number of students' enrollment in colleges/universities, holistic view reveals that still only a meager of the total population has access to higher education. Globalization and privatization are imposing new challenges but the nations are still entangled in solving the basic problems of accessibility to higher education for all. In the wake of the transition from elitist to mass education, universities worldwide are under pressure to enhance access and equity, on the one hand, and to maintain high standards of quality and excellence, on the other. Today the notion of equity not only implies greater access to higher education, but also opportunities for progress. In recent debates on higher education, the notions of equity and access go beyond minority to diversity. Affirmative action, too, has become race-exclusive and gender-neutral.

Prof. Sukhadeo Thorat, Chairman of UGC has recently stated that expanding the higher education system through establishment of new universities, increase in intake capacity with prime importance to inclusive education and quality would be the key areas of focus for higher education in the Eleventh Five Year Plan. In this research paper an attempt has been made to study the major issues the higher education sector is facing at present and suggest suitable measures to correct and rejuvenate it in the coming years.

Objectives of the Study

1. To analyze the higher education system in India.

2. To describe the problems faced by the higher education sector in India.

3. To analyze the growth and present status of higher education sector in India.

4. To suggest corrective measures to strengthen the higher education sector in India.

This research work is primarily based on secondary data published in various journals and government reports. It is descriptive in nature.

While delivering the convocation address at the 18th convocation of Pondicherry University on May 20th 2008 the Chairman of the University Grants Commission Prof. Sukhadeo Thorat, expanding the higher education system through establishment of new universities, increase in intake capacity with prime importance to inclusive education and quality would be the key areas of focus for higher education in the Eleventh Five Year Plan. He said higher education has been neglected in the last few decades and certain issues need to be addressed immediately. In the early 1950's the enrolment ratio was less than one per cent. Today, it has increased to 10 per cent. Yet this is low when compared to the world average of 23 per cent. Countries falling in the middle income group have a ratio of 35 to 37 per cent, while Europe and United States have over 40 per cent he has stated.

EDUCATIONAL DEVELOPMENT IN INDIA

India's education has a long history dating back to institutions such as Nalanda.India, being a developing nation, struggles with challenges in its primary education. Literacy rate has increased from around 3% in 1880 to around 65% in 2001. Net enrollment of 6-10 years old Indians increased from 68 percent to 82 percent between 1992/93 and 1998/99. Yet great challenges remain as The Economist reports that half of 10-year-old rural children can't read at the basic level, over 60% is unable to do simple division, and half drop out by the age 14. Fewer than 40 percent of adolescents in India attend secondary schools. Around 1 in 10 young persons has access to tertiary education. Mercer consulting estimates that only a quarter of graduates are "employable". All levels of education in India, from primary to higher education, are overseen by the Ministry of Human Resource Development, Department of Higher Education, India and Department of School Education and Literacy, and heavily subsidized by the Indian government, though there is a move to make higher education partially self-financing. The Indian Government is considering allowing 100% foreign direct investment in Higher Education.

Higher Education in India has evolved in distinct and divergent streams with each stream monitored by an apex body, indirectly controlled by the Ministry of Human Resource Development. The 415 universities/ institutions are mostly funded by the state governments. However, there are 24 important universities called Central universities, which are maintained by the Union Government and because of relatively large funding, they have an edge over the others. The engineering education and business schools are monitored and accredited by the All India Council for Technical Education (AICTE) while medical education is monitored and accredited by the Medical Council of India (MCI). Like-wise, agriculture education and research is monitored by the Indian Council for Agriculture Research. Apart from these, National Council for Teacher Education (NCTE) controls all the teacher training institutions in the country.

Higher Education System in India

Higher Education in India is one of the most developed in the entire world. There has in fact been considerable improvement in the higher education scenario of India in both quantitative and qualitative terms. In technical education, the IITs, and in management, the IIMs have already marked their names among the top higher educational institutes of the world. Moreover the Jawaharlal University and Delhi University are also regarded as good higher educational institutes for doing postgraduates courses and research in science, humanities and social sciences. As a result, students from various parts of the world are coming today for higher education in India. Higher Education system in India: There are at present 227 government-recognized

Universities in India. Out of them 20 are central universities, 109 are deemed universities and 11 are Open Universities and rest are state universities. Most of these universities in India have affiliating colleges where undergraduate courses are being taught. According to the Department of higher Education, Government of India, there are 16,885 colleges, 99.54 lakh students and 4.57 lakh teachers in various higher education institutes in India.

India has one of the largest 'Higher Education System in the world. Main players in the higher education system in the country are: University is responsible for coordination, determination and maintenance of standards, release of grants. Professional Councils are responsible for recognition of courses, promotion of professional institutions and providing grants to undergraduate programmes and various awards. Central Government is responsible for major policy relating to higher education in the country. It provides grants to the UGC and establishes central universities in the country. The Central Government is also responsible for declaration of Educational Institutions as 'Deemed to be University' on the recommendation of the UGC. Presently there are sixteen (18) Central Universities in the country. In pursuance of the Mizoram Accord, another Central University in the State of Mizoram is planned. There are 99 Institutions which have been declared as Deemed to be Universities by the Govt. of India as per Section of the UGC Act, 1956. State Governments are responsible for establishment of State Universities and colleges, and provide plan grants for their development and non-plan grants for their maintenance.

The coordination and cooperation between the Union and the States is brought about in the field of education through the Central Advisory Board of Education (CABE).

Special Constitutional responsibility of the Central Government: Education is on the 'Concurrent list' subject to Entry 66 in the Union List of the Constitution. This gives exclusive Legislative Power to the Central Govt. for co-ordination and determination of standards in Institutions of higher education or research and scientific and technical institutions.

India is today one of the fastest developing countries of the world with the annual growth rate going above 9%. In order to sustain that rate of growth, there is need to increase the number of institutes and also the quality of higher education in India. Therefore the Prime

Minister of India has announced the establishment *of 8 IITs, seven Indian Institutes of Management (IIMs) and five Indian Institutes of Science, Education and Research (IISERs) and 30 Central Universities in his speech to the nation on the 60th Independence Day.* The outlay for education during the 11th Five Year Plan, which runs from the current fiscal to 2012-13, represents a four-fold increase over the previous plan and stands at Rs 2500 billion.

The thrust of the policy underlying the Eleventh Five Year Plan for Higher Education is on increasing access to quality higher education while ensuring equity. A new Scheme for Reduction in Regional Imbalances, Social Gaps and Promotion of Inclusiveness in Higher Education has been introduced by the University Grants Commission (UGC) in the XI Plan, which will serve the rural and tribal areas as well. Central Universities have been established in all the states in the North-Eastern Region including in states with predominately tribal population. In addition, during the XI Plan a Central University will be established in each of those states where there is no Central University. 374 new colleges are proposed to be established one in each district where the Gross Enrolment Ratio (GER) is lower than the national average (Union human resource development minister *Kapil Sibal has stated that our aim is to achieve a Gross Enrolment Ratio (GER) is 12.4%, government's target is around 30% by 2020.* In the XI Plan, a target has been set to increase the GER of students in the eligible age group of 18-24 years in higher education by 5 percentage points by the end of the Plan. Provision for infrastructural and other requirements for this purpose is required to be made by Central and State Governments.

Growth of Higher Education in India

Since ancient times, India has been a centre of excellence in the field of higher education. Nalanda, Vikramashila and Takshashila were few of the oldest universities in the world and were the most renowned seats of higher education during their time. Students' from far off countries came to study in these universities. Today India has one of the largest higher education systems in the world and also some world-class institutions for higher education. The present system of higher education dates back to Mountstuart Elphinstone's minutes of 1823, which stressed on the need for establishing schools for teaching English and the European sciences. Subsequently, the universities of Calcutta, Bombay and Madras were set up in 1857, followed by the University of Allahabad in 1887. The first attempt to formulate a national system of education in India came in 1944, with the Report of the Central Advisory Board of Education on Post War Educational Development in India, which recommended the formation of a University Grants Committee, which was formed in 1945 to oversee the work of the three Central Universities of Aligarh, Banaras and Delhi. After independence, a full-fledged Ministry of Education was established on 29th August 1947. In 1952, the Union Government decided that all cases pertaining to the allocation of grants-in-aid from public funds to the Central Universities and other Universities and Institutions of higher learning might be referred to the University Grants Commission (UGC). The UGC was formally established in November 1956 as a statutory body of the Government of India through an Act of Parliament for the coordination, determination and maintenance of standards of university education in India.

India has significant advantages in building a large, high quality higher education system. It has a large higher education sector – the third largest in the world in student numbers after China and the United States. It uses English as a primary language of higher education and research. It has a number of high quality institutions that can form the basis of a world-class higher education system. Nevertheless, the system only enrolled 9 million students in 2003/04 (equivalent to a 9-10 percent enrolment rate as estimated by the Ministry of Human Resource Development). This compares to with more than half of the young people in major developed countries and about 20 per cent in China. Similarly, the *world-class institutions in India that are known globally — mainly the IITs and the IIMs – are small, enrolling well under 1 per cent of the student population.*

The Government will take strong steps in the 11th Five Year plan to increase opportunities in Higher education, relieve skill shortages in the economy, and increase competitiveness. *The goal for the 11th Five Year plan for 2007-2012 is an increase of five percent in the enrolment rate of higher education equivalent to the creation of approximately 8 million new seats in Indian higher and technical education.* Some of the steps are: (i) establishment of a central autonomous university in each state, (ii) higher education institutions in each district of the countries, (iii) private institutions may be granted deemed university status, (iv) creation of more Inter-University Centers, and (v) funding of up to 150 new polytechnics autonomous colleges. Further, all institutions are asked to make higher education more inclusive, more responsive to economic needs, and raise quality. Therefore, the public and the government are likely to increase investment into higher education, and in return demand accelerated change in the higher education sector.

The governance of the Indian Higher education sector is changing. Like the Indian economy underwent a liberalizing in the 1990s, the education system is gradually being opened up for change and decentralization. In particular, the federal and state governments are gradually giving higher education institutions more decision and spending power. This represents a move away from detailed government control over spending, teaching, and curriculum decisions, which required frequent approval from federal or state government officials. Besides the 11th Five Year Plan, several facts pay witness to this movement:

- Many institutions have become autonomous during the 10th plan Five Year Plan through an increase in the number of autonomous institutions: Central Universities (2), State Universities (39), "deemed-to-be" Universities (50), and Private Universities (10).
- Two recent reports from the Central Advisory board of Education (CABE) on respectively the 'autonomy of higher education institutions" and 'financing of higher and technical education' recommend changes to governance of the higher education institutions.
- The Oversight Committee on the Implementation of the New Reservation Policy in Higher Educational Institution equally recommends increased autonomy to institutions within recruitment and remuneration of faculty and admission policies to find the right balance between equity and excellence for each institution.

Forum on Governance of Higher Education in India: How Best to Strike the Balance between Autonomy and Accountability?

Higher education in India has grown large since the country's independence in 1947. Starting from a small base, the pace of growth was initially rapid. Initially, the pace of growth was rapid. Enrolments grew by 13 to 14 per cent per annum during the 1950s and 1960s. Over the past few decades, the growth rate has declined noticeably. Since then it has remained stable between 4 and 5 per cent.

EXPENDITURE ON EDUCATION

The world's most developed economies, such as the US, the UK and France allocate 6-7 per cent of their national budgets on public education and health. India by contrast, allocates just 3 per cent for education. When we made education a Constitutional right, at par with the right to life, it hardly befitted the spirit of the Constitution to take such a minimalist approach to child rights. The 2009-2010 Budget ratifies the minimalist approach, by not increasing the Sarva Shiksha Abhiyan allocation (it remains, as in the previous year, at Rs 13,100 crore).To make any real impact on children's lives, the country needs to spend at least 10 per cent of GDP on school education and health. Currently, the spending on schooling is 1.28 per cent (the total government outlay is 3.3 per cent) of GDP. Instead of investing public resources, we, as a country, are opening up a core sector to private players — a move that goes against both the short- and long- term interests of children (Puja Marwaha, 2009).

Public Spending on Education and Health : An International Comparison

Country	Public Expenditure on Education as % of GDP (2002-04)	Public Expenditure on Health as % of GDP (2003)
France	6	7.7
U.K.	5.5	6.9
U.S.	5.9	6.8
Brazil	4.1	3.4
South Africa	5.4	3.2
Mexico	5.8	2.9
S. Korea	4.6	2.8
Bangladesh	2.2	2.3
Malaysia	8	2.2
India	3.3	1.2

Source:UNDP, Human Development Report 2006.

Public Expenditure on Education as a percentage of GDP

Year	Education Expenditure to Expenditure on all sectors	Education Expenditure to GDP
1999-00	14.60	4.19
2000-01	14.42	4.28
2001-02	12.89	3.80
2002-03	12.60	3.77
2003-04	11.98	3.49
2004-05	12.13	3.39
2005-06	12.68	3.58

Source:http://www.thehindubusinessline.com/2009/07/24/stories/2009072450160800.

NATIONAL KNOWLEDGE COMMISSION

Assocham Press Trust of India has suggested that Government should deregulate higher education in India: It has stated that The National Knowledge Commission's report on higher education is one in the series that started with the report of the Dr.Radhakrishnan Commission (1948). It recommended that 1.5 to 2 per cent of GDP for higher education from .7 per cent at present, assuming a provision of 6 per cent for education and the observation that implicit politicization has made governance of universities exceedingly difficult and much more susceptible to non-academic intervention from outside are worth emphasizing. In order to increase the gross enrolment ratio to 15 per cent, the Commission suggests that India needs as many as 1500 Universities by 2015.

The knowledge commission found the following problems related to higher education.

1. With 90 per cent of the undergraduate students and 66 per cent of the postgraduate students studying in affiliated colleges, we have today a system that is overwhelmed by affiliated colleges which are in many cases only marginally better than good higher secondary schools.
2. We have in the affiliated colleges 84 percent of the total faculty in higher education, comprising only lecturers of different grades who do not, and are not expected to pursue any research. Consequently only the faculty members in the Universities who constitute a mere 16 per cent of the total are expected to do research.
3. Universities which are to be the prime centers of scholarship and where there is an uninterrupted flow of young minds, play an insignificant roles in generating a base for creating new knowledge and technologies. This is regrettable. While China published 72,632 research papers with citation in 2005, in India the number was 25, 227. The progressive decline in Indian research can be seen from the fact that the corresponding figures in 1990 were 6991 for China and 11563 for India. Prof. V.C.Kulandai Swamy has reported that the research potential of Indian Universities is alarmingly poor. The urgent step that is needed to improve the health

of higher education and research which is really anemic is to increase the number of universities and transfer higher education from affiliated colleges to University campuses.

The number of Universities that has been suggested is not too large. Japan with a population 128 million has 726 universities, Germany with 82 million has 350, UK with 62 million has 116 and the U.S.A with a population of 300 million is reported to have 2466. China, according to National Knowledge Commission has created 1250 new Universities in the previous three years. Having suggested a massive increase in the number of universities, the commission has broadly outlined acceptable measures to achieve it, namely, the establishment of 50 national universities, the up gradation of deserving colleges in the deemed universities, and the establishment of new universities by the Central and State governments and private provides.

The role of the private sector in higher education has been stressed by the commission in unambiguous terms. Consequent to the increase in demand and inadequate response on the part of governments, there has been in recent years a quite but steady increase in private participation in general and professional education. The world is also witnessed a gradual transformation of higher education from public to private good. The commission recommends," there is a clear need to establish an Independent Regulatory Authority for Higher Education (IRAHE). Such regulatory authority is both necessary and desirable.

India's government will create 12 new central universities, adding to the 18 that currently exist. This is a mammoth undertaking and the equivalent of US$73 million has been allocated from the central government budget to it. Earlier this year India announced it would create 30 'world class' Universities, eight new Indian institutes of technology and seven Indian institutes of Management in the coming five years (India will soon set up 14 unique Innovation Universities, each based on a different model and concept, to address future education requirements of India). On the recommendation of the National Knowledge Commission, the central government is planning massive investment to upgrade and expand higher education. Other plans include enhancing the salaries of college and university academics - boosting salaries by as much as 70 per cent. This prospect represents welcome news since India currently lacks world class universities according to the international rankings, and Indian academics, when compared internationally, are rather poorly paid. Students also suffer an immense shortage of places in India's top academic institutions and throughout the higher education system.

India today educates only half as many young people from the university age group as China and ranks well behind most Latin American and other middle income countries. India exhibits a special problem at the top of its higher education hierarchy. With the notable exceptions of the institutes of technology and institutes of management, and a small number of outstanding non-university research and training institutions - such as the All India Institute of Medical Sciences - top-notch schools are rare. Indeed, none of India's 348 universities is ranked in the top 100 in the world. Generally, when India has wanted to innovate in the higher education sector, it has side-stepped the universities and has started entirely new institutions such as the institutes of technology. However, if India invests large amounts of money and human capital into academic improvement and expansion without undertaking strategies to ensure that the investment will yield results, resources will be wasted and failure will be assured. Despite a discussion of organizing some of the new universities based on the American model, so far neither the ideas nor the funding seems adequate. Yet, a newspaper reported that one official said: "The view was that there should be no hierarchy or disparity in standards amongst universities, and the reforms and changes suggested for world class universities should be applied to all universities." This attitude shows a complete misunderstanding that the American system institutes significant hierarchy among the public universities. Just pumping money and resources into a fundamentally broken university system is a mistake. Establishing new universities, especially those intended to be innovative, requires careful planning and an understanding of the weaknesses of the current system.

PROBLEMS ASSOCIATED WITH HIGHER EDUCATION IN INDIA

Philip G. Altbach in his work on 'higher education in India' has described the bad shape of India's higher education system. India has significant advantages in the 21st century knowledge race. It has a large higher education sector — the third largest in the world in student numbers, after China and the United States. It uses English as a primary language of higher education and research. It has a long academic tradition. Academic freedom is respected. There are a small number of high quality institutions, departments, and centers that can form the basis of quality sector in higher education. The fact that the States, rather than the Central Government, exercise major responsibility for higher education creates a rather cumbersome structure, but the system allows for a variety of policies and approaches.

Yet the weaknesses far outweigh the strengths. India educates approximately 10 per cent of its young people in higher education compared with more than half in the major industrialized countries and 15 per cent in China. Almost all of the world's academic systems resemble a pyramid, with a small high quality tier at the top and a massive sector at the bottom. India has a tiny top tier. None of its universities occupies a solid position at the top. A few of the best universities have some excellent departments and centers, and there are a small number of outstanding undergraduate colleges. The University Grants Commission's recent major support of five universities to build on their recognized strength is a step toward recognizing a differentiated academic system – and fostering excellence. At present, the world-class institutions are mainly limited to the Indian Institutes of Technology (IITs), the Indian Institutes of Management (IIMs) and perhaps a few others such as the All India Institute of Medical Sciences and the Tata Institute of Fundamental Research. These institutions, combined, enroll well under 1 per cent of the student population.

India's colleges and Universities, with just a few exceptions, have become large, under-funded, ungovernable institutions. At many of them, politics has intruded into campus life, influencing academic appointments and decisions across levels. Under-investment in libraries, information technology, laboratories, and classrooms makes it very difficult to provide top-quality instruction or engage in cutting-edge research.

Even the small top tier of higher education faces serious problems. Many IIT graduates, well trained in technology, have chosen not to contribute their skills to the burgeoning technology sector in India. Perhaps half leave the country immediately upon graduation to pursue advanced study abroad – and most do not return. A stunning 86 per cent of students in science and technology fields from India who obtain degrees in the United States do not return home immediately following their study. Another significant group, of about 30 per cent, decides to earn MBAs in India because local salaries are higher — and are lost to science and technology. A corps of dedicated and able teachers work at the IITs and IIMs, but the lure of jobs abroad and in the private sector makes it increasingly difficult to lure the best and brightest to the academic profession.

Few in India are thinking creatively about higher education. There is no field of higher education research. Those in government as well as academic leaders seem content to do the "same old thing." Academic institutions and systems have become large and complex. They need good data, careful analysis, and creative ideas. In China, more than two-dozen higher education research centers, and several government agencies are involved in higher education policy.

Higher education is necessary for one to achieve excellence in the line one is best. But one should be selected for higher education on the basis of merit only. Further, fees for education in general should not be high; especially, the fees for higher studies should be within the reach of every class of people in the nation.

A recent study by Thomson Reuters titled Global Research Report: India concluded that, given ideal conditions, India's research productivity would be on a par with that of most G8 nations within seven to eight years and that it could probably overtake them in 2015-2020. In the last decade, India has seen its annual output of scientific publications grow from roughly 16,500 in 1998 to nearly 30,000 in 2007. Before we pat ourselves on the back, it would be good to consider things in perspective. Although India produces about 400,000 engineering graduates and about 300,000 computer science graduates every year, just about 20,000 master's degree holders and fewer than 1,000 Ph.Ds in engineering graduate each year (Compared to India and China, the United States produces only 70,000 engineering graduates every year. All of Europe produces just 100,000).

In 2007-08, India had about 156 researchers per million in the population, compared with 4,700 per million in the United States. In terms of sheer numbers, in 2007 China had 1,423,000 researchers, second internationally to the United States, which had almost 1,571,000. India by comparison had 154,800. India's spend on R&D in 2007-08 was about US$ 24 billion compared with China's investment of about US$ 104 billion back in 2006 and the United

States' US$ 368 billion. These comparative allocations, which have not changed much since then, reveal the gross inadequacy in India's commitment to research, considering our scientists' potential and our aspirations as a nation.

A survey of 47 universities conducted by the University Grants Commission in 2007-08 revealed vacancy levels as high as 51 per cent. It is evident that the majority of India's graduating engineers, particularly the cream, are going directly into the job market - affecting the number and quality of those available for research. This trend is partly because of the widespread notion that remuneration in a research career is below par and partly because of the lack of adequate encouragement and direction for young potential researchers.

Not enough Ph.Ds graduate in India — be it in number or excellence — to meet the growing staff requirements of its universities. As a result, even the quality of faculty has shown a declining trend and this is bound to have serious repercussions on the country's intellectual edge. Add to this the issues of politicization of the Indian scientific establishment, particularly in according due recognition, the lack of adequate funding and infrastructure and the disparity in research funds and facilities available to universities (Narayana Murthy, 2009)

Ramesh (2007) in his work on *Analysis* Present System & Higher Education in India has stated that the present system of higher education does not serve the purpose for which it has been started. In general education itself has become so profitable a business that quality is lost in the increase of quantity of professional institutions with quota system and politicization adding fuel to the fire of spoil system, thereby increasing unemployment of graduates without quick relief to mitigate their sufferings in the job market of the country. So, the drawbacks of the higher education system underscore the need for reforms to make it worthwhile and beneficial to all concerned.

Next to China, India is the most populated country in the world. Naturally there is too much rush and competition in every field. So, rush to technical and higher education has increased as scope for arts and science has become lesser and lesser due to lack of reforms and up gradation in the course structure and materials according to the developments of the world. Also, qualification in higher education gives added advantage to face successfully competition in the job market. Purpose of Education. All round development of personality is the purpose of education. But the present day education is neither imparting true knowledge of life, world and helping one stand on one's own leg nor improving the talent of a student by which one can achieve laurels in the field one is interested. So, combination of arts subjects and computer science and science and humanities or literature should be introduced so that such courses could be useful for the students to do jobs after recruitment in some companies which would reduce unnecessary rush to higher education.

Professor Philip G Altbach has outlined some of the problems with respect to establishing world class Universities in India that need fixing before resources are given.

India is world famous for sclerotic bureaucracy, and higher education fits into that mold. Few decisions can be made without receiving permission from an authority above, and the wheels of decision-making grind slowly. Fear of corruption or of a loss of control entrenches bureaucracy. Teachers and academic leaders at colleges and universities have little incentive to innovate higher education - indeed quite the opposite. It is completely impossible to build world class universities in this bureaucratic context. If the new institutions must tolerate responsibilities to both the central government and the states in which they are located, the bureaucratic burden will be completely overwhelming.

2. Great universities need to be located on friendly soil. In general, the best universities worldwide are in or near major urban centres or in places with intellectual traditions and strength. While it is entirely appropriate to have a good university in each of India's states, the idea of a truly world class university (an institution that can compete with the best universities in the world) in cities like Guwahati or Bhubaneshwar is simply unrealistic. It would be extraordinarily difficult to attract top professors or even the best students, and the 'soft' infrastructures, such as most cultural amenities, are missing. High-tech industry is also absent in these locations and world be difficult to lure. No amount of money will guarantee the establishment of a world class university in such a place.

3. Indian academics deserve higher salaries, and the current move to dramatically improve remuneration is a positive step. It would be a serious mistake to simply give more money to the professoriate

without at the same time demanding significant reforms in the structure and practices of the profession. Indian academics are rewarded for longevity, rather than productivity, and for conformity rather than innovation. The most productive academics cannot be rewarded for their work, and it is almost impossible to pay 'market rates' to keep the best and the brightest in the universities. World class universities require a salary structure that rewards productivity.

4. Indian universities are enmeshed in a culture of mediocrity, with little competition either among institutions or academics. Universities are subject to the whims of politicians and are unable to plan for their own futures. Academics are seldom involved in the leadership and management of universities. Bureaucracy governs everything and holds down innovation. Without essential and deep structural change in how universities are governed and in the culture of institutions, there is little possibility for improvement. An additional challenge is that some of the world class universities are to be created by improving existing state universities. This will be extraordinarily difficult, since these institutions are, with very few exceptions, mired in mediocrity and bureaucracy, and hardly amenable to change and improvement, even with the carrot of additional resources. An element of corruption exists at many levels of the higher education system, from favouritism in admissions, appointment to faculty positions, exam cheating, questionable coaching arrangements, and many others. Damaging at all levels; corruption destroys a research culture and makes a world class university impossible.

5. World class universities are deeply meritocratic institutions. They hire the best professors, admit the most intelligent students, reward the brightest academics, and make all decisions on the basis of quality. They reject - and punish - plagiarism, favouritism in appointments, or corruption of any kind. Much of Indian academe, unfortunately, does not reflect these values. Some of the problem is structural. The practice of admitting students and hiring professors on the basis of rigid quotas set for particular population groups - up to 49% - however well intentioned or justified virtually precludes meritocracy. Deeply ingrained in Indian society and politics, the reservations system may well be justified - but to have successful world class universities, meritocracy must be the primary motivating principle.

6. World class universities are research-intensive. All highly

ranked universities in the world exhibit this characteristic. India faces several problems in developing a research culture. It is fair to say that no Indian university today is, as an institution, research-intensive. India's universities can claim a small number of departments that have a high level of research - and many highly accomplished professors work in the system. And some institutions, such as institutes of technology and some non-university agencies like the Tata Institute of Fundamental Research and the All India Institute of Medical Sciences produce impressive research and are respected internationally. The creation of a research-intensive university is mandatory to achieve world class status.

7. Rs 3,280 crores for the 12 new central universities, plus the other impressive amounts announced for related projects, sounds like a lot of money. In fact, it is very inadequate. Creating a world class research university that can play in the best international leagues is an expensive undertaking - to establish and then to sustain. As an example, one large research-intensive new Chinese university cost around US$700 million to build and has a total annual budget of close to US$400 million.

In comparison with China, India probably has more opportunities because of the knowledge of English. The Chinese government, however, has invited more than 50,000 Indians to teach English. But the other advantage for India is its young population. But not only young people, a modern economy need a highly educated and creative population. Reports and research studies on the position of the 11 million students in the 18,000 Indian colleges and universities show that they receive inferior training. Students, educators and business leaders state that there is a heavy stress on obeisance and a neglect of marketable skills. It is not only a lack of knowledge and skills; it unveils the mental behaviour of the graduates. The class room environment infantilizes students up till the age of around 25 years. The emphasis in universities is note-taking and discipline in stead of analysis, debate and persuasion. Except students from the more elite universities, graduates are considered unemployable by top global and national companies. The Indian educational system is locking millions of students in the bottom berth of a two-tier economy of the fullest expression of their talents and denying students a chance to share in the fruits of reform,' writes Anand Giridharadas in the International Herald Tribune (November 20, 2006). Dr. Pratap Bhanu Mehta, a former Harvard professor and former member of the National Knowledge Commission wrote: The University has become a place-holder. My own experiences over the last decades are in accordance with the critical reports.

In a report this association stated that just 10 percent of Indian graduates with generalist degrees were considered employable. In the current situation colleges and universities are depriving the country of the fullest expression of the students' talents and denying them a chance to share in the fruits of reform. The government approach to protect local universities by implementing bureaucratic rules for foreign universities is contradicting the democratic principles and the academic basis concerning free exchange of information. It will certainly not protect Indian Universities, and is not stimulating economic growth. It might prevent individuals and the Indian society from fully participating in the international community. Reports and the many jobless graduates show a fundamental problem in Indian higher education. This is a worrying problem for the expanding Indian economy.

Based on various reports and personal experiences, one can list the following main problems:

a. an old-fashioned didactical method and out-dated approach of students'

b. An important gap between what universities offer and what the society needs

c. Lack of learning soft skills

Pawan Agarwal (2006) has put forwarded the following suggestions (1) the need for clear definition of goals and purposes; (2) emphasis on the preservation of inherent quality and diversity; (3) spread of community/junior colleges across the nation; (4) the establishment of open universities; (5) advancement of social justice; (6) that associate in arts degrees be made generally available after the two years of post-10-year school education, to be followed by two- or three-year-degree courses in different faculties (a mix of the U.S.S.R. and U.S. systems); and (7) that all postsecondary education be properly coordinated and systematized. A listing of the universities in India is appended, and a bibliography and index are provided.

. Higher education in India suffers from several systemic deficiencies. As a result, it continues to provide graduates that are unemployable despite emerging shortages of skilled manpower in an increasing nu mber of sectors. The standards of academic research are low and declining. Some of the problems of the Indian higher education, such as – the unwieldy affiliating system, inflexible academic structure, uneven capacity across various subjects, eroding autonomy of academic institutions, and the low level of public funding are well known. Many other concerns relating to the dysfunctional regulatory environment, the accreditation system that has low coverage and no consequences, absence of incentives for performing well, and the unjust public funding policies are not well recognized. Driven by populism and in the absence of good data, there is little informed public debate on higher education in India.

Abhishek Behl (2006) in his paper on Higher Education has analysed the defects of higher education in India and suggested a lot of policy measures to correct it.The number of Indian students attending higher education institutions in the United States is the highest from a foreign country.Likewise, the number of Indian students going to United Kingdom is increasing and so is the case with Canada, Australia and NewZealand. In monetary terms, Indians are burning millions of dollars to get quality ducation in these countries. And mind you the boys and girls going to foreign shores are not only from the metropolitan cities but also from places like Patiala, Shimla, Karnal, Jammu, KoziKhode, Andamans, Aligarh, Gaziabad and little towns of moffusil India. The reason behind this mass exodus of quality students, willing to shell ten times the amount which they need to spend to get similar education in India perhaps lies in the failure of our education system which has not been able to offer viable and creative solutions meeting emerging demands.

Indian universities were designed by erstwhile European rulers and they functioned on the principles laid by Lord Macaulay and the famous Woods Despatch tabled in 1854. These institutions were basically fashioned to produce clerks, who were adept in bureaucratic work and could assist their colonial masters in their plunder.Unfortunately the British legacy was not laid to rest as soon as we attained freedom. Instead of taking on the gargantuan task of reforming the education system, the country under the leadership of a Cambridge educated Nehru decided to create islands of excellence choosing perhaps the easier way out. As a result of this ham-handed socialist policy, we find ourselves in a mess as our educational institutions have failed to come to terms with the needs of a post-colonial country with a burgeoning population. The Indian Universities particularly outside the Metros remained totally out of sync with the ground realities. Mired in the processes and systems which served the British and the socialist Indian state they continue till date to churn Babus, who are of no use to the Indian industry, picularly, post-privatization, when the role of the Indian government as well as its size has shrinked in the public domain.

In the increasingly knowledge and skill based society slowly evolving amidst us, there was and still is, no need for the millions of graduates and postgraduates, who flaunt their degrees but have vastly underrated skills. Perhaps the Indian system has failed to arm the youth with a skill-set which could empower the learners and enable them to perform their jobs in a better way.In this way, these people have been unable to earn their livelihood and failed to become an asset to the economy. Due to this failure, millions of educated youth in this country are facing stagnation and despite spending lakhs on education, they find themselves in the unemployed ranks. And the reason for this failure is obvious-it lies in the way our higher education institutions function. Instead of imparting skills, they have turned simply into examination centres, where students enter to pass exams and earn their degrees. Learning, meanwhile, has no role to play in this entire process barring a few institutions. Why this happened-again the answer is simple-education for the last fifty years and even earlier has been the last refuge of those, who were a failure in everything they tried their hands on. Bored wives of politicians and bureaucrats, unsuccessful sons of eminent men and educationists and even the progeny of university clerks, officials and even peons managed to get highly paying teaching jobs in these institutions. For these jobs guaranteed lifelong security of tenure, no responsibility and virtually zero accountability. Naturally, the entry of these people, who had no inclination for teaching and research led to an unmitigated disaster which is hurting India more than any political or financial scandals.

The great Indian universities have become mafia rackets where the teachers are the great mafiosi holding the future of the youth and the country to ransom.The syllabus which is being taught here to the undergraduates and post-graduates is the same which was being taught to their grandfathers and great-grandfathers. The so-called Professors do not know what is happening in their respective fields because they are busy in petty intrigues and politics. Instead, of teaching they prefer to become administrators and like to hold posts such as Deans, Registrars and the much touted Controller of Examinations. Lack of accountability and responsibility has been witnessed highest in departments such as Managment and Computer Sciences, where the University run institutes have failed to compete with private sector, despite the fact that they are way ahead in terms of resources. This is perhaps due to the fact that a University teacher has no stake in the future of the students. His job is secure, his promotions secure and his pension all the more secure-so where does teaching come in. Naturally, wealthy Indian students are taking recourse to migrating to the West for higher education.

But, where does this leave us— Just take the example of Jammu University, the University is on an expansion spree, opening new campuses and affiliating numerous B.Ed colleges run by politicians and businessmen in tandem. The Graduates and Postgraduates being churned by this university are facing a universal dilemma-although they have degrees but they dont have the skills to be successful in the job market. But, for the ubiquitous state government jobs, these students have no where to go. The problem is well known, but no one wants to bell the cat. This University is the last refuge of the mediocre teaching talent in the state verging on inferiority.

The syllabus is stale and has not been changed for the last twenty years, except few cosmetic changes. Neither the teachers nor the administrations wants to take the pains of changing the rules of the game as every one is enjoying the power and the pelf. The students, ignorant of the fact that they are being taken for a ride are happy with their degrees and life goes on smoothly. Till they face the harsh realities of the job market.

Similarly, the politics in this academic institution is so virulent that teachers are even in their departments are divided into camps as if they are India and Pakistan. You can imagine the affect it has on the quality of education. As far as research and development is concerned, the university might have produced hundred of PhDs, but not a single world class work has come out of the science or social sciences labs. However, the Indian universities take the lead in one sphere-that is for organizing seminars, lectures and symposiums which earn for the participants lot of TA/DA, earned leaves, visits to exotic locations on government expenses, lavish dinners and the chance to bask in glorious sea of mediocrity. Except for the yearly or half-yearly ritual of conducting exams- most of the Indian universities do little concrete to justify the millions of rupees being spent on them yearly. What is the benefit of a Managment Department or a law Department or a Department of History, when the students passing out are simply not having the skills needed to be a successful manager, lawyer or a art historian. If by reading books one could become a doctor or an engineer or a historian than what is the need of the Universities and their highly paid teachers. All this muddle has led to an acute disenchantment with the higher education system and soon the civil society and the government will have to find a way to clean this mess or else India again will lose the race to become a developed country. We must realize that handful of IIMs and IITs will not make India a superpower and the sooner, we do so, the better it will be.

Engineering education is in a shambles in India. The number of engineering aspirants is much higher than the available seats in good colleges. Owing to poor salary levels, qualified and capable professionals do not take up teaching positions. This has impacted the quality of education: 75 per cent of engineering graduates are unemployable, according to a McKinsey study. While the scenario seems daunting, it is however, possible to ensure that quality education becomes accessible and affordable to all. The total number of children who reach the college-going age every year is two crore. About six lakh of them, or 3 per cent of the age group, take up engineering. These students can do well if there are good teachers. However, most colleges, even those that charge a tuition fee of more than Rs 50,000 a year, lack good teachers. In contrast, IITs remain islands of excellence. However, there are only 5,000 seats in IITs. This amounts to 0.025 per cent of the age group of two crore (At present IIT's have 6992 seats). Owing to the paucity of seats in good colleges, many go overseas for higher studies. These programmes cost a lot of money. Students who pursue undergraduate engineering degrees overseas pay more than Rs 10,000 crore a year Good corporate and bodies should be invited to get into this sector. Two types of career options should be available in colleges: contract appointments for periods of about five years, at salaries suggested in this article, and permanent positions at a much lower pay.

At present we have only regulatory bodies, such as the All India Council of Technical Education. We also need rating agencies, such as CRISIL, that can rank the colleges by performance. Students should be allowed to change their programmes and colleges. Insurance schemes should be available to protect the students. As an example, the Tata group, which has a long and historical association with quality science education, could perhaps take over about a hundred colleges and run them efficiently. The approach suggested here has the potential to firmly establish India as a high-tech education provider for the entire world, providing increased job opportunities for our graduates. It also has a far greater potential than the solutions attempted so far. For example, even if we succeed in doubling the numbers at IITs at a great effort, we will end up upping the number of graduates from 0.025 per cent to only 0.05 per cent of the age group. Reservations to OBCs and other sections in IITs help only a small fraction of the target communities. Strict controls and lack of flexibility discourage good organisations from entering education. Corruption and political interference have resulted in unscrupulous operators cornering most of this sector. Deregulation and the resulting competition will greatly improve the quality of education while keeping the prices under check (Kannan Moudalya, 2009.)

David Malone, who was Canada's High Commissioner to India from 2006-2008, and is now the president of Canada's International Development Research Centre (IDRC), a funder of global development research, has outlined a new capacity building initiative to increase the ability of research institutions to shape economic and social policy. He has stated that in higher education and research, as in all else, India displays a range of contradictions. Its first Prime Minister, Jawaharlal Nehru, deeply believed in the importance of science and of education, launching India on to the path of innovations that were to serve it well in its development trajectory and that today place it among the leading nations of, for example, satellite delivery in space. He believed passionately in greater access to education at all levels, a commendable response to the highly selective colonial policies that had left much of India illiterate. In subsequent decades, literacy rates climbed, and significant progress was made on access to primary and secondary education. As well, the numbers of institutions of higher learning and of university students grew, but, perhaps as a by-product of the priority devoted to wider access, the quality of teaching and student support did not always follow. In contrast to the Indian Institutes of Management and the Indian Institutes of Technology (IIMs and IITs) and other elite institutions gaining international fame, many universities, colleges and deemed universities barely bumped along, serving their students poorly. Student discontent, in these circumstances, was altogether rational — although, manifested in excess, it further weakened the fragile capacity of many such institutions (David Malone, 2009).

UGC REVIEW COMMITTEE

The Government should deregulate higher education in the country to prevent repatriating over Rs 50,000 crore per annum as nearly five lakh students still go abroad to acquire better skills, as stated by industry body ASSOCHAM. The chamber said that higher education in India is so subsidized that on average, an IIT or an MBA student in reputed institutions shell out $120 per month as fees, while people who go for studies abroad spend between $1,500 and $5,000 fee per month for getting engineering or management degrees in the U.S., Canada, Australia and the U.K.. "If higher education is deregulated, there is no reason why India cannot earn $50-100 billion per year and provide at least 10-20 million additional jobs in the field of education alone," it said. Countries like Singapore are planning to have 1, 50,000 foreign students. Australia has about four lakh, which earns for the country a$12 billion per year, it said, adding that India has only 27,000 foreign students and has no plans for any regulated increase because of controls in higher education. The primary reason why a large number of Indian students go out of the country is mainly lack of capacity as domestic institutions are constrained in that respect. About 99 per cent of those who appear in entrance examinations at the IITs and IIMs get rejected. Over 1,50,000 students every year go overseas for university education, which costs India a foreign exchange outflow of $10 billion per annum. This amount is sufficient to build many IIMs and IITs, in India.

Prime Minister Manmohan Singh, while addressing the National Education Day celebrations on 11th November 2009 to commemorate the birth anniversary of the first Union Education Minister, Maulana Abul Kalam Azad, dwelt upon the difficulties being faced by his government in finding teachers for the newly created institutions of higher education and made out a strong case for restoring the prestige and status of the teaching profession. While referring to the shortage of faculty at every stage of education, the Prime Minister focused on the difficulty in finding top-level professors and lecturers in the newly created Indian Institutes of Technology, the Indian Institutes of Science Education and Research, and other such institutions. "This state of affairs cannot be allowed to persist, and I urge all of you to work to address these problems of deficiency in the quality of teaching in our schools, in our colleges and in our universities," Dr. Singh stated. He has stated that the Right to Education (RTE) was one such step, but was quick to point out that its implementation depended equally on expansion of educational infrastructure and availability of trained and qualified teachers. "The RTE alone would require an additional one million teachers," Union Human Resource Development Minister Kapil Sibal said the RTE would take quality education to about 160 million students who were presently out of school.

According to Mr Krishan Khanna, who is doing a study on the education process in India, the country sends abroad over 150,000 students every year for higher education, and, in the process spends $10-$12 billion.

SUGGESTIONS

Human Resource Development Minister Arjun Singh informed the Lok Sabha that there are "significant disparities in the availability of colleges in the rural and urban areas in the country". "Over three fifths of colleges imparting courses in general education are located in urban areas. This figure is over 80 per cent in the case of technical and professional colleges,". He said the government is working to bring improvement in the situation. It has been proposed to start 370 colleges in districts where the enrolment ratio is very low, he said. "Most of these districts also have a concentration of Scheduled Castes, Scheduled Tribes and minorities,". The ministry is also planning to support over 6,000 colleges, which were not given any funding by the University Grants Commission (UGC).There is also a proposal to launch incentive-based schemes for state governments for expanding and starting new institutions of higher education. The UGC provides special grants to universities and colleges located in backward areas to improve their infrastructure to a level where they are able to introduce innovations and meet challenges of globalization of higher education. On the vocational education side, the HRD ministry is planning to establish 600 polytechnics on public-private partnership basis. Similarly, another 400 polytechnics in the private sector are on the anvil, the minister said." The above proposal will ensure support for starting a polytechnic in every district which does not have a polytechnic," the minister added. Only 20 per cent of professional colleges are in rural India. Rural India, where 65 per cent of the population lives, has less than 20 per cent of the country's professional colleges to fulfill their skill-based educational needs.

Stressing the need for quality up gradation of higher education, Kerala Governor R S Gavai while addressing the Republic Day parade after unfurling the national flag at the central stadium in Thiruvananthapuram, on January 26, 2009 stated universities in the state had to be transformed into centers of excellence in research and development and converging the latest trends in knowledge industry". Innovative academic policy and creation of more employment opportunities for the youth is the need of the hour." Promoting discipline and traditional respect for education and the Guru will strengthen India as the choice destination for higher education evoking the traditions of the oldest universities in the world such as those at Takshashila and Nalanda.

When efforts are on to build the nation into a strong and vibrant knowledge economy in coming years through initiatives such as National Knowledge Commission, youth and students of the youngest nation of the world have to become partners in sustaining and nurturing the traditional values of respect for education, which is a great civilizational value. In these testing times, it is our dharma to uphold the tradition exemplified by the great tenet: aano bhadraah krtavo yantu vishvatah (let noble thoughts flow from all sides).

The Ananthamurty Committee, which was entrusted with drafting a policy on the State Higher Education by the Kerala Government, has recommended various policy measures from setting up a college service commission for recruitment of teachers to constituting a scholarship fund for quality improvement in the higher education sector. The report holds that quality is premised on equity. Peaks of excellence arise from a broad base. It steers clear of populist and elitist approaches to higher education and tries to evolve an ambitious model of development within the limits of ground realities. The report tries to balance the claims of the mother tongue and English in the learning process; autonomy and accountability; private and public initiatives in higher education; and functional efficiency and-democratization of administration. Stating that democratization of the administration of universities and colleges would compensate to a great extent the shortcomings of administrators; Dr. Ananthamurthy urged the government to set up a college service commission for the appointment of teachers to government, aided and unaided institutions. While appointment to government institutions could be made by the commission directly, private institutions can appoint teachers from the list prepared by the commission.

The Ananthamurthy Committee (drafted a policy) on higher education has proposed a five-year action plan for revitalizing the higher education sector in Kerala. This can be treated as a model for the entire country. The major 'recommendations made by the committee are:

1. Student should get opportunities for acquisition of existing knowledge and generation of new knowledge. Written assignments, seminars, problem solving sessions, projects, field studies and so on should become integral to any reform in pedagogy. Through a dialogic process, the teacher should induce the student to think, innovate and challenge existing ideas and generate new knowledge.
2. The method of evaluation should be progressively changed to continuous internal evaluation by evolving an open, transparent and fool-proof system with an appropriate mechanism for effective grievance redressal. The credit and semester mode should be preferable to the uniform, annual mode, as the former would give the students an opportunity to select subject combinations of their choice and to encourage more focused learning by dividing the content into manageable chunks.
3. While English may continue as the medium of instruction in the universities and colleges, there has to be some provision for the production of knowledge and its dissemination in the mother tongue -in the-University. This is because there is a greater possibility for the production of knowledge, especially in humanities and social sciences, in the mother tongue than in other languages.

4. Autonomy should be linked up with accountability. We need a decentralized democratic system of academic governance that would translate the ideal of socially accountable autonomy into a living reality:
5. All institutions for higher education, including universities and colleges, should set up Social Accountability Cells (SACs). A system of academic audit and compulsory disclosures should be put in place through these cells.
6. The Right to Information Act (RTI) should be implemented in all higher education institutions. Each institution and each individual teacher should maintain a web site in which basic data regarding the institution, individual and self-assessment reports should be compulsorily posted and updated at regular intervals.

YASH PAL PANEL REPORT

The HRD Minister, Kapil Sibal who has been put on introducing reforms in the higher education system has welcomed that Yaspal Committee report calling the recommendations 'serious'. Terming the report as a roadmap for the Centre to initiate reforms in higher education, Human Resources Development Minister Kapil Sibal said it would be considered for implementation within the next 100 days. He also stated that "Inclusive and excellent quality education is every child's right and we are committed to that issue."

The Committee to Advise on Renovation and Rejuvenation of Higher Education, headed by Professor Yash Pal, expressing concern over the "character and value" of the mushrooming deemed universities, engineering and management colleges – "which are mere business entities dispensing very poor quality education" –, has recommended the establishment of a National Commission for Higher Education and Research (NCHER) as an advisory body responsible for comprehensive and continuous reforms in higher education.

To reduce possibilities of interference, this Commission should be established as a central statutory body through a constitutional amendment and, subsume the existing regulatory bodies such as the University Grants Commission (UGC), the National Council of Teacher Education (NCTE) and the All-India Council for Technical Education (AICTE), the report suggested.

All of higher education cannot be detached from general education. Professional education cannot be detached from general education. It would be, therefore, imperative that all higher education, including engineering, medicine, agriculture and law be brought within the purview of a single, all-encompassing higher education authority.

Rather than acting as bodies giving licenses to professional institutions, professional bodies such as the AICTE, the NCTE, the Medical Council of India, the Bar Council of India, the Council of Architecture, and the Pharmacy Council of India should be looking at whether the people who wish to practice in their respective fields are fit to do so.

They should conduct regular qualifying tests for professionals in their respective fields. Universities should be made responsible regarding the academic content of professional courses, the committee said. The report expressed hope that the proposed Commission would also act as a facilitator and catalyst for joint programmes between different universities and institutions.

Further, recommending that universities should become self-regulating partners in managing the overall education system, the committee said continuous monitoring and inspections caused delays and led to corruption. Asserting that the NCHER would respect the autonomy of universities and not enforce uniformity, the committee stressed on management system within a university while pointing out that some of the best-run central universities, Indian Institutes of Technology and Indian Institutes of Management could show the way to others.

Importantly, the committee favoured the idea of inviting from abroad a substantial number of potentially great academics and scientists to work with students and teachers here (Aarti Dhar, 2009).

Existing institutes should be given three years to develop as universities and fulfill the prescribed accreditation norms. IITs and IIMs should be encouraged to diversify and expand their scopes to work as full-fledged universities. Apart from recommending setting up a seven-member Commission for Higher Education and Research (CHER), it also suggested doing away with multiple regulatory bodies like the University Grants Commission (UGC), All India Council of Technical Education (AICTE) and Medical Council of India (MCI). The proposed

CHER, the report said, should first identify India's 1,500 top colleges for up gradation as universities and then create clusters of potentially good colleges to evolve as universities. Also, all levels of teacher education should be brought under the purview of higher education.

Kaushik Basu (2009) has stated that if we want to attract top talent to research and teaching, we have to allow for pay differentials. The exact modality of this will entail discussion and debate. Two ways of doing this are: First, designating, say, 20 universities, as centers of excellence and putting them on a higher funding scale. The list of top 20 should be evaluated and revised every three years so that all universities stand a chance of getting there. The second option is to select a small number of professors in each field from the entire nation and place them on a higher salary and research support.

Third, we should allow private sector money to come into higher education. Surreptitious privatization is already a fact of life. It will be better to let this happen openly; there can then also be open monitoring. The purely-private colleges should of course not be subsidized by the state. They should be allowed to set college fees as high as they choose (as long as this is made transparent). It is true that such private colleges will end up teaching mainly commercially-viable subjects and cater to relatively rich students. There is no harm in this and some advantages, since the state will now be able to allocate more money to the colleges and universities under its charge and provide good education to the remainder at a lower cost.

Finally, this is the time to consider steps to make India into the world's major hub for higher education. If India can build some good universities with high quality residences for students and advertise globally, India can give this market tough competition.

Narayana Murthy, President of the Infosys Science Foundation, stated that the key to continued success for India in a globalised knowledge-driven economy is building a higher education system that is superior in quality and committed encouragement of relevant research in science and technology. What is needed is an environment where the government, universities, companies, venture capitalists, and other stakeholders come together for the enablement of the entire science eco-system with an eye on future sustainability. The IIT model of success needs to be replicated on a far larger scale. Providing the requisite autonomy to research institutions is an important necessity. Professors, scientists, and institution heads are often the people best informed on the necessary conditions required for the advancement of research goals. They must be enabled with the autonomy to create those conditions. With industry often being the downstream beneficiary of several research efforts, increased interaction between industry and research establishments is important. There needs to be a sound incentive system for the corporate sector involved in scientific R&D as well, with infrastructure and financial benefits, as is the case with the IT industry. This includes viable incentives such as tax breaks for corporate R&D efforts and special economic zones and technology parks for R&D establishments.

In an age where issues of research interest are often global in nature, we must encourage active interaction and exchange with international research institutions. Cross-continental research cooperation and knowledge sharing was at the base of the story of the three winners of the Chemistry Nobel for 2009, among who was Dr Venkataraman Ramakrishnan, of Indian origin. Creating partnerships with relevant peer institutions in India and abroad, hosting events and conferences and getting eminent researchers and scientists to shed light on progress in key research areas and supporting related publications—these measures will go a long way not only in enriching India's research eco-system but also in enticing potential young researchers to the cause. For instance, it should be a practice to invite Nobel Prize winners or similar eminent international scientists for seminars with selected young research minds and students in India at least annually. This could prove a valuable source of insight and inspiration to young potentials. In this regard, I would suggest the creation of an institution like the National Science Foundation, endowed with a suitable corpus from key public and private stakeholders, conferred with the responsibility of regularly undertaking such initiatives.

The importance of rewards and recognition for scientific research cannot be understated as a measure to encourage talented youngsters to consider careers in research. There is a need to recognize and applaud the accomplishments of our researchers and scientists, just as we applaud the achievements of our sportspersons. This must include measures such as financial support to encourage students to adopt research careers, suitable incentives, and awards for scientific achievement. For example, the best and brightest top 1000 students across India with the potential and inclination for research could be provided guaranteed funding for their further education and early careers in research. And the private sector could play the role of a patron here.

The present government has avowed goals to reduce poverty and stimulate development. The Human Resource Development Ministry's efforts to improve the higher education system and the establishment of five new Indian Institutes of Science Education and Research in the past three years will provide a vital boost to the cause of scientific research in India. The need for a strong science eco-system based on a sound research foundation has an integral connect with India's development as a world power. India needs the best intellect available for government, business, military, or any aspect of society to strive for global excellence. Their accomplishments need to be lauded and brought to the forefront. Globally, there are several prestigious awards that ensure due recognition, visibility, and reward for outstanding achievements in research. There is a need to emulate this in India to encourage higher levels of research work with an impact on India's development.

The University Grants Commission (UGC) has framed a regulation making it mandatory for all universities and colleges to be certified by the National Assessment and Accreditation Council (NAAC). UGC Chairman Professor Thorat has stated that the move is an attempt to assess and thereafter ensure the quality of education offered in institutions of higher education in the country. The move is an attempt to assess and thereafter ensure the quality of education offered in institutions of higher education in the country. Currently, certification from the NAAC, an autonomous body with its headquarters in Bangalore established by the UGC in 1994, is voluntary. "While there has been progress in the absolute numbers of students with access to higher education since the time of Independence, the enrolment rate of about 11 percent in India is much less than the world average of 23 percent and not much higher than the *7 percent of Africa,"*. The problem has been addressed in the 11th Five-year Plan, with the government announcing the creation of 1440 new institutions including seven Indian Institutes of Technology (IIT) and seven Indian Institutes of Management (IIM), which he described as the "second wave of higher education in the country." The government's allotment of Rs. 47,000 crore in the 11th plan, instead of the Rs. 400 crore previously has given adequate attention to higher education which was "neglected for the last 40 years,". He also enumerated vast inequalities in gender, religion, caste and income groups, inconsistencies in quality and the lack of relevance to industry among the problems that ail higher education in the country. According to Professor Thorat, "There is a considerable presence of the private sector in higher education," at a session on 'Private Participation in Education – Implications for Equity' organised by the Calcutta Chamber of Commerce. In 1991, there was only one State Private University, whereas today there are 42. Of the 130 deemed universities, 90 are private universities and 95 percent of all colleges are private colleges, he stated adding that in the coming years the numbers were only going to rise (Ananya Dutta, 2009)

A Higher Education Scholarship Fund was launched by the Prime Minister in Thiruvananthapuram early in 2010 and three college clusters were established in as many locations in the State. The draft Ananthamurthy Committee report had also recommended that the system of employing guest faculty in institutions of higher learning be abolished. The committee also recommended that all existing vacancies of teachers in colleges be filled "on a priority basis" (Mahadevan, 2010).

INNOVATION UNIVERSITY

India plans to launch 14 Innovation universities across the country. These 14 new 'innovation varsities' the government has decided to set up will be unique in the context that each university's financial, academic and research structure will be different from the other."These universities will be innovative in their governance, in their financial structure, in their academics and research structure, in their content and in every other way," The varsities will be unique institutions which will set benchmarks in academics, and more importantly, in research comparable to the best in the world, he said speaking at the golden jubilee celebration of IIT Delhi. The rational behind setting up these universities is to support innovation and nurture a different mindset among students. The government wants mentors from leading universities in the US and UK. They include the Massachusetts Institute of Technology, Harvard, Yale and George Washington universities, and Imperial College, London. The 14 innovation universities are to be centers of excellence along the lines of Harvard and Oxford. The government wants the universities to be autonomous entities with no 'regulation from outside'. At present, universities are governed by the University Grants Commission and have limited powers to fix fees or sanction teaching posts. But a 'concept note', prepared by the Education Ministry and circulated to other government departments, says the universities will be allowed to frame their own rules for academics and the qualifications needed for teaching positions. They will have freedom to decide their fees, curricula and rules for the appointment of faculty. The innovation universities are meant to fill a gap in research and also tackle new areas or problems significant to India. These include urbanization, green energy, environmental sustainability and public health.

CONCLUSIONS

According to Prof. Anandakrishnan, all those who are genuinely interested in higher education have articulated the core concerns of the sector often enough. Ever since the nation recognized the value of higher education for promoting economic growth and social development, the pressure for reforms has been escalating. This has been formally embodied in two eminent reports brought out in recent years, one by the National Knowledge Commission headed by Sam Pitroda and the other by the Committee on Renovation and Rejuvenation of Higher Education headed by Yash Pal. The four Bills are: Foreign Educational Institutions (Regulation of Entry and Operation) Bill, 2010; Prohibition of Unfair Practices in Technical, Medical Educational Institutions and Universities Bill; the Educational Tribunal Bill and the National Accreditation Authority Bill. Of them, the Bill on the entry and operation of foreign institutions has created the most controversy. Unfortunately, the criticism of the Foreign Institutions Bill is based on uninformed misapprehensions. Most of the critics tend to ignore the ground reality that more than 200 foreign programmes are offered in India in various modes. The basic premise of the Foreign Institutions Bill is that every foreign educational service provider engaged in offering programmes leading to degrees and diplomas, whether it already operates in India or intends to do so in future either on its own or in collaboration with an Indian partner, must register itself with a designated authority, giving all the necessary information. The apprehension that the legislation will open the floodgates to all kinds of foreign educational institutions is unfounded.

On the contrary, the provision in the Bill against the repatriation of surpluses will effectively prevent the entry of commercially motivated institutions. The requirement that these institutions must have a track record of 20 years in offering recognized and accredited degree programmes in their home country will help weed out fly-by-night operators. They have to comply with the relevant laws of the land. They should deposit Rs.50 crore to meet any liability to students, faculty and others in case they quit or their registration is withdrawn. Beyond the issues covered in these Bills, there are certain fundamental concerns in the reports of the National Knowledge Commission and the Yash Pal Committee which take a long-term view of the higher education scenario. They draw critical attention to fundamental academic weaknesses such as compartmentalization and fragmentation of knowledge systems, absence of innovation in learning methods, disconnect with the society, and excessive emphasis on a multitude of harmful entrance and qualifying tests.

Speaking at the 90th Annual Convocation of the Benaras Hindu University (BHU), our Prime Minster has stated "Only 10 per cent of India's youth go to college as against 40-50 percent in the developed Western countries". "What is even more serious is that two-thirds of India's universities are providing sub-standard education while 90 per cent colleges are below average". "The Green revolution and IT revolution in the country were the results of the growth in higher education;" However, we still have a long way to go to meet the challenges thrown by the developed western world." If any country has to attain an important place in the international community and wants to progress there are three requisites - a strong base of science and technology, a strong defense system and a strong economy". The Prime Minister also emphasized the need for universities to play a larger role in disseminating knowledge to the rural areas. "Universities must realize their responsibility in this regard". He called for improving higher education. Prime Minister expressing concern over the availability and quality of higher education asked colleges and Universities to raise their standards to meet the challenges.

REFERENCE

1. Affirmative Action in Higher Education in India and the US: A Study in Contrasts Asha Gupta, Coordinator, UGC Major Research Project; Visiting Scholar, Center for Studies in Higher Educationhttp://repositories.cdlib.org/cshe/CSHE-10-06/.

2. Education in India http://en.wikipedia.org/wiki/education_in_india
3. Higher Education in India, http://www.academics-india.com/
4. Department of Higher education, Ministry of Human Resource Development, Government of Indiahttp://education.nic.in/higedu.asp
5. Higher Education in India http://www.indiaedu.com/education-india/higher-education.html.
6. Promotion of Higher Education in India, November 04, 2008 http://indiaedunews.net/in-focus/november_2008/promotion_of_higher_education_in_india_6494/
7. Higher Education http://india.gov.in/citizen/higher_education.php
8. http://web.worldbank.org/wbsite/external/wbi/wbiprograms/kfdlp/0,,contentmdk:21812442~menupk:461215~pagepk:64156158~pipk:64152884~thesitepk:461198,00.html
9. Government should deregulate higher education in India: Assocham Press Trust of India New Delhi, January 26, 2009 http://www.hindustantimes.com
10. Philip G Altbach and N Jayaram, "The title of their article in International Higher Education is "India's Effort to join 21st Century Higher Education". INDIA: Effort to join 21st Century higher educationhttp://www.universityworldnews.com
11. Higher education in India Philip G. Altbach, April 12, 2005.http://www.hindu.com/2005/04/12/
12. http://papers.ssrn.com/sol3/papers.cfm?abstract_id=1063601
13. Analysis Present System & Higher Education in India by TA Ramesh February 3, 2007, http://www.boloji.com/analysis2/0181.htm
14. Philip G Altbach, The title of their article in International Higher Education is "India's Effort to Join 21st Century Higher Education". INDIA: Effort to join 21st Century higher education http://www.universityworldnews.com/
15. Pawan Agarwal (2006), ED200145 - Problems of Higher Education in India. An Approach to Structural Analysis and Reorganization. http://eric.ed.gov/ERICWebPortal/custom/portlets/recordDetails/detailmini.jsp?_nfpb=true&_&ERICExtSearch_SearchValue_0=ED200145&ERICExtSearch_SearchType_0=no&accno=ED200145, ICRIER Working Paper No. 180 HIGHER EDUCATION IN INDIA: THE NEED FOR CHANGE http://www.icrier.org/publication/working_papers_180.html

16. Has Higher Education Failed India?Abhishek Behl May 17, 2006 Tags: Higher education http://www.chowk.com/articles/10591
17. Govt. should deregulate higher education in India: Assocham Monday, January 26, 2009 :2000 Hrshttp://www.hindu.com/
18. IANS http://education.in.msn.com/
19. http://www.newkerala.com/topstory-fullnews-81577.html
20. http://www.petitiononline.com/vidya/petition.html
21. Krishnakumar.G,(2009), Aiming for quality change', education plus, the Hindu, February 3, http://www.hindu.com
22. David Malone (2009), "Higher education & research in India: David M. Malone" July 8, 2009: The Hindu, "http://www.youthforequality.com
23. Marwaha (2009)," Right to Education Bill, 2009: Will it help all Indians make the grade? http://www.thehindubusinessline.com
24. Kannan Moudgalya, (2009), "Deregulate engineering education", Wednesday, Aug 12, Education, The Hindu, Business Line, P8.http://www.thehindubusinessline.com/
25. David M.Malone (2009), Higher Education and Research in India, Wednesday, July 8, the Hindu, Kochi, Central Page.
26. Aarti Dhar (2009), Sibal: Yash Pal panel report will be implemented in 100 days Thursday, Jun 25, 2009 http://www.thehindu.com
27. Kaushik Basu (2009) Broad aims, but... Friday, Jun 26, 2009 http://www.thehindubusinessline.com
28. Action on Yashpal panel report in 100 days: Sibalhttp://www.deccanherald.com/
29. The Hindu and Business Line, Various issues.
30. Narayana Murthy (2009), Securing India's Science Future, The Hindu: Opinion / Editorials : Friday, November 13, 2009, www.hindu.com
31. Ananya Dutta (2009) NAAC certification must for all universities and colleges: UGC chief Ananya Dutta, Education, Calcutta, 2009beta.thehindu.com/
32. Mahadevan (2010), Whither higher education reforms?, www.hindu.com/edu/2010/06/22/

❑❑❑

14

Impact of Education in India

P. Ramakrishnan

INTRODUCTION

Efforts have been taken by various educational theorists to compress into a phrase or two, the essential meaning of the term 'education' with its vast implications. *Pestalozzi,* Swiss pedagogue and educational reformer, defined education as a "a natural, harmonious and progressive development of man's innate power.*G.H.Thomson,* taking a biological viewpoint, identifies education with the influence of the environment on the individual with a view to producing a permanent changes in his habits of behaviour,of thought and of attitude. The Spens Report on Secondary Education defines education from rather a functional and practical point of view. According to it, education consists in developing specific habits, memories, ideals, forms of manual and mental skill, intellectual interests, moral ideas and a knowledge not merely facts and conclusions, but also of methods. With education increasingly becoming the primary determinant of overall development in the emerging knowledge economy, India education seeks to become a meeting point for students, teachers, and all those who are concerned.

Basic Education, formerly known as the Wardha Scheme of education, is one of those factors which have exerted a great influence on educational thought today and which has gone a long way towards a new orientation of the aims, ideals and methods of our education in free India. This scheme developed and shaped by the Zakir Hussain Committee which gains importance for other reason also. It attempts for the first time, to relate education to national needs and problems. It visualizes education, not from the point of view of a small privileged community, but from the view point of the masses that have been denied the benefits of education under a system which has been functioning for the last 150 years. This scheme is based on the four resolutions passed at the Wardha Education Conference held in October, 1937.the four resolutions which became the fundamental features of the scheme are:

- Free and compulsory education for seven years
- Mother- tongue to be the medium of instruction
- Process of education to centre round some form of manual and productive work in the shape of a craft
- Self –supporting to the extent of covering teacher's pay.

The Conference appointed a Committee with Dr.Zakir Hussain as its Chairman. This Committee submitted its report after 2 months. It is this report which embodies the detailed plan of basis education, the education that is expected to form the basis of our national life and culture.

The word 'basic' also implies the minimum of learning to be acquired by an average Indian student. Another implication of this word is that education will be linked with the basic needs and urges of human life. One such urge is the basic for creative work. Since education will be basic because it to be correlated with the basic occupations of community life.

The scheme, at first point out the defects of the British system of education it hopes to eradicate these impacts:

- The British system of education has failed to organize and direct its forces tendencies into proper channel
- It does not teach the child to adapt himself to his social and material surroundings because it is divorced from life.
- One of the serious drawbacks is that it is too literary and does not train individual to become useful productive members of society.

- The present educational system is not inspired by any life giving ideal.
- The system benefits only a few privileged beings, hardly 10 % of the teeming millions.
- Our primary education is not enough to create and confirm literacy.

Education in India is mainly provided by the public sector, with control and funding coming from three levels: federal, state, and local. The Nalanda University was the oldest university-system of education in the world. Western education became ingrained into Indian society with the establishment of the British Raj. Education in India falls under the control of both the Union Government and the states, with some responsibilities lying with the Union and the states having autonomy for others. The various articles of the Indian Constitution provide for education as a fundamental right. Most universities in India are Union or State Government controlled.

With the arrival of the British Raj in India a class of Westernized elite was versed in the Western system of education which the British had introduced. This system soon became solidified in India as a number of primary, secondary, and tertiary centres for education cropped up during the colonial era..

Following independence in 1947, Maulana Azad, India's first education minister envisaged strong central government control over education throughout the country, with a uniform educational system. However, given the cultural and linguistic diversity of India, it was only the higher education dealing with science and technology that came under the jurisdiction of the central government.

The National Council of Educational Research and Training (NCERT) is the apex body for curriculum related matters for school education in India. The NCERT provides support and technical assistance to a number of schools in India and oversees many aspects of enforcement of education policies. In India, the various curriculum bodies governing school education system are:

- The state government boards, in which the majority of Indian children are enrolled.
- The Central Board of Secondary Education (CBSE) board.

- The Council for the Indian School Certificate Examinations (CISCE) board.
- The National Institute of Open Schooling (NIOS) board.
- International schools affiliated to the International Baccalaureate Programme and/or the Cambridge International Examinations.
- Islamic Madrasah schools, whose boards are controlled by local state governments, or autonomous, or affiliated with Darul Uloom Deoband.
- Autonomous schools like Woodstock School, Auroville, Patha Bhavan and Ananda Marga

PRIMARY EDUCATION

The Indian government lays emphasis to primary education up to the age of fourteen years (referred to as Elementary Education in India. The Indian government has also banned child labour in order to ensure that the children do not enter unsafe working conditions.However, both free education and the ban on child labour are difficult to enforce due to economic disparity and social conditions. 80% of all recognized schools at the Elementary Stage are government run or supported, making it the largest provider of education in the Country. However, due to shortage of resources and lack of political will, this system suffers from massive gaps including high pupil teacher ratios, shortage of infrastructure and poor level of teacher training. Education has also been made free for children for six to 16 years of age or up to class X under the Right of Children to Free and Compulsory Education Act 2009.

There have been several efforts to enhance quality made by the government. The District Primary Education Programme (DPEP) was launched in 1994 with an aim to universalize primary education in India by reforming and vitalizing the existing primary education system. 85% of the DPEP was funded by the central government and the remaining 15 percent was funded by the states. The DPEP, which had opened 160000 new schools including 84000 alternative education schools delivering alternative education to approximately 3.5 million children, was also supported by UNICEF and other international programmes. This primary education scheme has also shown a high

Gross Enrollment Ratio of 93-95% for the last three years in some states. Significant improvement in staffing and enrollment of girls has also been made as a part of this scheme. The current scheme for universalization of Education for All is the Sarva Shiksha Abhiyan which is one of the largest education initiatives in the world. Enrollment has been enhanced, but the levels of quality remain low.

SECONDARY EDUCATION

The National Policy on Education (NPE), 1986, has provided for environment awareness, science and technology education, and introduction of traditional elements such as Yoga into the Indian secondary school system. Secondary education covers children 14-18 which covers 88.5 million children according to the Census, 2001. However, enrolment figures show that only 31 million of these children were attending schools in 2001-02, which means that two-third of the population remained out of school. A significant feature of India's stem is the emphasis on inclusion of the disadvantaged sections of the society. Professionals from established institutes are often called to support in vocational training. Another feature of India's secondary school system is its emphasis on profession based vocational training to help students attain skills for finding a vocation of his/her choosing A significant new feature has been the extension of SSA to secondary education in the form of the Madhyamik Shiksha Abhiyan.

India's higher education system is the third largest in the world, after China and the United States. The main governing body at the tertiary level is the University Grants Commission (India), which enforces its standards, advises the government, and helps coordinate between the centre and the state. Accreditation for higher learning is overseen by 12 autonomous institutions established by the University Grants Commission.

As of 2009, India has 20 central universities, 215 state universities, 100 deemed universities, 5 institutions established and functioning under the State Act, and 13 institutes which are of national importance. Other institutions include 16000 colleges, including 1800 exclusive women's colleges, functioning under these universities and institutions. The emphasis in the tertiary level of education lies on science and technology. Indian educational institutions by 2004 consisted of a large number of technology institutes. Distance learning is also a feature of the Indian higher education system.

Some institutions of India, such as the Indian Institutes of Technology (IITs), have been globally acclaimed for their standard of education. The IITs enroll about 8000 students annually and the alumni have contributed to both the growth of the private sector and the public sectors of India. Besides top rated universities which provide highly competitive world class education to their pupil, India is also home to many universities which have been founded with the sole objective of making easy money. Regulatory authorities like UGC and AICTE have been trying very hard to extirpate the menace of private universities which are running courses without any affiliation or recognition. Students from rural and semi urban background often fall prey to these institutes and colleges. Three Indian universities were listed in the Times Higher Education list of the world's top 200 universities — Indian Institutes of Technology, Indian Institutes of Management, and Jawaharlal Nehru University in 2005 and 2006. Six Indian Institutes of Technology and the - Pilani were listed among the top 20 science and technology schools in Asia by . The Indian School of Business situated in Hyderabad was ranked number 12 in global MBA rankings by the *Financial Times* of London in 2010 while the All India Institute of Medical Sciences has been recognized as a global leader in medical research and treatment.

CURRICULUM ISSUES

Modern education in India is often criticized for being based on rote learning rather than problem solving. *BusinessWeek* denigrates the Indian curriculum saying it revolves around rote learning and *ExpressIndia* suggests that students are focused on cramming.

Central Government Involvement

Budget

As a part of the tenth *Five year Plan* (2002–2007), the central government of India outlined an expenditure of 65.6% of its total education budget of Rs. 438250 million, or (Rs. 287500 million) on elementary education; 9.9% (Rs. 43250 million) on secondary education; 2.9% (Rs. 12500 million) on adult education; 9.5% (Rs. 41765 million) on higher education; 10.7% (Rs. 47000 million) on technical education;

and the remaining 1.4% (Rs. 6235 million) on miscellaneous education schemes.

CONLUSION

Thus the government is compelled to show its soft corner towards the development of higher education only rather than primary and secondary educations in India. Scientific knowledge and technological skills play a significant role in shaping the contemporary world scenario. These advancements are a consequence of higher education leading to the genesis of what is known as a Knowledge Society. Man is now better equipped in understanding the genesis of the universe. Geographical and national boundaries of modern world are fast getting erased with flashing of information at an unimaginable rate and accuracy. Man is now better equipped in understanding the genesis of the universe. But somehow he or she is obviously influenced by the consequence of higher secondary education in one's life. Each and everyone is dispensed with such an indomitable kind of knowledge at the beginning of a true learning where it begins with the college studies that is during one's under graduate level of studies. Before getting into the domains of knowledge, a student is supposed to analyse basic components of the given subject. But what happens in course of school or higher secondary education, they are simply asked to memorize the prescribed materials and make them to reproduce the same thing in the upcoming examination or test. So what sort of mentality the students will have? In such an occasion they are forced to indulge in the process of mere memorization without understanding the essence of the subject given to them. Since Information technology brought about a contraction of spatial dimensions molding the knowledge society to a global village for the past one decade yet they didn't attained their objective of true learning. This is due to the poorly qualified teachers of higher secondary education and their lesson plan. They are also reproducing the same thing which is given in prescribed text book and are unable to give out their own example relevant to that exercise. Let us take for example, the teaching of English to school level that is secondary and higher secondary, they are not at all interested in teaching them the basic nuances of school grammar. Hence higher secondary education evidently exerts a profound influence rather than the secondary education in the current milieu which leads to great social changes.

Though India is a developing country, it posses a lion's share of highly eminent young scientists, scholars, teachers, assistant professors, doctors, physicians, managers, CEO's and so on. But at present, in India there is not even a single guide to lead them in the path of light. Because most of the senior guides were simply the imitator of what they did in their school studies of mere a machine does it now. They don't know how to face a problem or a doubt triggered by a student. In India there are more than 100 crore people but only a third part of them are able to read. In case of other nation Indian education is falling behind. This is a country where maximum people are in a economical and social problem due this reason the Indian education program is continuing under fall. The education system of rural area is too poor. Many student of rural area receive a poor education and more of them are supposed to leave the school before the 5th standard due to some social factor which may act as a hurdle in continuous development of education. As a result of their incapability to explain certain things may lead a good student to curtail his or her creative thinking which on a large scale plays a vital role in an innovation of ideas.

REFERENCES

1. B.D.Bhatia, The Theory and Principles of Education (Philosophical & Sociological Bases of Education). New Delhi: Doaba House Book Sellers & Publishers, 1981.
2. http://egovindia.wordpress.com/2006/06/24/some-aspects-of-higher-education-in-india-and-its-impact-on-the-north-eastern-region/
3. http://india_resource.tripod.com/britishedu.htm

□□□

15

Spread of the Innovative Approaches of Rishi Valley Rural Education Project to the Schools of Tamil Nadu

S. Ramya Devi

Recent years have been marked by widespread dissatisfaction with public education system and attempts were made to find more successful approaches in educating the children. Not surprisingly, educators have sought to offer innovative and alternative schooling models. Individuals and organisations since then are getting involved with improving the quality of education in government schools. They are seeking to make teaching-learning more innovative and relevant, to ignite the students' natural desire to learn and prepare them for a rapidly changing world. Therefore, the introduction of innovative approaches came from the concerns to make compulsory education a meaningful and relevant experience for the child.

In India, the need for innovative approaches in the formal schools has been felt by various providers of education and has a fairly long history. Some of these innovations have continued for a few years only while others have managed much longer periods of existence, even getting legitimately assimilated or institutionalized by the larger 'mainstream'. The Rural Education programme (RIVER) of Rishi Valley Education Trust (Andhra Pradesh) is an interesting example of how an innovation started by responding to local specific needs developed into a "model" that is being adopted in different parts of the country and even spread to other countries.

The innovative approaches of the RIVER have become a model to many of the states in improving the teaching-learning experience for the past two decades. Started in 1986, 12 satellite schools have been established so far, where learning happens through the teaching-learning methodology called **'Learning Ladders'**[1] developed uniquely to address multi-grade classrooms for the rural children. Inspired by the principles of pedagogy, this innovative approach was later adapted in different states under different names. Their significance is not just in running the program, but the extent to which it had spread in the other systems. Their efforts to make school education innovative have spread to different places because of their proven effectiveness. Such interventions have received support and also endorsement from the Ministry of Human Resource Development and other central and state departments. In addition, the governments' educational policies have played a decisive role in determining its innovation and wider expansion. This innovative and alternative approach was adopted and implemented by Tamil Nadu government in its primary schools.

'Activity Based Learning' (ABL) in Tamil Nadu has been developed based on the Rishi Valley experience and initially adapted on an experimental basis in 13 corporation schools in Chennai in 2003. Further it has been up-scaled to 37,500 schools in the state by the State Department of Education with the support of Sarva Shiksha Abhiyan (SSA) and UNICEF. Many adaptations in this new design have been made in order to fit into the spaces, which was hitherto untouched. Rishi Valley Model has been adopted in several other states, including Kerala, Uttar Pradesh, Rajasthan, Gujarat and Madhya Pradesh (UNICEF, India). **'Nali Kali'** in Karnataka is one of the initiatives drawn from the RIVER. While the rest of the states have limited their expansion only to few districts, Tamil Nadu has adapted it in a large-scale, extending to the whole state.

The present paper aimed to understand how an innovation of Rishi Valley School model is developed, carried, modified and institutionalized into system-wide practice in Tamil Nadu, with special consideration to the factors that facilitate and inhibit the development of innovation, which includes ideas, people and context over time in the field of education. This required an understanding of the processes, events and relationships in the context of innovation. In order to do this, various secondary sources were used to trace the movement of innovation from Rishi Valley Rural Education Center to the schools of Tamil Nadu. The field work was also conducted at three places to trace the movement of innovation: Rishi Valley Rural Education Centre in the state of Andhra Pradesh, Chennai district and Tiruppur district of Tamil Nadu. Major inputs on the various aspects of innovation have been collected through observation, semi-structured interview and informal discussions from various stakeholders involved in the process of innovation.

WHY NEW IDEAS ARISE?

When the existing system is not satisfying, or could not respond to the newly emerging challenges, new ideas or innovation arises. J. Krishnamurthi states that, *'Unless we voluntarily bring about a radical change in education, we are directly responsible for the perpetuation of chaos and misery'* (1992:31). This deep sense of discontentment, with the existing system of education leads to the development of Rishi Valley School in 1929. The Rishi Valley School (RVS) has over the years developed a "culture" which has kept the rural children from nearby villages out of reach. Another important reason is that, the tiny villages were without primary schools and the children have to walk several miles to attend schools. This further necessitated starting an educational programme separately for the rural children. But how to transact education in the rural school became another issue of concern.

The development of new ideas or innovation in the rural school also rose with the deepest discontentment with the existing system. In a close study and analysis of elementary schools nearby Rishi Valley School, it has identified some of the major problems like high dropout rate, low rate of learning, teacher-directed and multi-grade situation with high student-teacher ratio. The discontentment became apparent to them with the mono-level learning material, in which all children are expected to be at the same stage of learning at a given time, was not suitable to the rural classroom. Also the real situation of the classroom is multi-grade, but the teachers are trained for mono-grade classroom situation. This helped in developing a framework for redesigning the whole outlook towards curriculum of the village schools.

It was found from the experience of Rishi Valley (Andhra Pradesh) that, innovation was born out of strong discontentment with the existing system. The process reflects the critical way in which the organizations responded to the perceived challenges. Nohria and Gulati rightly points out that innovation are vital for the organizational adaptation and renewal (1996: 1245). It helps in refining one's own system to address the challenges it is facing. Also, an innovation does not have to be a completely new idea; it may be just new to those that are pursuing it for the first time (Van De Ven, 1986). Though the ABL methodology is perceived as new to the people involved, it is an "innovation' in Tamil Nadu, even though it may appear to others to be an "imitation" of RIVER methodology.

Innovation is always perceived as a new idea and it is often viewed as a "good thing" because the new idea must be useful-profitable, constructive, or solve a problem. The MGML methodology at REC is a new idea because, the regular textbook was replaced by carefully designed 'study cards' and 'work cards' supported by a pictorial 'achievement ladder' which gave a clear sequential organization of this self-learning material. The innovation was not just limited to the classroom process, but it also tried to bridge classroom learning to the outer world. Thus, the learning transcended the boundaries of school to the community. It had another important objective of bringing in community participation in education process.

DEVELOPMENT OF INNOVATION

The ideas before getting mainstreamed goes through various stages. Initially, ideas got institutionalized when the Rural Education Centre was set up in mid 1970s. Thus, Institutional framework provided this idea to develop from mere "abstract" to a "concrete" reality. In the next stage, the ideas were shared with different people. Various people were involved in carrying these ideas through different stages. As Van De Ven (1986) also points out that these ideas are developed and implemented by people who over time engage in transactions with others within an institutional context. The methodology got confirmation from various people which further propelled the movement. The confirmation became even stronger when other individuals and organizations appreciated and showed interest in adopting it in their settings.

Various steps were taken in managing this idea into "good currency"[2] so that it is implemented and institutionalized. Firstly, for any ideas to spread in a useful manner, application of those ideas (innovation) has to happen. The living culture of REC has given a right platform for the development of innovation. Also, it cannot be denied that those who were involved in the development of RIVER to a great extent were/are influenced by J. Krishnamurthi's philosophy. Secondly, the methodology wouldn't have gained good currency if it had not been designed on the line of the national curriculum. The methodology has taken in various aspect of J.Krishnamurti's philosophy, but carefully brought it down to the practice to fit within the framework of the "regular" school curriculum.

For J. Krishnamurti, the real issue in education was "to see that when the child leaves the school, he is well established in goodness, both outwardly and inwardly... The child is to be open, aware and fearless" (Krishnamurti, 1992). The result was the opening of Rishi Valley School (RVS). To him, the purpose of education is not merely to pass examinations after learning a few facts and acquiring some skills, but to understand the complexity of life. He urged the students to appreciate their role in the creation of a 'new' world without fear, conflict or contradiction. This could only be done if there was 'right education' in an atmosphere of freedom, without fear or authority, where intelligence and goodness could be nurtured (Krishnamurti, 1992).

The invention of the new ideas (methods) may be an individual activity but pushing and riding those ideas into good currency becomes a collective activity (Schon, 1971). The multi-grade methodology did not gain good currency until the community was "involved" in the schooling process. It has made a deeper connection with the community and the nature by bring it close to their 'local' culture. Each community has a sense of "ownership" in the satellite schools as they have actively participated in various activities of the schools. The methodology gained support also because of the "perceived" effectiveness. This had helped in building enough justification for the methodology.

MOVEMENT OF INNOVATION

The ideas of RIVER have been adopted in Tamil Nadu as 'Activity Based Learning', and it has been introduced in all the government and government-aided primary schools of Tamil Nadu. Though the ideas have travelled to all the schools in 2007, the experiments on ideas started way back in mid nineties. It has crossed various stages to get to this place. Though the development of idea began in 2003, but the efforts to make the idea to reach public consciousness and gain attention started way back in 1993, in Vellore District of Tamil Nadu, when 20 special schools were started for the children who had been freed from being bonded labor. Most of the officials are aware of the stage, when idea entered the formal system in Chennai District in 2003.

In the case of Tamil Nadu, the search for innovative approaches in education had started in mid-nineties as an effort to provide quality education for the children, who had been freed from bondage in Vellore Districts of Tamil Nadu. Looking at the abysmal situation of these children, 20 special schools were started for these children under the central government scheme for the child labors, "*Kulanthai Tholilaral Nalvalvu Iyakkam*" (Child Labor Welfare Association) in 1993. These special schools were also called as Non-Formal Centers, started with Special schools were started because these children of varying ages from 6 to 14 did not get admitted in the regular schools. In the special schools, teachers and volunteers were appointed keeping the student-teacher ratio as 1:20-25. Those who were educated and unemployed were specially appointed as teachers for those schools. The method of teaching in the regular schools was found to be unattractive.

There were various methods tried on an experimental basis in those Non-Formal centers. The methods and materials, which were devised by Tamil Nadu Science Forum (TNSF), to help the children catch up on the lost years of childhood, seemed both appropriate and attractive. TNSF prepares subject books, based on activities and games to make learning interesting and enjoyable. To give training to those teachers, a team of 20 were formed comprising members from TNSF, 'Arivoli Iyakkam' (Literacy Movement) and government teachers under '*Karpathu Karkande*'. Some of the teachers, gaining the support of the District administrators, this initiative started initially with 20 special schools further got extended to 60 special schools.

This initiative became well known and gained momentum as public became aware of it. To begin with, 60 head masters of the regular schools came for the training. Further, 7000 teachers from more than 2000 schools from all over the Vellore district were given training, which was sponsored by UNICEF. Later, the district level initiative gained momentum and became a state level initiative. It was introduced in all the primary schools of Tamil Nadu with the help of UNICEF under the name '*Katralil Inimai*' (Joyful Learning). In 2003, with the initiative of Tamil Nadu Education Department, a group of 30 teachers- two each from the selected 13 schools across zones and supervisory staffs were sent to Rishi Valley for a training program. They implemented the methodology on a pilot basis for a year in these 13 schools.

The event marked the initial movement of the innovation from the non-formal system to the formal system. One important thing to note here is that, on returning to Vellore, the teachers of the special schools did not wonder if such a joyful learning programme would be possible in the Non-Formal centers. They might have wondered, if they have to introduce it in the formal schools. The non-formal setups were more flexible for the new experiments. So, enough justification was initially "built" in the non-formal setup in Vellore district of Tamil Nadu before it got to the formal set up. Further, the experiment began in 13 model schools of the Chennai District. These schools were the forerunners for the others to follow. It shows clearly that, the innovation (ABL) which has been tried out on pilot basis in 13 schools are likely to be accepted more readily, since there is less risk involved. It is helpful for the system to try out innovations on a small scale, and carefully monitor and evaluate them, before proceeding further to implement it on a large scale. These schools are serving as the demonstrating site of the innovation. The schools that represent the original idea are still joining the list of model schools. Since the commitment to an innovation has been made and much time, energy and effort expended in its development and implementation, there is a strong reluctance to discontinue it. They served as a nodal school for reflection, experimentation and interaction which helped in further up-scaling of the process.

It was clear from the experiences of Tamil Nadu that the users were active participants and not a passive receiver. They searched for solutions, from which one was selected and applied. When the solution was an appropriate one, it lead to a reduction of the originally felt need. When it was not the right solution, the search was repeated until RIVER methodology was found as an appropriate need-reducing solution. Also, during any of the intermediate stages between initial awareness of the innovation and ultimate use the receiver in Tamil Nadu was free to adopt or reject it.

The innovations in Tamil Nadu which were in peripheral areas began to surface to the mainstream as a result of the efforts of people who supplied the energy necessary to raise the ideas over the threshold of public consciousness. They, in turn, exerted their own influence on the ideas by further developing them and providing them with a "catchy slogan" and "new names" that provided emotional meaning and energy to the idea (Schon, 1971). At each point of departure the name of the innovation in Tamil Nadu has been changed viz. *Karpathu karkande, Katralil Inimai* and Activity Based Learning. In addition to that, various international organizations also provided a support system by "recognizing" and "promoting" the innovation. These recognitions gave a "validation" for the innovation and in turn provided greater chance for the promotion of the innovation. As the results were encouraging, the innovation was extended to all 264 schools in Chennai Corporation during 2004 in the extension phase. Finally in June 2007, out of the Chennai Corporation experience, ABL was scaled up to the extent that covers the entire State. Thus, the ideas were absorbed in to the entire primary education in Tamil Nadu.

While taking a long journey from one place to another and from one hand to another, the idea undergoes changes. The original idea gets modified during the adaptation process, but it also gets diluted in the large scale adoption process. Activity Based Learning in Tamil Nadu is not the exact replication of RIVER methodology. In the ABL, "there are significant departures from and improvements on the Rishi Valley materials" (Anandalakshmi). Also, the flexibility in the RIVER methodology leaves more space for adaptability of the same in the different context. When the methodology was adopted in Tamil Nadu it was flexible enough to be able to incorporate the local context. The teachers adapted Telugu materials to Tamil and researched into suitable folk and local cultures to include in the curriculum. Thus, strong sense of 'ownership' over the methodology has been developed during the process of adaptation. By changing the methodology to address the local context, a sense of belonging was also built.

KEY ACTORS IN THE PROCESS OF INNOVATION

'Key actors' were the people who played an important role in each stage in the process of innovation. Innovators, core group, interest groups, administrators, politicians, principals and teachers are the key actors in the process of innovation. Firstly, innovators were responsible for the innovation (new idea or method or device) which may be originally developed or at times may be adopted. The main task of the innovator is to show as effectively as he/she can the validity of the innovation in terms of the gains to be achieved by adopting it. Not everyone who produces new ideas or methods becomes an innovator. Which means the innovation experimented by various people either did not address the problem of the situation or the motivation and commitment level was not strong. When the "need" for developing an innovative methodology for the rural schools in Rishi Valley and special schools in Tamil Nadu has been met by the innovators: Mr. Padhmanaba Rao & Mrs. Rama Rao and M.P.Vijaya Kumar at the respective places, their arrival itself has marked as a "turning point".

The innovators reacted to the innovations presented to them and it's the nature of their reaction which determined subsequent stages of adoption. Having been made aware of various innovations, they showed interest in it, there followed a series of stages which culminated in acceptance of some of the innovations and rejection of the other innovations. Finally, they proposed innovative methods for these schools to make learning relevant and interesting. They were convinced of the benefits of the proposed innovation and they communicated these to their colleagues to "convince" and therefore adopted the innovation.

The actor's motivation and energy played an important role in transacting the innovation into a system. The innovator is generally self-motivated to make a change in the society. The self-motivated innovators were able to collect "motivated" and "like-minded" individuals for the development of the innovation. Only minimum resistance was created by them. The process of adoption became easier with the minimum resistance at the initial stage. For example, in addition to M.P. Vijaya Kumar, there were many more motivated individuals who joined the process of adoption of the innovation at different levels in Tamil Nadu. Their motivation alone could not have brought a change in the system, but also the "time and place" which provided "right" atmosphere to cultivate their motivation. Outside agencies also provides motivation which places a sense of responsibility to the actors to carry forward the innovation. The appreciation and support of many individuals and agencies further motivated them for the expansion.

The innovator was constantly engaged in finding better ways of meeting the needs of the schools. He used many means for making the teachers of the school increasingly aware of what constitutes a good adoption. With his leadership style he was able to identify the teachers of a school who were creative and committed, who had ideas for change with which they experimented, and who were thus instrumental in bringing new procedures to the school. He used them effectively for the adoption of innovation. Also the break down of hierarchy and a dynamic interchange of ideas triggered the movement of innovation.

The "dynamic" approach of the leader could convince the higher officials to the teachers. With the strong commitment and the hard work the leader could trigger the people around. These innovations were dependent on the quality of leadership. Initially, the system faced problem in internalizing it, as a new innovation introduced. Till it got internalized, a strong support system has been established. Supportive leadership was, therefore, equally essential to create a core that carried the process forward within the organization.

PROVIDING MOTIVATIONAL AND ENERGY INPUT

Innovations demand one or more actors whether individuals or groups to become bearers of change. Therefore, innovation identified by the innovator was communicated to the core group consisting of dedicated people and further various interest groups were evolved during the process. Some of them, who were trained at Rishi Valley, became the core group. Others were trained by the core group. It is very important to notice that a handful of "dedicated" people were collected for the initial training and adaptation who were easily convinced of the innovation and triggered the movement by further involving others for the cause.

Some individuals and groups were effectively organized and engaged in collective action when they became members of the interest groups. These Interest groups received dues and contributions from its members in order to accomplish its agenda. Some people likely joined the movement to express an ideological or moral value that they believed in. Media also encouraged the dissemination by selectively favouring the innovation. The analysis of Newspaper clipping shows that the media attended "selectively" to the most favourable aspects of ABL. These groups provide necessary energy and motivation for propelling the movement.

Institutionalization of the Innovation

The innovation might have discontinued, if the innovator merely introduced the innovation to the schools. Such innovators appear to regard innovation as a single act rather than as a process and appear to be concerned with merely introducing innovation and not with the more difficult tasks of development and maintenance. By involving the educational administrators and other officials helped in implementing the methodology and there by institutionalizing the innovation. They help in creating the structures and systems necessary to sustain and make the innovation an integral part of the system. The ABL programme has been internalized to an extent that most of the higher officials of the education department visualize it as "their" program. Various departments were also interlinked to seek support for the adoption of innovation.

In order to survive, innovation must be supported by those with political power in an active way rather than through merely formal or legal channels. These political conditions may be understood as being the extent of the 'political will' that supported ABL project, from the specific combinations of forces, specifically those agents and groups that support this innovation and those who were indifferent and antagonistic. Education Minister of the state is the instrumental for state-wide adoption of ABL. He was able to convince the Chief Minister. Though it was a team work, the government's support was a key factor for making an attempt to convince the whole state for the innovation. The 'Government Order' for implementing in all government primary schools and aided schools shows the extent of the support. They also helped during the adjustment process while the project was implemented. It was important to gain the 'political will' of those responsible for its approval, as well as granted necessary resources and staffs to undertake the planned activities.

INVOLVEMENT OF PRINCIPALS AND TEACHERS

Educational innovations diffused at a considerable rate from their sources to the educational institutions, but this did not ensure their adoption in the school system unless and until the teacher developed a very favorable attitude towards them. The principal also occupied a key position so far as implementation of a new practice in the school was concerned. So the class-room teachers as well as their principal have to be fully exposed to educational innovations. The success of adoption and adaptation of any innovation ultimately depended on them.

It was usually the Principal who took the initiative in introducing innovations into the school, and even where this was not the case his/her support was necessary for any innovation proposed by a member of staff either within the school or outside the school. Along with other factors the principal aided the adaptability of her school by doing more to turn the sentiment of her teachers to one which favoured ABL. Teachers utilized every means at her command to create a situation most stimulating to the teachers who were high in initiative and creativity. Wherever the principal was less motivated to adopt the innovation, the schools tend to do just the mechanical transfer of ABL.

The principal are able to recognize the problems created by the present educational methods and to device solutions for these problems. The recognition of educational issues offers the best opportunity for creating a more adaptable school. There are many factors which influence the ability of a school to eliminate out-worn practices and to be on the alert for innovation. The willingness on the part of the principal to effect the changes needed to bring his/her school to meet the desired objective. If this is done there will be little question as to whether the principal is an obstacle in the path of adoption of innovation for her school or the driving force that makes adoption possible.

An innovation that is appropriate for one school may not be so for another and what works in one school may not in another. Though the rate and degree of adoption and of an innovation adaptation depends on various factors, the involvement of Principal and teachers becomes the key element. The teachers were more inclined to favor adoption of innovation in their school once they were supported by the Principal. This indicated that the bulk of initiation of adaptations must still remain the concern of the administrator. Some teacher adopted it eagerly, quickly and with enthusiasm, while others were more cautious, reluctant and hesitant and were under circumstances, rejected them in their own way, if not obvious.

The tasks of planning and implementing innovations brought work in addition to the normal teaching duties of teachers. Some teachers found participation in innovation so stimulating and exciting that they willingly accepted the extra work. In case of a model school, such teachers were in the forefront to showcase their school's innovation to the visitors. In addition, the principal used these teachers for sloughing off outmoded practices and gained support of other teachers for the adaptation of ABL in their school. There were other teachers, however less enthusiastic about innovation or perhaps deriving their professional satisfaction from their classroom activities, who were much less willing to take on the additional task of adapting the innovation.

SUPPORTING POLICIES AND DISCOURSES

Different situations present different opportunities for innovation. "Time" and "place" played an important role in providing the "right" platform for the innovation to develop. The time period and the context gave rise to spaces that were susceptible to the adoption of ABL programme. Many critics in this period have condemned the rigidity of the present education system. This dominant discourse is the collection of expectations on the quality of schools which are generally taken for granted. It provided crucial platform for this innovation to happen.

Among many critics, Paulo Freire (1972) has stimulated worldwide interest and discussion on the oppressive nature of formal education. Rabindranath Tagore also pointed out limitations in the conventional schools set up in India by colonial authorities. He favored, Mahatma Gandhi's call for noncooperation with contemporary education, saying: "There are times when it may be more educative to boycott schools rather than joining them." (Chakrabarti, 1993) This thought was echoed many years later, in Ivan Illich's *Deschooling Society* (1971).

The founders and pioneers of education such as John Dewey, Maria Montessori, among others, have examined education from alternative perspectives and insisted that education should be understood as the art of cultivating the moral, emotional, physical, psychological and spiritual dimensions of a developing child. Similarly, Tagore set up his own alternative to the prevailing system: Vishva Bharati, in Santiniketan, located in the eastern Indian state of West Bengal. Classes here were and still are held in the lap of nature (Chakrabarti, 1993). Gandhi developed *Nai Taleem* or New Education. In Gandhian schools, a few hours a day are devoted to reading and writing, and another few to the performance of 'bread labor'—crafts-work, agriculture, cooking, cleaning (Singh, 2008)

Gujrat-based Gijubhai Bhadeka set up Dakshinamurti Bhavan, a school in Gujarat. Gijubhai worked with children in the village context, teaching them history, geography and other subjects in a way that would appeal and be relevant (Aggarwal & Gupta, 2008). Sri Aurobindo and the Mother developed their idea of education for the whole person. The Mother worked closely with children, evolving a philosophy of 'Free Progress', each child developing and flowering in an absolutely spontaneous, inwardly centered and self-directed, process (Aurobindo, 1995).

The trend is highlighting the ills of the formal system developed mainly due to the pressures brought on the system by the humanist-deschooler lobbies who effectively articulated the arguments in favour of reforming formal education. They demanded that the learning system be made more open, participative and interesting. Some of their experiments serve as the demonstrating ground for the innovative practices. This had created a "sound" platform for the educational reformation to take place.

Apart from the educational critics, there has been a general concern for the educational administrators and policy makers that the quality of education in government schools were bad, when one teacher was expected to manage multi-grade classes- even in schools with two or more teachers. The state level administrators were open to innovative methods to revitalize primary schools. The idea of joyful learning was not new and has been accepted as an important dimension of educational reform. Policies have also played a role in determining innovation and spread. Some of the policies have highlighted the "child-centred" and "joyful learning" which provided a strong base for the adoption of ABL in the State.

The National Policy on Education (NPE) 1986 emphasized the need for a 'child-centred approach' at the elementary school level. Another important policy initiative was the effort of the National Advisory Committee appointed by the MHRD in 1992 to advice on how to reduce the burden on school students while improving the quality of learning (Learning without Burden). Following that Yashpal committee report prepared in 1993 suggested burden free education, emphasizing child-centred education at a large scale. Very recently, Right to Education Act, 2009 has further substantiated a child-friendly education.

With a great lobby of critics and policy makers debating on the poor quality of government schools, the ABL system has brought in a sea change in classroom environment by addressing various needs of the time. It has transformed the classroom from a set of passively learning children and a commanding teacher to a mainly self-learning system. The in-built flexibility in the methodology gave space for the teachers to be innovative and thereby teacher gained the ownership feeling over ABL. The various aspects of ABL methodology address important issues that have been raised in the education sector and thus it seemed to be appealing to various stakeholders in the field of education. The visual appeal and the strengths of the methodology has even attracted the administrators and thereby favouring the adoption to the whole state.

While looking at the "favourable" aspects of ABL methodology, one may ignore the "reality" in the schools. Not all schools are similar in adopting the methodology. At an ideological level every educational institution is innovative. But at a practical plane, only very few select schools tend to be so; only some schools are known for their innovative proneness and practices while others are not. So, it is also very important to question why some schools are always in the fore front of educational modernization and progress, while others lag behind.

RESISTANCE FOR THE ADOPTION OF INNOVATION

There was vociferous protest from many of the teachers about sitting on the floor, the seemingly chaotic classroom, the variety of symbols used, about multi-grade classroom. Moreover, it would be extremely naive to expect no resistance to proposed innovations. Some of them are most conformist to tradition and are not easily convinced of the utility of an innovation. They do not want to make any changes, even if these changes appear to be for the better. Many feel that new ideas for improving education are fine in theory but do not work out in practice.

Initial resistance to change was a widespread and strong. Establishing causes for the resistance proved to be extremely difficult, because in some cases teacher felt that it was not in their best interest to admit to feelings of inadequacy or insecurity and so the reasons given may not be the real ones. So the resistance was present but not openly expressed. It was very superficial to take just the face value of the causes presented by the teachers. Some of them were found to be most conformist to tradition and were not easily convinced of the utility of an innovation. Many felt that new ideas for improving education are fine in theory but do not work out in practice. Individuals also tend to resist most strongly at the point where the pressures of change were greatest because they look at the change as a threat.

When the innovation proved to be successful, early skepticism turned into recognition of its utility. If the positive side of the resistance was considered, the idea of overcoming resistance was no longer appropriate. It becomes more appropriate to think in terms of taking account of resistance. The members of an organization showed resistance to an innovation unless they had been involved in its formulation. Participation in decision-making found to be a means of coping with resistance to innovation.

CONCLUSION

The transformation of innovation as an idea into the practices in the classroom situation has taken different forms. It has also traveled beyond the place of origin to different places and cultures. The development of innovation and it spread to different places did not happen on its own without key actors and supporting context. Thus the findings of the study provided an insight on the various aspects that go in making the innovation from a 'model' to a state-wide practice. This has important implications for educational administrators and the researchers to understand that there are a number of interlocking elements that make an innovation become best practices. The overarching message from this study may help all those who are engaged in the gigantic task of bringing about desired change in our existing system of education.

REFERENCES

1. Aggarwal, J.C & Gupta, S. (2008) *Great Philosophers and Thinkers on Education*, Shipra Publications, New Delhi.
2. Anandalakshmy, S. (2007) *Activity based learning – a report on an innovative method in Tamilnadu*, Government of Tamil Nadu Publication, Chennai.
3. Aurobindo, Sri. (1995) *Sri Aurobindo and The Mother on Education: A*

New Education For A New Consciousness, Sabda Sri Aurobindo Ashram, Pondichery.

4. Chakrabarti, Mohit. (1988), "Philosophy of Education of Rabindranath Tagore", Atlantic Publishers & Distributors: New Delhi.
5. Carlson, R.O. (1965), "Adoption of educational innovations". Eugene, *Center for the Advanced Study of Educational Administration.*
6. Chakrabarti, Mohit. (1993), *Tagore and Education: For Social Change*, Gyan Books, Delhi.
7. Freire, Poulo. (1972). *The Pedagogy of the Oppressed*, Penguin: London.
8. Fullan, M. (2001). *Leading in a culture of change.* San Francisco: Jossey-Bass
9. Funk & Wagnalls. (1980). Standard *Dictionary.* New York: Harper.
10. Farnsworth, Philo T. (1944), *Adaptation Process in Public School Systems*, New York: Teachers College.
11. GoTN, (2007), Silent Revolution in Tamil Nadu, A Documentary, Government of Tamil Nadu, Chennai.
12. Illich, Ivan. (1971), *Deschooling Society*, Harper and Row: New York.
13. Jagannathan, Shanti (2001), "The Role of Nongovernmental Organizations in Primary Education: A Study of Six NGOs in India", *Policy Research Working Paper* 2530, under Robert McNamara Fellowship Programme of the World Bank Institute, World Bank
14. Knight, E. E. (1967), "A Descriptive Model of the Intra-Firm Innovation Process" *Journal of Business*, 40, 478-496.
15. Krishnamurti, J. (1992), *Education and the Significance of Life*, Krishnamurthi Foundation India: Chennai.
16. Kumar, M. & Sarangapani, Padma M. (2005 Ed.). *Improving Government Schools: What has been Tried and What Works*, Books for Change, Bangalore.
17. Kumpf, Carl H. (1952), *The Adaptable School*, New York: The Macmillan Company.
18. Little, W. Angela. (2006). "Education for All and Multigrade Teaching: challenges and opportunities", New York: Springer
19. Mahapatra, Amukta. "Activity Based Learning Program in Schools of Chennai Corporation", in Kameshwari Jandhyala and Vimala Ramachandran (eds.), *Enabling most Deprived Children to Learn: Lessons from Promising Practices.* New Delhi: ILO, 2006 (unpublished mimeo).
20. Mort, Paul R. (1951), *Educational Adaptability*, New York: Metropolitan School Study Council.

21. Mort, Paul R., and Cornell, F.G. (1938), *Adaptability of Public School Systems*, New York: Teachers College.

22. Mort, Paul R., and Cornell, F.G. (1941), *American schools in transition: How our schools adapt their practices to changing needs, a study of Pennsylvania*. New York: Teachers College.

23. NCF (2005), National Curriculum Framework, 2005, National Council for Educational Research and Training, New Delhi.

24. Nohria, Nitin & Gulati, Ranjay. (1996) "Is Slack good or bad for innovation?" *Academy of Management Journal*, 39(October): 1245-1265.

25. National Policy on Education 1986, Ministry of Human Resource Development, New Delhi.

26. Rao, Padmanabha, Y.A. (2005). "Quality Schooling: Enriching the commons". Paper delivered at the 8th UKFIET *International Conference on Education and Development*, Oxford, 13-15 September, 2005.

27. Rogers, E.M. & Shoemaker, F.F. (1971), *Communication of innovations-A cross-cultural approach*. New York: The Free Press.

28. Ross, D.H. (Ed.). (1951), *Administration for adaptability* (Vol. 3). New York: Metropolitan School Study Council.

29. Rogers, E. M. (1995). *The diffusion of innovations* (3rd ed.). New York: The Free Press.

30. Rogers, E. M., & Jain, N. C. (1968). Needed research on diffusion within educational Organizations. (ERIC Document Reproduction Service No. ED 017 740).

31. Rishi Valley Education Centre. (2000) 'Report of the Second National Workshop on Planning and Implementation of Multigrade Programmes'. Rishi Valley, Andhra Pradesh: Rishi Valley Education Centre, Krishnamurti Foundation, India.

32. Schon, D. (1971), *Beyond the Stable State*, Norton: New York.

33. Singh, M K. (2008), *Gandhi on Education*, New Delhi: Rajat Publications

34. Thapan, Meenakshi. (1991), *Life at School: An Ethnographic Study*, Oxford University Press, New Delhi.

35. Van de Ven, A. (1986), *Central Problems in the Management of Innovation*. Management Science. 32(5): 590-607, INFORMS

36. Yashpal (1993): "Report of the National Advisory Committee on Learning Without Burden" (1992-93), *Ministry of Human Resources Development*, Government of India.

□□□

16

Learning in Education : A Social Constructivist Approach

Anamika Rai

INTRODUCTION

Learning is the process through which people obtain their education throughout life. A popular notion is that education is something carried out by one person, a teacher, standing in front of a class and transmitting information to a group of learners who are all willing and able to absorb it. The successful educator must be one who understands the complexities of the teaching learning process and can draw upon the knowledge to act in ways which empower learners both within and beyond the classroom situation. Learning is certainly part of the process of education, but to be truly educative it must give a broader value and meaning to the learner's life.

Learning is not an essentially individual process in the class. It is essentially social. But the rule against side talk is part of a general system of beliefs that ignores this. It presumes that each student learns as an isolated individual, even though part of a group. Even in our traditional classroom setting it is expected from students that they will accept unquestioningly the words of the teachers and the text they produce for their students, which makes the students a passive receiver of ideas. Learning is seen as a product of teaching or of adults' provision of information. Adults see themselves as responsible for filling children up with knowledge, as if children are receptacles and knowledge is a product. Children are seen as receivers of a body of knowledge, but not active participants in learning. The children have little role except to be receptive, as if they could just open a little bottle cap to let adults pour the knowledge in.

As we know that childhood is the period of growth and change, involving and developing one's physical and mental capacities to the fullest. That's why there is a need to make them a natural learner or active receiver of ideas, that they can participate actively in class, join in interactive language learning tasks and become autonomous learners. In such situations social constructivism is a ray of hope which opens the door of a new approach of learning.

Earlier, in learning theories, behaviorist theories were concerned with the use of appropriate rewards and punishment. After this, cognitive perspective has shaped the field of education and has been given the importance to organism and their mental process. These learning theories were looking individual as a passive learner. After cognitivism constructivist approach came into assistance which views learning as a process where individual actively construct their knowledge. The whole picture is providing insight that all these three approaches are lacking individual's social and cultural aspects. This lack is fulfilled by social constructivist approach which says learning basically takes place with in a web of social relationships as teachers and pupils interact both formally and informally. Play and scuffle with one's friends on the school grounds, free time to sit on the benches and chat with one's friends during breaks, gathering together for morning assembly and other festive and significant occasions in the school, all these are activities bringing the community together.

Social constructivism emphasizes the importance of culture and context in understanding what occurs in society and constructing knowledge based on this understanding. This perspective is closely associated with many contemporary theories, most notably the developmental theories of Vygotsky and Bruner. Social constructivism emphasizes education for social transformation and reflects a theory of human development that situates the individual within a socio cultural context. Individual development derives from social interactions within which cultural meanings are shared by the group and eventually internalized by the individual (Richardson, 1997). Individuals construct knowledge in transaction with the environment, and in the process both the individual and the environment are changed. The subject of study is the dialectical relationship between the individual and the social and cultural environment.

THEORIES OF LEARNING

Learning is a basic psychological process, and is defined as a gradual change in behaviors or beliefs that results from experience. The ability to learn provides every living organism with the ability to adapt to a changing environment. Learning theories can be defined with in the parameters of one or other of the broad theoretical approaches in which social constructivist approach is one of them. To understand the social constructivist approach there is need to understand other learning theories also, which begins from behaviorist approach.

BEHAVIORISM

Behaviorism as a theory was most developed by B. F. Skinner and J.B.Watson. It includes the work of such people as Thorndike, Tolman, Guthrie, and Hull. What characterize these investigators are their underlying assumptions about the process of learning. In essence, three basic assumptions are held to be true. First, learning is manifested by a change in behavior. Second, the environment shapes behavior. And third the principles of contiguity (how close in time two events must be for a bond to be performed) and reinforcement (any means of increasing the likelihood that an event will be repeated) are central to explaining the learning process. For behaviorism, learning is the acquisition of new behavior through conditioning (Baron, 2005).

There are two types of possible conditioning:

(1) Classical Conditioning (Respondent Conditioning) is a form of associative learning that was first demonstrated by Ivan Pavlov. The typical procedure for inducing classical conditioning involves presentations of a neutral stimulus along with a stimulus of some significance. The neutral stimulus could be any event that does not result in an overt behavioral response from the organism under investigation. Pavlov referred to this as a Conditioned Stimulus (CS). Conversely, presentation of the significant stimulus necessarily evokes an innate, often reflexive, response. Pavlov called these the Unconditioned Stimulus (US) and Unconditioned Response (UR), respectively. If the CS and the US are repeatedly paired, eventually the two stimuli become associated and the organism begins to produce

a behavioral response to the CS. Pavlov called this the Conditioned Response (CR) (Baron, 2005).

(2) Operant conditioning is the use of consequences to modify the occurrence and form of behavior. Operant conditioning is distinguished from classical conditioning (also called respondent conditioning, or Pavlovian conditioning) in that operant conditioning deals with the modification of "voluntary behavior" or operant behavior. Operant behavior "operates" on the environment and is maintained by its consequences, while classical conditioning deals with the conditioning of respondent behaviors which are elicited by antecedent conditions. Behaviors conditioned via a classical conditioning procedure are not maintained by consequences. Reinforcement and punishment, the core tools of operant conditioning, are either positive (delivered following a response), or negative (withdrawn following a response). This creates a total of four basic consequences (positive reinforcement, negative reinforcement, positive punishment, and negative punishment), with the addition of a fifth procedure known as extinction (i.e. no change in consequences following a response) (Baron, 2005).

The strongest reflection of behaviorism has been that it is only concerned with observable behavior. In choosing to concentrate only on that which is observable, behaviorism denies the importance of fundamental element in the learning process, the sense that learners themselves seek to make of their words, and the cognition or mental processes that they bring to the task of learning .In order to explore this aspect of learning further, we now turn to the field of cognitive approach.

COGNITIVISM

In contrast to behaviorism, cognitive approach is concerned with the way in which the human mind thinks and learns. Cognitive theories look beyond behavior to explain brain-based learning. Cognitivists consider how human memory works to promote learning. We can say that cognitivism is a theoretical approach in understanding the mind, which argues that mental function can be understood by quantitative, positivist and scientific methods, and that such functions can be described as information processing models. Cognitivism has two major components, one methodological, the other theoretical.

Methodologically, cognitivism adopts a positivist approach and the belief that psychology can be fully explained by the use of experiment, measurement and the scientific method. This is also largely a reductionist goal, with the belief that individual components of mental function can be identified and meaningfully understood. The second is the belief that cognition consists of discrete, internal mental states (representations or symbols) whose manipulation can be described in terms of rules or algorithms. In this school of thought there are several cognitive psychologists. It has its foundations in the Gestalt psychology of Max Wertheimer, Wolfgang Kohler, and Kurt Koffka, and in the work of Jean Piaget, who provided a theory of stages/phases that describe children's cognitive development. In a cognitive approach, the learner is seen as an active participant in the learning process, using various mental strategies.

The main issues that interest cognitive psychologists are the inner mechanisms of human thought and the processes of knowing. Cognitive psychologists have attempted to throw light on the alleged mental structures that stand in a causal relationship to our physical actions.

CONSTRUCTIVISM

Constructivism goes beyond the study of how the brain stores and retrieves information to examine the ways in which learners make meaning from experience. Rather than the transmission of knowledge, learning is an internal process of interpretation. Constructivism views learning as a process in which the learner actively constructs or builds new ideas or concepts based upon current and past knowledge. In other words, "learning involves constructing one's own knowledge from one's own experiences." Constructivism is generally attributed to Jean Piaget, who articulated mechanisms by which knowledge is internalized by learners. Through processes of accommodation and assimilation, individuals construct new knowledge from their experiences. When individuals assimilate, they incorporate the new experience into an already existing framework without changing that framework. This may occur when individuals' experiences are aligned with their internal representations of the world, but may also occur as a failure to change a faulty understanding. When individuals' experiences contradict their internal representations, they may change their perceptions of the experiences to fit their internal representations.

According to the theory, accommodation is the process of reframing one's mental representation of the external world to fit new experiences. Accommodation can be understood as the mechanism by which failure leads to learning: when we act on the expectation that the world operates in one way and it violates our expectations, we often fail, but by accommodating this new experience and reframing our model of the way the world works, we learn from the experience of failure, or others' failure. Constructivism is often associated with pedagogic approaches that promote active learning, or learning by doing. The purpose of education as educating the individual child in a fashion that supports the child's interests and needs, consequently, the child is the subject of study, and individual cognitive development is the emphasis. Learning is primarily an individualistic enterprise. This is a child-centered approach that seeks to identify, through scientific study, the natural path of cognitive development.

SOCIAL CONSTRUCTIVIST APPROACH

Social constructivism provides a psycholinguistic explanation for how learning can be fostered effectively through interactive pedagogical practices. It emphasizes that learning takes place in a socio-cultural environment and views learners as "active constructors of their own learning environment" (Mitchell & Myles, 1988). We learn not as isolated individuals, but as active members of society. Vygotsky, the father of social constructivism, believed that all higher cognitive processes have their origins in social interaction. Through joint activities with more mature members of society, children come to master activities and think in ways that have meaning in their culture. A special concept, the zone of proximal development, explains how this happens. It refers to a range of tasks that the child cannot yet handle alone but can accomplish with the help of adults and more skilled peers.

As children engage in cooperative dialogues with more mature partners, they take the language of these dialogues, make it part of their private speech, and use this speech to organize their independent efforts in the same way. Although Vygotsky was not very explicit about the features of these dialogues that promote transfer of cognitive processes to children, contemporary researches believe that at least two characteristics are important. The first is intersubjectivity. It refers to the process where by two participants who begin a task with different understandings arrives at a shared understanding. Intersubjectivity creates a common ground for communication as each partner adjusts to the perspective of other. Adults try to promote it when translate their own insights in ways that are within the child's grasp. For example, an adult might point out the links between a new task and ones the child already knows. As the child stretches to understand the interpretation, he is drawn into a more mature approach to the situation.

A second feature of social experience that fosters children's development is scaffolding. It refers to a changing quality of social support over the course of a teaching session in which adults adjust the assistance they provide to fit the child's current level of performance. Direct instruction is offered when a task is new; less help is provided as competence increases.

THE NATURE OF THE LEARNER

In social constructivism each learner is a unique individual having his or her own unique needs and backgrounds. Having various needs and backgrounds they seen as complex and multidimensional. Social constructivism not only acknowledges the uniqueness and complexity of the learner, but actually encourages, utilizes and rewards it as an integral part of the learning process (Wertsch 1997).

This approach encourages the learner to arrive at his or her own version of the truth, influenced by his or her background, or culture. Historical developments and symbol systems, such as language, logic, and mathematical systems, are inherited by the learner as a member of a particular culture and these are learned throughout the learner's life. This also stresses the importance of the nature of the learner's social interaction with knowledgeable members of the society. Without the social interaction with other more knowledgeable people, it is impossible to acquire social meaning of important symbol systems and learn how to utilize them. Social constructivism also emphasizes the importance of the learner being actively involved in the learning process, unlike previous educational viewpoints where the responsibility rested with the instructor to teach and where the learner played a passive, receptive role.

Another crucial assumption regarding the nature of the learner concerns the level and source of motivation for learning. Motivation to learn is strongly dependent on the learner's confidence in his or her potential for learning. These feelings of competence and belief in potential to solve new problems are derived from first-hand experience of mastery of problems in the past and are much more powerful than any external acknowledgment and motivation (Prawat and Floden 1994). This links up with Vygotsky's "zone of proximal development" (Vygotsky 1978) where learners are challenged within close proximity to, yet slightly above, their current level of development.

THE ROLE OF THE INSTRUCTOR

According to the social constructivist approach, instructors have to adapt to the role of facilitators and not teachers (Bauersfeld, 1995). Where a teacher gives a didactic lecture which covers the subject matter, a facilitator helps the learner to get to his or her own understanding of the content. A teacher tells, a facilitator asks; a teacher lectures from the front, a facilitator supports from the back; a teacher gives answers according to a set curriculum, a facilitator provides guidelines and creates the environment for the learner to arrive at his or her own conclusions; a teacher mostly gives a monologue, a facilitator is in continuous dialogue with the learners. A facilitator should also be able to adapt the learning experience 'in mid-air' by using his or her own initiative in order to steer the learning experience to where the learners want to create value.

THE NATURE OF THE LEARNING PROCESS

Social constructivists view learning as an active process where learners should learn to discover principles, concepts and facts for themselves, hence the importance of encouraging guesswork and intuitive thinking in learners (Brown et al.1989). In fact, for the social constructivist, reality is not something that we can discover because it does not pre-exist prior to our social invention of it. Kukla (2000) argues that reality is constructed by our own activities and that people, together as members of a society, invent the properties of the world.

Vygotsky (1978) also highlighted the convergence of the social and practical elements in learning by saying that the most significant moment in the course of intellectual development occurs when speech and practical activity, two previously completely independent lines of development, converge. Through practical activity a child constructs meaning on an intrapersonal level, while speech connects this meaning with the interpersonal world shared by the child and her/his culture. A further characteristic of the role of the facilitator in the social constructivist view point, is that the instructor and the learners are equally involved in learning from each other as well. This means that the learning experience is both subjective and objective and requires that the instructor's culture, values and background become an essential part of the interplay between learners and tasks in the shaping of meaning. Learners get a new, socially tested version of truth through comparing their own version of the truth with the instructors and fellow learners (Kukla 2000). The task or problem is thus the interface between the instructor and the learner which creates a dynamic interaction between task, instructor and learner. For this dynamic interaction there is a need in learners and instructors that they should develop an awareness of each other's viewpoints and then look to their own beliefs, standards and values, thus being both subjective and objective at the same time.

COLLABORATION AMONG LEARNERS

Every individual or learner is different in their skills and backgrounds, so that they should collaborate in tasks and discussions in order to arrive at a shared understanding of the truth in a specific field. Most social constructivist models, stress the need for collaboration among learners, in direct contradiction to traditional competitive approaches. One Vygotskian notion that has significant implications for peer collaboration is that of the zone of proximal development. Defined as the distance between the actual developmental level as determined by independent problem-solving and the level of potential development as determined through problem-solving under adult guidance or in collaboration with more capable peers, it differs from the fixed biological nature of Piaget's stages of development. Through a process of 'scaffolding' a learner can be extended beyond the limitations of physical maturation to the extent that the development process lags behind the learning process (Vygotsky 1978).

The social constructivist paradigm also gives importance to the context in which the learning occurs as central to the learning itself. Underlying the notion of the learner as an active processor is "the assumption that there is no one set of generalized learning laws with each law applying to all domains" (Di Vesta 1987:208). Decontextualised knowledge does not give us the skills to apply our understandings to authentic tasks because we are not working with the concept in the complex environment and experiencing the complex interrelationships in that environment that determine how and when the concept is used. One social constructivist notion is that of authentic or situated learning, where the student takes part in activities which are directly relevant to the application of learning and which take place within a culture similar to the applied setting.

Holt and Willard-Holt (2000) emphasize the concept of dynamic assessment, which is a way of assessing the true potential of learners that differs significantly from conventional tests. Here the essentially interactive nature of learning is extended to the process of assessment. Rather than viewing assessment as a process carried out by one person, such as an instructor, it is seen as a two-way process involving interaction between both instructor and learner. The role of the assessor becomes one of entering into dialogue with the persons being assessed to find out their current level of performance on any task and sharing with them possible ways in which that performance might be improved on a subsequent occasion. Thus, assessment and learning are seen as inseparably linked and not separate processes (Holt and Willard-Holt 2000).

According to this viewpoint instructors should see assessment as a continuous and interactive process that measures the achievement of the learner, the quality of the learning experience and courseware. The feedback created by the assessment process serves as a direct foundation for further development.

Learners should constantly be challenged with tasks that refer to skills and knowledge just beyond their current level of mastery which will capture their motivation and build on previous successes in order to enhance the confidence of the learner. This is in line with Vygotsky's zone of proximal development which can be described as the distance between the actual developmental level (as determined by independent problem-solving) and the level of potential development (as determined through problem-solving under adult guidance or in collaboration with more capable peers) (Vygotsky 1978).

Vygotsky (1978) further claimed that instruction is good only when it proceeds ahead of development. Then it awakens and rouses to life an entire set of functions which are in the stage of maturing, which lie in the zone of proximal development. It is in this way that instruction plays an extremely important role in development.

It is also important for instructors to realize that although a curriculum may be set down for them, it inevitably becomes shaped by them into something personal which reflects their own belief systems, their thoughts and feelings about both the content of their instruction and their learners (Rhodes and Bellamy 1999). Thus, the learning experience becomes a shared enterprise. The emotions and life contexts of those involved in the learning process must therefore be considered as an integral part of learning. The goal of the learner is central in considering what is learned? (Brown et al., 1989).

It is important to achieve the right balance between the degree of structure and flexibility that is built into the learning process. If the learning environment is very much structured it will be harder for the learners to construct meaning based on their conceptual understandings. A facilitator should structure the learning experience just enough to make sure that the students get clear guidance and parameters within which to achieve the learning objectives, yet the learning experience should be open and free enough to allow for the learners to discover, enjoy, interact and arrive at their own, socially verified version of truth.

TEACHING METHODS BASED ON SOCIAL CONSTRUCTIVISM

Learners learn by experimentation, and not by being told what will happen. They are left to make their own inferences, discoveries and conclusions. Social constructivism also emphasizes that learning is not an "all or nothing" process but that students learn the new information that is presented to them by building upon knowledge that they already possess. It is therefore important that teachers constantly assess the knowledge their students have gained to make sure that the students' perceptions of the new knowledge are what the teacher had intended. Teachers will find that since the students build upon already existing knowledge, when they are called upon to retrieve the new information, they may make errors. It is known as reconstruction error when we fill in the gaps of our understanding with logical, though incorrect, thoughts. Teachers need to catch and try to correct these errors, though it is inevitable that some reconstruction error will continue to occur because of our innate retrieval limitations. In most teaching methods based on constructivism, the teacher's role is not only to observe and assess but to also engage with the students while they are completing activities, wondering aloud and posing questions.

Finally we can say that a social constructivist learning approach is thus an intervention where contextualized activities (tasks) are used to provide learners with an opportunity to discover and collaboratively construct meaning as the intervention unfolds. Learners are respected as unique individuals, and instructors act as facilitators rather than as teachers.

EVALUATION OF SOCIAL CONSTRUCTIVIST APPROACH

While evaluating this approach we can say that this approach of learning is unique from other approaches in helping us to understand the wide variation in cognitive skills across cultures. It leads us to expect highly variable development, depending on the child's specific cultural experiences. For example the reading, writing, and mathematical activities of children who go to school in literate societies generate cognitive capacities that differ from those in preliterate cultures.

Allowing students to work independently is an essential aspect of social constructivist approach. There is a need to set tasks which allow students to read in areas which interest them and for purposes which are important to them is the best motivator. However freedom without support is a recipe for disaster. So that, scaffolding before and during individual or small group tasks is essential.

Although, this approach is unique in itself, but we can not say that all teaching methods based on this approach efficient or effective for all learners. Students centered instruction and the collaborative process will work well only with motivated, high achieving students. Where as those students who are not motivated, are not as quick as picking things up as students or who might be shy and timid will not benefit from this environment.

CONCLUSION

In conclusion, social constructivist approach to learning offers tools and principles for teachers or educators to draw students into energetic participation in text events, not as outsiders, but as active participants. In many ways this approach may challenge the traditional beliefs of learning.

REFERENCES

1. Baron, R.A. (2005): Learning: How We're Changed by Experience, *Psychology*, Fifth Edition, Pearson Education (Singapore) Pte. Ltd. 166-207.
2. Brown, J. S., Collins, A., & Duguid, P. (1989): Situated Cognition and the Culture of Learning. *Educational Research*, 18(1), 32-41.
3. Di Vesta, F. J. (1987): The Cognitive Movement and Education. In J. A. Glover & R. R. Ronning (Ed.), *Historical Foundations of Educational Psychology*, New York: Plenum Press, pp. 203-233.
4. Holt, D. G. & Willard-Holt, C. (2000): *Lets Get Real–Students Solving Authentic Corporate Problems. Phi Delta Kappan, 82 (3).*
5. Kukla, A. (2000): Social Constructivism and the Philosophy of Science. New York: Routledge.
6. Mitchell, H., & Myles, F. (1988): *Second Language Learning Theories.* London: Arnold. *Prawat,*
7. R. S., & Floden, R. E. (1994): Philosophical Perspectives on Constructivist Views of Learning. Educational Psychologist, *29(1), 37-48.*
8. Richardson, V. (1997): Constructivist Teaching and Teacher Education. Theory and Practice. In V. Richordson (Ed.), *Constructivist Teacher Education: Building New Understandings,* Washington, DC: Flamer press, pp.3-14.
9. Vygotsky, L.S. (1978): *Mind in society: The development of higher mental processes. Cambridge,* MA: Harvard University Press.
10. Wertsch, J.V. (1997): *Vygotsky and the Formation of the Mind.* Cambridge.
11. Williams, M., and Burden, R. L., (undated): An Introduction to educational psychology: Behaviorism and Cognitive psychology. *Psychology for Language Teachers: A Social Constructivist Approach,* Cambridge University Press, pp.5-29.
12. http://books.google.co.in/books?id=lSWiKzjuFf4C&printsec=frontcover&lr
13. http://people.ischool.berkeley.edu/~duguid/SLOFI/Situated_Learning.htm
14. http://books.google.co.in/books?id=RxjjUefze_oC&printsec=frontcover

□□□

17

Women Empowerment Through Education : A Sociological Study

T. MURUGESAN AND I. SINGARAM

"Education is one of the most important means of empowering women with the knowledge, skills and self-confidence necessary to participate fully in the development process."

STATUS OF WOMEN

Women account for generally partially the world's population, perform two-thirds of the hours worked, receive one-tenth of the world's income, and have less than one hundredth of the world's property registered in their names. Female deprivation is particularly acute in the developing countries with high levels of poverty, though in affluent nations women also suffer low status due to conservative attitudes. The most dramatic and telling statistic of women's status is the sex-ratio in the population, that is, the number of females per 100 males. It is a well-known fact that life-expectancy at birth favors females. The overwhelming reason why 100 million women are missing in the world is excess female mortality. In the developed world, women outlive men by an average of six years; by contrast, in large parts of society, men can expect to live longer than women.

Differential mortality is only the most dramatic manifestation of systematic discrimination against females. Women and girls are more likely to be impoverished than men and boys. Also, studies have found that girls are fed less than their brothers and that their illnesses are less likely to be treated. It should come as no surprise then that, in most regions of the world, female literacy and education fall far short of male literacy and education, while poverty and cultural factors must surely influence the extent of female deprivation, they do not explain it entirely.

RISING LEVEL OF EDUCATION

With the introduction of the new Constitution in 1946 and the Fundamental Law of Education that followed, the equal opportunity for education for boys and girls at all levels was legally promised and co-educational school system was disseminated throughout Japan. The enrolment rates for both boys and girls on the level of primary education (elementary and junior high/secondary schools) became almost 100% as early as in the 1940s. The enrolment rate for girls on the level of secondary education (senior high schools) started lower than that for boys but increased rapidly in the 1960s and exceeded the rate for boys in 1969 to sustain the trend till today. The enrolment pattern in higher education has been gender- discriminatory. The enrolment rates for both boys and girls increased drastically in the late 1960s and early 1970s to reach the levels of 40% for boys and over 30% for girls, but nearly two-thirds of the girls were enrolled in junior colleges where the principle of women-' s education was in line with the pre-world-war-II ideology. It was only in the late 1990s, that girls' enrolment in the 4-year universities increased considerably to reach the point of 31.5% in the year 2000 in comparison with 47.5% for boys while the girl's enrolment in junior colleges began to decrease.

FACTORS TO PROMOTE EDUCATION

Major pushing factors for promoting higher education in the formal school system were the introduction and institutionalizations of the democratic ideology in the school system and in society in general, and the economic growth which expanded the need for better-educated labour supply when the number of children per couple declined. In the process of rapid urbanization and the growing middle class population, the social class distinction became blurred and the equality of opportunity became seemingly an a priori. The ideology of democracy and the economic affluence jointly worked to break a discouraging climate towards women to receive a higher education.

Also, Their expectation, however, was in accordance with the general social norm and tended to be gender-specific: education for boys was considered a core resource and qualification for their success as the breadwinner and the citizens in the public sphere while education for girls was appreciated as an important qualification for their successful mate-selection which would determine their adult life style as the housewife in the private sphere. The notion of education as an investment shifted from the standpoint of national development to that of personal development but the route to personal development was gender- differentiated.

Making Changes in Gender Stereotype in Education

Gender stereotypes in education are the product of various factors such as the attitudes of family members and the community, the mind-set of the people in the school environment, the opportunity structure of society particularly in education and occupation, and the gender norm embedded in the reward and compensation system of a society.

The parents' expectations for their children's education has been growing and more parents are expressing their desire for their daughters to have education on the university level than ever before, and yet a considerable gender gap still exists (33% for girls and 65% for boys). As for the fields of study in the universities, there has been a high concentration of female students in humanities, social sciences and education, though social sciences are gaining popularity while others have lost gradually. Again, we find a big gender gap in the preference of the academic discipline. The slowing changing patterns of gender gaps in the above two indicators reflect the normative gender stereotypes of our society that are directly linked with the breadwinner-housewife division of roles.

Education and Women Empowerment

Education is the process of instruction aimed at the all round development of boys and girls. Education dispels ignorance. It is the only wealth that cannot be robbed. Learning includes the moral values and the improvement of character and the methods to increase the strength of mind.

Once the first Prime Minister of India, Jawaharlal Nehru said, "you can tell the condition of a nation by looking at the status of its women". This is absolutely true. Woman of any nation is the mirror to its civilization. If women enjoy good status it shows that the society has reached a level of maturity and sense of responsibility while a decadent image conjures up if the opposite is true. The story of Indian women is as old as the history of Indian civilization.

Kumud Sharma of the Centre for Women's Development Studies in New Delhi traced the correlation between education and domestic violence to patriarchal attitudes. "Educated women are aware of their rights," she said. "They are no longer willing to follow commands blindly. When they ask questions, it causes conflicts, which, in turn, leads to violence. In many Indian states, working women are asked to hand over their paycheck to the husband and have no control over their finances. So, if they stop doing so or start asserting their right, there is bound to be friction." Women constitutes half of the total population in the world and they perform an estimated 60 per cent of the world's work but own only one percent of the world's land and earn just 10 percent of the world's income. Further, they are denied with the right to education, intellectual obscurantism in the patriarchal society. Even though they are contributing for the national development, their work is unrecognized and uncounted. As a result of this, they lagged behind in all spheres of life and suffering from chronic malnutrition, hygiene in the home and ignorance heightens their conditions. Recognizing their potentialities and to convert them as active human resources, the Government of India has formulated and implemented education and welfare programmes. Inspire of these efforts their position has not altered significantly. An attempt has been made in this volume to document the various strategies adapted for women sustainable education and their empowerment.

Education Opportunity for Women

In India, the increase in the educational facilities and opportunities for women and the removal of traditional bars on entry of women to particular branches and levels of education came to be supported by all champions of women's emancipation from the 19th Century onwards. However, the Indian reformers of the 19th Century wanted to educate women to perform their role as good wives and mothers and not to make them as direct active participants in the process of national development of the country. The colonial authorities generally supported this limited view-point of women's education. The expansion of education and health services in the 20th Century, however, precipitated a need for women teachers and doctors which resulted in the incorporation of these two vocations in the programme of women's education.

Planning for Women Education System

After independence, the Constitutional guarantee of equality changed the conceptual thinking of educational development of women and gave a call to women to play multiple roles in the polity, the economy and the society and the educational development of women began in that broad direction. This is amply evident in the Government's policy, reports of various commit- tees and commissions set up for this purpose and in the objectives of Development Plans formulated after Independence. The National Policy of Education provides that "The Education of girls should receive emphasis not only on grounds of social justice but also because it accelerates social transformation". The very First Five Year Plan of Education stated "The general purpose and objective of Women's education cannot, of course, be different from the purpose and objectives of the men's education .... At the Secondary and even at the University stage women's education should have a vocational or occupational bias". Similarly, the Secondary Education Commission (1953) sated that "In a democratic society where all citizens have to discharge their civic and social obligations, differences which may lead to variations in the standard of intellectual development achieved by boys and girls can be envisaged". The Re- port of the Committee on Differentiation of Curricula for boys and girls (1959) also emphasized on the same type of educat on and same role of men and women in the society. The Education Commission (1964-66) endorsed the recommendations of all committees and commissions about the equality in the educational development of women. The Government's national policy also laid down that "The education system must produce young men and women of character and ability committed to national services and development. Only then will education be able to play its vital role in promoting national progress, creating a sense of common citizenship and culture and strengthening national integration".

In spite of the constitutional provision of equality and the recommendations of the committees and commissions about the provision for the same type of education for women as for men, the traditional limited view point of women's education, with a separate role of women in the society. Has had a great influence on the planning for women's education. Before, however, we review the accelerated growth and progress of women's education and analyse the problems of their future development after independence, it will be interesting and informative to trace very briefly the history of women's education during British regime.

FEMALE LITERACY IN INDIA

According to last census held in 2001, the percentage of female literacy in the country is 54.16%. The literacy rate in the country has increased from 18.33% in 1951 to 65.38% as per 2001 census. The female literacy rate has also increased from 8.86% in 1951 to 54.16%. It is noticed that the female literacy rate during the period 1991-2001 increased by 14.87% whereas male literacy rate rose by 11.72%. Hence the female literacy rate actually increased by 3.15% more compared to male literacy rate.

Integration in Decision Making Power for Women

Women's contribution to local and community development is significant, but rural women everywhere are in a minority in decision-making and planning, particularly at regional and national levels. This is in part due to women's multiple roles and workload, but is also due to the persistence of traditional views about women's and men's roles in society. The low level of participation by women in decision making inevitably leads to biases in the priorities and policies pursued by development organizations. A balanced participation by women and men in decision making is important for local democracy and for the quality of decisions taken on developments that affect the life and future of rural communities and economies.

Decision-Making Women's Through Education

This section addresses development organizations and professional associations, as well as local and regional authorities. They are asked to actively encourage and support women in planning and decision-making, both as members of management boards and committees and at senior staffing levels. Aspects that could usefully be reviewed, with an eye to gender-orientation, include:

- Organizational culture and structure

- Recruitment procedure and promotion of staff
- Terms and conditions of employment (working time)
- The selection and nomination of board and committee members
- Procedures used for making decisions
- The timing and location of meetings and events. At local, regional and national level special steps could be taken
- The establishment of associations and networks of rural women
- The involvement of existing women's associations in committees and partnerships
- Encouraging women's groups to apply for funding for development initiatives
- Linking up women's associations with development organizations

As a lack of spare time is a reason frequently given by rural women for their not being more involved, every effort should be made to eradicate obstacles and ensure their participation. It may be necessary to provide transport and childcare facilities, and men may need encouraging taking more responsibility for family tasks.

The Economic and Social Gains from Women Education

Equality of the sexes - in terms of men and women's command over resources, their access to education and health, and in terms of freedom to develop their potential - has an intrinsic value in its own right. The equal treatment of the sexes for intrinsic reasons is, in the parlance of welfare economics, the equity reason for reducing gender-imbalances. A second important reason in favour of reducing gender-imbalances is what might be termed the instrumental reason, that is, the gains to be had from granting equality. For example, if with equal education, women's contribution to economic development (or to other desirable goals) is comparable to men's, then reducing gender-imbalances in education will enhance women's capacity to contribute to economic progress.

Economic Efficiency

Human capital theory suggests that just as physical capital

(machines) augments people's economic productivity, so human capital acquired through education improves the productivity of individuals. Studies of the sources of economic growth demonstrate persuasively that education plays a major role as a factor in the rise of output per worker. The new growth theories in economics place education and human resource development at the centre of their explanation for long-term economic growth. Confidence has grown in the belief that education affects economic growth because many studies have shown the positive correlation between a country's educational effort and its economic status, and causality has been attributed to education.

If female schooling raises human capital, productivity, and economic growth as much as male schooling does, then women's disadvantage in education is economically inefficient. Research world-wide shows that, in general, the economic benefits from women's education - calculated as the economic rate of return to education - are comparable to those from men's education.

Social Efficiency

While the economic benefits of educating girls are similar in size to the economic benefits of educating boys, recent findings suggest that the social benefits from investing in female education are far greater than those from investing in male education. Specifically, female education has powerful effects on the total fertility rate (and hence on population growth), the infant mortality rate, the female disadvantage in child survival, and on child health and nutrition. By contrast, statistical analyses show that male schooling has relatively much smaller effects on these important social outcomes.

A similar exercise by Murthi, Guio, and Drèze for India using district level aggregated data shows that whereas the district female literacy rate had a strong inverse correlation on the district average total fertility rate, on under-five child mortality rate, and on the female disadvantage in child survival, the district male literacy rate had no significant effect on each of these outcomes. Moreover, district per capita income, urbanisation, and the spread of medical facilities were not statistically significant determinants of total fertility rate. While these latter three variables do have positive effects on child survival levels, their effects were relatively small compared with the powerful effect of female literacy.

Simulations show that the benefits from expanding female education are far greater than the benefits from other public interventions such as improving family planning service provision or increasing the number of physicians in the population. For example, Subbarao and Raney (footnote 12) found that a doubling of the 1975 average secondary school enrolment ratio in the 72 sample countries from 19% to 38% would have reduced the average number of births in 1985 by 29% compared to the actual number in 1985, whereas a doubling of the family planning provision would have reduced the number of births by only 3.5%.

The gains in terms of deaths averted are also striking. Simulations predict that doubling the female secondary school enrolment ratio from 19% to 38% in 1975 reduces infant deaths in 1985 by 64% while doubling the number of physicians reduces the number of infant deaths by a mere 2.5%. Doubling per capita income (or GDP) from the average of $650 in the 72 sample countries to $1300 would have no effect on the number of infant deaths!

CONCLUSION

The challenge of providing higher education to rural Indian women must be put in the context of the demographics and cultural traditions of the country. While great efforts have been made at population control resulting in a rate of population increase of just 1.8% per year, in a country of 1 billion people, that still means an annual population increase of some 18 million people who require all the essentials of life as well as education at all levels. The population increase in and of itself presents a staggering educational and financial challenge.

The need for education of women, and in particular of rural women, is overwhelming. It is recognized by the Government to be essential to the country's development and population control. Much has been done, but there is a long way to go. The main policy prescriptions of this paper are that governments and other organizations should attempt to educate people about the equity and efficiency benefits of female education and that public policy should encourage girls' access to schooling by extra subsidies in order to compensate for the asymmetry in parental incentives to educate sons and daughters in poor societies. I have also argued that education *per se* is not sufficient. It is clear that societies which have achieved universal education are currently extremely deficient socially despite their economic prosperity.

REFERENCES

1. M. Murthi, A. Guio, and J. Drèze, "Mortality, Fertility, And Gender Bias In India," in J. Drèze and A.Sen (eds.), *Indian Development: Selected Regional Perspectives*(Delhi: Oxford University Press, 1997).

2. Pruthi, Raj Kumar; Rameshwari Devi and Romila Pruthi (2001). Status and Position of Women: In Ancient, Medieval and Modern India. Delhi : Vedam books.

   See review of studies in T.P. Schultz, "Returns to women's education," chapter 2 in E. King and M. Hill (eds.), *Women's education in developing countries* (Washington D.C.: Johns Hopkins Press for the World Bank, 1993).

4. "Women in History". National Resource Center for Women. 2006.

5. "National Policy for the Empowerment of Women (2001)". Andhra Pradesh Sri Padmavati University, Tirupati, Delhi

6. Jyotsna Kamat (2006-12-19). "Gandhi and Status of Women". http://www.kamat.com/mmgandhi/gwomen.htm. Retrieved 2006-12-24.

❑❑❑

PART-IV
ENVIRONMENTAL REALITY

18

Seawater Intrusion – A Major Threat for Water Crisis in India

S. RAMESH AND N. SUKUMARAN

INTRODUCTION

National water policy (2002) of India states that "water is a prime natural resource, basic human need and precious national asset". India is rich in water resources, being endowed with network of rivers; there is unfortunately mismatch between the endowment of natural resources and the population to be supported. Our country accounts for 2% of the world's geo-graphical area and 4% of its fresh water, it has to support 17% of world's population and 15% of its livestock. Apart from water available in the various rivers of the country, the ground water is also an important source of water for drinking, agricultural, industrial and domestic use. It accounts for about 80% of domestic water requirement and more than 50% of the total irrigation potential of the country (Kumar *et al.*, 2005). With rapid growing population and improving living standards, the pressure on water resources is increasing and per capita availability of water resources is reducing day by day. As per the International norms, now our country is categorized as water stressed (< 1700 m^3/capita/year) and likely to be water scarce (< 1000 m^3/capita/year) by 2050 (Gupta and Deshpande, 2004). The continuous high demand of water resources leads to the depletion of groundwater table which causes saline intrusion in the freshwater aquifers that degrades quality and quantity of water resources (Kumar *et al.*, 2005; Khayat *et al.*, 2006)

Saline intrusion is one of the widespread problems all over world. Because, almost two-thirds of the world's population lives within 400 km of the ocean shoreline, just over half lives within 200 km, an area only taking up 10% of the earth surface (Hinrichsen, 2007). Most of the coastal regions rely on groundwater for main source of fresh water for various purposes. Hence, an urgent need for proper monitoring of saline intrusion and management of groundwater resources in the coastal areas is recognized for sustainable utilization of water resources.

SALINE INTRUSION – AN OVERVIEW

Saline intrusion is the movement of saline water into the freshwater aquifer which causes salinization of groundwater resources. It is an irreversible event occurring as groundwater table declines below some threshold level. Saline water is water that contains high levels of dissolved solids and is generally considered unsuitable for human consumption. Saline water contains more than 1,000 parts per million (ppm) of dissolved solids of any type. Table 1 shows the general classification of water based on Total dissolved solids (TDS).

Classification of water based on the Total dissolved solids (Davis and Wiest, 1996)

Water type	TDS (mg/l)
Fresh	< 1000
Slightly Saline	1000 – 3000
Moderately Saline	3000 – 10000
Very Saline	10000 - 35000
Brine	> 35000

Besides the anthropogenic effects (e.g. fertilizers, waste deposits), the main origin of saline groundwater are seawater intrusion in the coastal areas, inter-aquifer exchange, salt domes and enhanced mineral concentration in groundwater by natural processes like rock-water interaction, leachates etc. Among them, seawater intrusion is a notable problem for groundwater salinization in India because Indian sub-continent has a dynamic coast line of about 7500 km of length.

HYDROLOGICAL ASPECTS OF SALINE INTRUSION

Saline intrusion occurs in virtually all coastal aquifers, where they are in hydraulic connectivity with sea water. Importantly, seawater intrusion may occur through a number of different processes, including lateral seawater intrusion, inter-aquifer exchange and upconing. Generally, sea water has a higher density (which is because it carries more solutes) than freshwater. This difference in density causes the pressure under a column of saltwater to be greater than the pressure under a column of the same height of freshwater. If these two columns are connected at the bottom, then the pressure difference would cause a flow of saltwater column to the freshwater column until the pressure equalizes. Under natural conditions, the flow of saltwater from sea to freshwater aquifer inland is limited in coastal areas. Further inland, the freshwater column is higher due to the increasing altitude of the land and is able equalize the pressure from the salt water, stopping the saltwater intrusion.

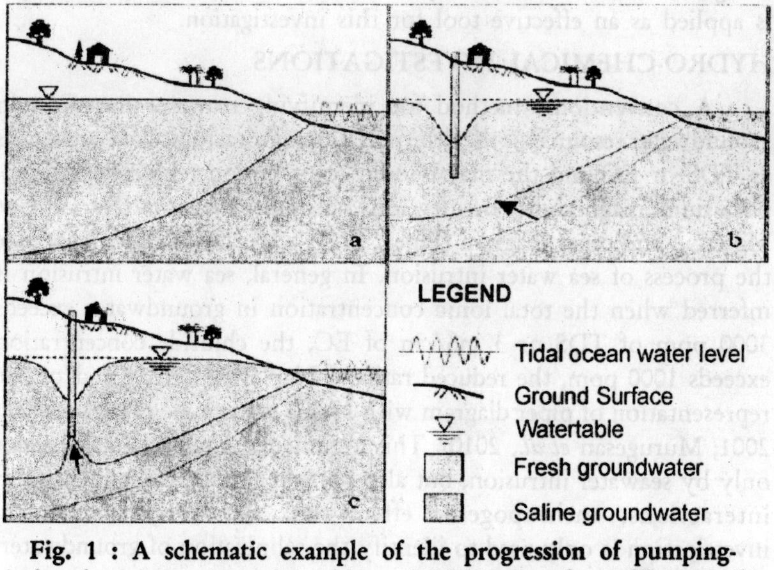

Fig. 1 : A schematic example of the progression of pumping-induced seawater intrusion: (a) an initial state of equilibrium, (b) lateral seawater intrusion, and (c) up-coning

Typically, groundwater flows from areas with higher groundwater table to areas with lower groundwater table. This natural movement (discharge) of freshwater towards sea prevents the movement of salt water from sea to freshwater coastal aquifers. The excessive pumping of groundwater can decrease the amount of freshwater flowing towards the coastal discharge areas, allowing sea water to be drawn into the freshwater zones of aquifer. Therefore, sea water inundates the freshwater aquifer (Khublaryan *et al.*, 2008). Due to increasing population, urbanization and industrialization in India, the rate of groundwater draft is continuously increasing, which leads to heavy exploitation of the aquifer. When the aquifer is disturbed due to excess pumping, the saline water will move until a new equilibrium is achieved. As a consequence of which, the transition zone moves inwards, increasing the extent of seawater intrusion.

MITIGATION OF SEAWATER INTRUSION

To sustain the use of groundwater resources, monitoring of seawater intrusion is essential by using effective tools. Conventionally, hydro-chemical investigations and geo-physical methods are used to mitigate the seawater intrusion processes. Now-a-days, isotope technique is applied as an effective tool for this investigation.

HYDRO-CHEMICAL INVESTIGATIONS

A conventional method for identifying seawater intrusion in groundwater resources is the determination of total ionic concentrations as TDS or EC and the major ionic contribution (chloride, sodium, potassium, magnesium). Besides, ions ratios of major ions (Na/Cl, Ca/Mg etc.,) and piper diagram (Piper, 1944) were also used to recognize the process of sea water intrusion. In general, sea water intrusion is inferred when the total ionic concentration in groundwater exceeds 3000 ppm of TDS or 3 mS/cm of EC, the chloride concentration exceeds 1000 ppm, the reduced ratio of Na/Cl & Ca/Mg and/or the representation of piper diagram with Na-Cl water type (Yingkai *et al.*, 2001; Murugesan *et al.*, 2010). This arguments, however, may be not only by seawater intrusion, but also by other process like rock-water interactions, anthropogenic effects etc. Thus, hydro-chemical investigation is only used to identify the salinization of groundwater.

GEO-PHYSICAL METHODS

In addition to the hydro-chemical investigation, there is a number of geo-physical methods have been used to monitor groundwater salinization. Recent studies reveal that use of Vertical Electrical Sounding (VES) and Time Domain Electromagnectics (TEM) methods successfully characterize the groundwater salinization (Wilson *et al.*, 2006; Neilson *et al.*, 2007). The salinization of groundwater may be inferred when low resistivities measured in the groundwater aquifers using these geo-physical methods. Use of these geo-physical techniques with geochemical sensors can provide resource managers with a powerful tool for the management of saline groundwater. These methods provide a number of benefits, including greatly improved groundwater models, a better understanding on how groundwater salinity responds to changes to parameters such as precipitation etc., and can provide a warning or alarm for degraded groundwater quality. The above said well known geo-physical methods alone can not clearly categorize the saline intrusion process in the groundwater resources.

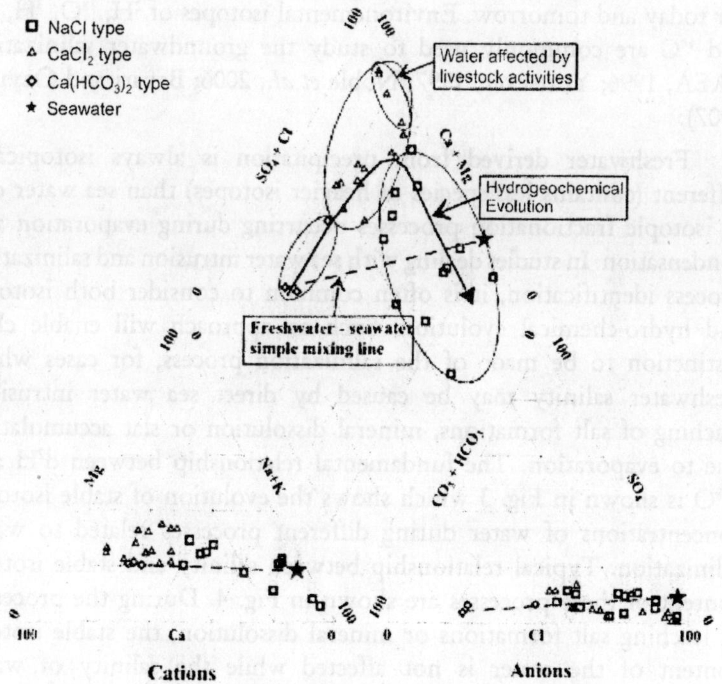

Fig. 2 : Shows the piper diagram which explains the seawater intrusion process

The interpretations of hydro-chemical and geo-physical investigations infer only the possibilities of saline intrusion for groundwater salinization, but not give conclusive inference about saline intrusion process. To resolve this problem, isotope technique is efficiently applied.

ISOTOPE TECHNIQUES

Application of the isotope technique has been revealed as one of the efficient tools to investigate underground sources of water, how they are recharged, whether they are at risk of saline intrusion or pollution (IAEA, 1981). Naturally, water is tagged with isotopic finger prints, which vary according to the history of a particular body of water and its route through the hydrological cycle. Thus, isotopes provide an effective label for sea water and fresh water to enable tracing of saline intrusion (Yurtsever, 1997). Isotope technique also provides critical information to make right decision on where to extract water for today and tomorrow. Environemental isotopes of ^{2}H, ^{18}O, ^{3}H, ^{11}B and ^{14}C are commonly used to study the groundwater salinization (IAEA, 1996; Yurtsever, 1997; Noble *et al.*, 2006; Bayari and Ozyurt, 2007).

Freshwater derived from precipitation is always isotopically different (contains less species of heavier isotopes) than sea water due to isotopic fractionation processes occurring during evaporation and condensation. In studies dealing with sea water intrusion and salinization process identification, it is often common to consider both isotopic and hydro-chemical evolution. Such an approach will enable clear distinction to be made of the salinization process, for cases where freshwater salinity may be caused by direct sea water intrusion, leaching of salt formations, mineral dissolution or slat accumulation due to evaporation. The fundamental relationship between $d^{2}H$ and $d^{18}O$ is shown in Fig. 3 which shows the evolution of stable isotopic concentrations of water during different processes related to water salinization. Typical relationship between salinity and stable isotope content of these processes are shown in Fig. 4. During the processes of leaching salt formations or mineral dissolution, the stable isotope content of the water is not affected while the salinity of water increases. This is a unique feature which enables the identification of such processes based on isotopic and chemical data.

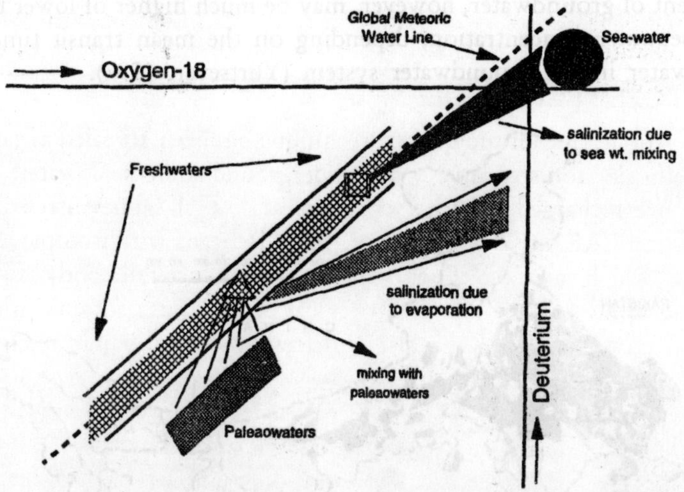

Fig. 3 : Evolution of stable isotopic composition of water for different water salinization processes (Yurtsever, 1997)

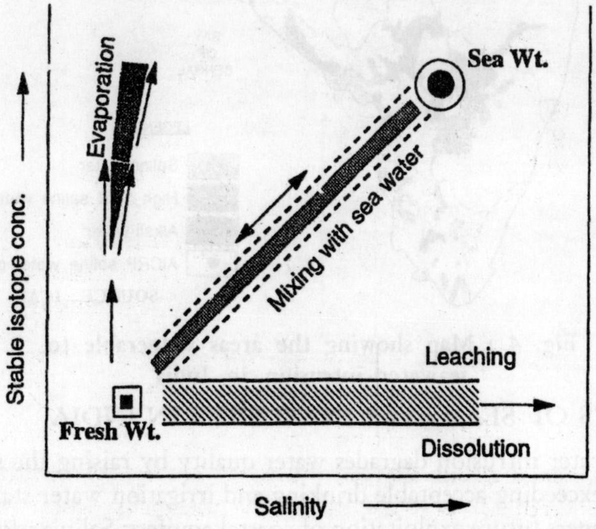

Fig. 3a : Relationship between salinity and stable isotope concentration for various salinization processes (Yurtsever, 1997)

The tritium content of sea water is usually in the range of 10-12 TU (tritium units) and radiocarbon content of seawater was around

85-95 pmc (percent modern carbon). Both tritium and radiocarbon content of groundwater, however, may be much higher of lower than the seawater concentration, depending on the mean transit time of the water in the groundwater system (Yurtsever, 1997).

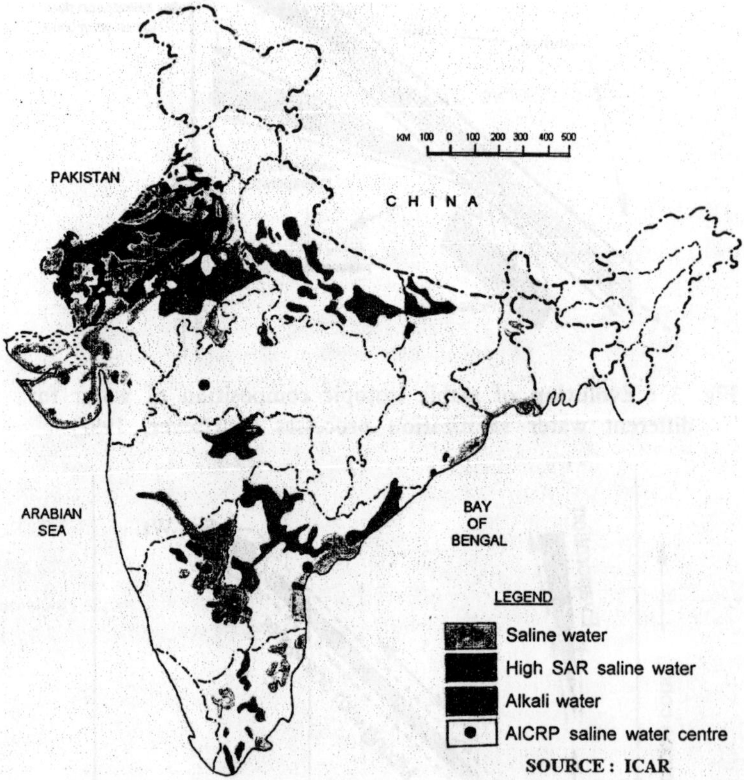

Fig. 4 : Map showing the areas vulnerable to seawater intrusion in India

IMPACTS OF SEAWATER INTRUSION IN INDIA

Seawater intrusion degrades water quality by raising the salinity to levels exceeding acceptable drinking and irrigation water standards, and endangers future exploitation of coastal aquifers. Salinization leads to an increase in the content of certain dissolved chemical species as well as affecting the over all water chemical composition (Ritcher and Kreitler, 1993). The deleterious impacts of groundwater salinization resulting from seawater intrusion have caused significant losses in potable water supplies and in agricultural production globally (FAO, 1997). In India, many parts of the coastal areas affected with saline water. Groundwater aquifers from Tamil Nadu, Andhra Pradesh, Orissa, West Bengal, Gujarat and Karnataka are facing the problem of seawater intrusion. If it is not managed, people shall struggle for water in future.

MANAGEMENT OF SEAWATER INTRUSION

Over-exploitation of groundwater resources should be avoided to prevent ingress of seawater into freshwater aquifers. To protect the aquifers from over-exploitation, an effective groundwater management policy oriented towards promotion of efficiency, equity and sustainability is required. Clearly, a joint management approach combining government administration with active people participation is a promising solution. There is need for increasing its availability of fresh groundwater. The availability enhanced by rejuvenation of dyeing lakes, ponds and tanks, rainwater harvesting and increasing the artificial means of groundwater recharge.

A well known recharge technique is rain water harvesting which is the process to capture and store rainfall for its efficient utilization and conservation to control its runoff, evaporation and seepage. Rainwater harvesting is the possible solution to water crisis. It has been used to provide drinking water, water for livestock, water for irrigation or to refill aquifers in a process called groundwater recharge. There are a number of types of systems to harvest rainwater ranging from very simple to the complex industrial systems. Generally, rainwater is either harvested from the ground or from a roof. Traditional rainwater harvesting, which is still prevalent in rural areas, is done by using surface storage like lakes, ponds, tanks etc. In urban areas, rain water will have to be harvested from the roofs of houses, tents and local institutions, or from specially prepared areas of ground, can make an important contribution to drinking water. Some of the benefits of rainwater harvesting are as, it increases water availability, it checks the declining water table, it improves the quality of water through dilution and it prevents soil erosion and flooding.

In addition, some preventive measures are also possible. If the thickness of fresh groundwater is only small it is better to pump many wells of small capacity than only few wells of large capacity. This is to avoid upcoming of saline groundwater. In a critically over-polluted area, bore well drilling should be regulated till the water table attains the desired elevation. Artificial recharge measures need to be urgently implemented in these areas. When applying artificial recharge in sand dunes, the inflow of saline water, below the freshwater lens is reduced by the lowering of the interface between fresh and saline groundwater and corresponding reduction of the height available for inflow of saline water between that interface and impermeable base.

CONCLUSION

Water is one of the essential natural resources for sustaining life and is likely to become critical source in the coming decades due to continuous increase in its demands and rapid increase in population. The over-exploitation of the groundwater resources lead to deteriorate the quality of water and to decline the groundwater table which causes groundwater salinization. For planning, design and manage the groundwater resources, regular water quality monitoring has to be launched for identifying the areas likely to be affected because of the saline intrusion problems especially in the coastal areas. For better management of groundwater resources in the coastal areas, water quality monitoring with efficient tools like isotope application is necessary for the management of seawater intrusion. Even though, prevention is better than cure. There is need for increasing its availability and reducing its demand. For increasing its availability, there is a better management of existing storages and creation of additional storages. The availability of water resources further enhanced by rejuvenation of dyeing lakes, ponds and tanks, rainwater harvesting and increasing the artificial means of groundwater recharge. "Sustainable use of water resources is a global responsibility". So that groundwater resources should be sustained for future of India, is a prime duty of every citizen.

REFERENCES

1. Bayari, C.S. and Ozyurt, N.N. 2007. Isotopic and chemical characterization of coastal and submarine karst groundwater discharges in Southern Turkey. In: Nuclear and isotopic technique for the characterization of submarine groundwater discharge in coastal zones. IAEA TECDOC – 1595, pp. 75–91.

2. Davis, S.N. and Wiest, D. 1996. Hydrogeology. John Wiley & Sons, New York, P. 463.

3. FAO (Food and Agricultural Organization). 1997. Seawater intrusion in coastal aquifers: Guidelines for study, monitoring and control, FAO Water Reports, Rome, P. 163.

4. Gupta, S. K and Deshpande, R.D. 2004. Water for India in 2050: first-order assessment of available options. Current Science, 86: 1216–1223.

5. Hinrichsen, D. 2007. Ocean planet in decline. Available (online). http.//www.people and planet.net/pdoc.php?id=429.Accessed July 10, 2010.

6. IAEA (International Atomic Energy Agency). 1981. Stable isotope hydrology – Deuterium and Oxygen in the water cycle. IAEA technical report series No. 210.

7. IAEA (International Atomic Energy Agency). 1996. Isotope field applications for groundwater studies in the Middle East. IAEA technical report series No. 890.

8. Khublaryan, M.G., Frolov, A.P. and Yushmanov, I.O. 2008. Seawater intrusion into coastal aquifers. Water resources, 35(3): 274-296.

9. Khayat, S., Hotzl, H., Geyer, S. and Ali, W. 2006. Hydro-chemical investigation of water from the Pleistocene wells and springs, Jericho area, Palestine. Hydrogeol. J., 14: 192–202.

10. Kumar, R., Singh, R.D. and Sharma, K.D. 2005. Water sources of India. Current Science, 89 (5): 794–811.

11. Murugesan, A.G., Sukumaran, N., Rajan, M.P., Ramesh, S., Sathesh Prabu, C. and George, T. 2010. Studies on physical, chemical, pathological and radiological quality of aquatic resources around Kudankulam Nuclear Power Project site covering 30 km radius. South Indian Coastal and Marine Bulletin, 2 (1): 6–9.

12. National Water Policy of India. 2002. Government of India, P. 5.

13. Neilsen, L., Jorgensemn, N. and Gelting, P. 2007. Mapping of the freshwater lens in a coastal aquifer on the Keta barrier (Ghana) by TEM. Journal of Applied Geophysics, 62 (1): 1-15.

14. Noble, J., Nair, A.R., Sinha, U.K., Joseph, T.S. and Navada, S.V. 2006. Isotope studies to understand the dynamic changes due to long term exploitation of groundwater systems in Western Rajasthan, India. In: Isotope assessment of long term groundwater exploitation. IAEA TECDOC – 1507, pp. 55–72.

15. Piper, A. M. 1944. A graphical procedure in geochemical interpredation of water analysis. Am. Geophys Union Trans., 25: 914–928.

16. Richter, B.C. and Kreitler, C.W. 1993. Geochemical Techniques for Identifying Sources of Ground-Water Salinization. CRC Press, P. 258.

17. Wilson, S., Ingham, M. and McConchie. 2006. The ability of earth resistivity methods for saline interface definition. Journal of hydrology, 316: 301-312.

18. Yingkai, X., Dezhong, Y., Weiguo, L., Qingzhong, W. and Haizheng, W. 2001. Boron isotope method for study of seawater intrusion. Science in China (Series E), 44 (1): 62-71

19. Yurtsever, Y. 1997. Role and contribution of environmental tracers for the study of sources and processes of groundwater salinization. In: Hydrochemistry (Proc. of the Rabat symposium April 1997). IAHS publication No. 244, pp 3-12.

□□□

19

Sustainable Development–A Vision for 21st Century

A. VELIAPPAN AND M. SADANANTHAN

INTRODUCTION

The recognition of and respect for the environment as the foundation of all life goes back several millennia in Indian thought. The world and its resources were seen not as being essentially for human existence but that each species had a right of its own. In traditions found throughout the country a natural resource, be it water or soil, would be respected, and often prayed to before it was used.

In contemporary India, Mahatma Gandhiji spoke of the need to conserve this unique life support system and to use its resources wisely. "The earth has enough for everyone's need but not for anyone's greed" he said long before the recognition of the environment crises. He was conscious of the development path India was embarking upon. In the late 1920s he warned, "God forbid that India should ever take to industrialism after the manner of the west....If an entire nation of 300 million took to similar economic exploitation, it would strip the world bare like locusts"(Gandhi, 1928).

Industrialization has provided humanity with many material and social benefits. At the same time it has brought in its many material and social problems. One of the major problems is the pollution of the environment. As the Stockholm Declaration (June,1972) has enunciated, man is both the creator and moulder of his environment, which gives him physical sustenance and offers him the opportunity for intellectual, moral, social and spiritual growth. The second principle of the Stockholm Declaration enunciates that the natural resources of the earth including the air, water, land, flora and fauna must be safeguarded for the benefit of present and future generations through careful planning and management.

SUSTAINABLE DEVELOPMENT

The idea of sustainable development was first used in an international forum in the world conservation strategy 1980. The strategy recommended the integration of conservation principles and objectives with social and economic development. It emphasized that Environmental Education and the participation of the public were critical support tools to achieve these objectives as they are indispensable to achieving the changes in the behaviour of individuals and societies with regard to the biosphere (Sarabhai, Pandya and Namagiri, 2007).

The Brundtland Report in 1987 by the World Commission on Environment and Development (WCED) provides the most widely operational definition of sustainable development. The report emphasized the need to promote sustainable development that would "meet the needs of the present without compromising the ability of future generations to meet their own needs". An important commitment to sustainable development came in the form of 187 countries signing the Rio Declaration during the 1992 United Nations Conference on Environment and Development (UNCED) in Rio de Janeiro. The declaration set out 27 principles for achieving sustainable development, and Agenda 21, a guiding document for sustainable development, was simultaneously adopted (UNESCO, 2005).

Principles for Sustainable Development

The following are some of the principles of sustainable development:

- Limit the human population to a level within the carrying capacity of the environment.
- Renewable resources harvesting rate should not be above the generation rate.
- In the case of non-renewable, rate of depletion should not be above the rate of generation of renewable substitutes.
- It brings people together with nature and gives better future.

Areas of Sustainable Development

Sustainable development includes three key areas of interaction: society, environment and economy with culture and values as underlying dimensions.

Society: an understanding of social institutions and their role in change and development, as well as the democratic and participatory systems which give opportunity for expression of opinion, selection of governments, forging of consensus and resolution of differences.

Environment: awareness of our dependence on the earth's resources, fragility of the physical environment and its effects on human activity and decisions along with a commitment to factoring in environmental concerns while delineating social and economic policy.

Economy: sensitivity to the limits and potential of economic growth and its impact on the environment and society, with a commitment to assess personal and societal levels of consumption with a concern for environment and social justice.

Thus, the well-being of these three components- environment, society and economy is intertwined and not separate. Sustainability means thinking about a future in which environmental, societal and economic considerations are balanced in pursuit of development and improved quality of life. A healthy, prosperous society would also need a peaceful environment for people from all parts of society to live and prosper in.

HUMAN SYSTEM - PART OF ECO-SYSTEM

It is the sharpening awareness of the impending environmental disaster, as a consequence of development, that made men understands that the human system is part of eco-system. The community of man is embedded in the natural environment, and there has to be an ecological balance for man's survival. This is called the new socio-biological approach to development. Now we were aware that flora and fauna, plants, birds, animals and micro organisms are the kith and kin of man and we all have to live together. As early as 1927, Mahatma Gandhi had warned against indiscriminate industrialization which destroys nature. But this warning of his was lost in the midst of work ship of the development.

EDUCATION FOR A SUSTAINABLE FUTURE

The first international event making the beginning of decade of education for sustainable development, an international conference organized by the Centre for Environmental Education (CEE) and held in Ahmedabad. The event discussed the role of the decade in re-orienting the vision of development that needs to be redefined but the paradigm of education also has to change in certain fundamental ways to achieve sustainability. Some of the changes as below:

- Learning rather than teaching.
- Lifelong and continuous rather than confined to a specific period.
- Multi-sourced and accessed rather than top down, controlled and orchestrated.
- Empowering rather than socializing.
- Global and yet locale specific.
- Capacity building to built abilities for critical thinking and problem solving.
- Multi-disciplinary approach as opposed to a single new discipline.
- Sensitive to gender, diversity etc.

Targets for Sustainable Development

- Stop imitating high energy consuming and resource depleting western pattern of development.
- Stop developmental patterns based on loans, subsides, imported resources and borrowed techniques.
- Move towards an eco-development using indigenous materials suited to our culture and traditions, at low costs.
- Depend on a sustainable development of energy and industry which,

  —Reduce annual emission of CO_2, SO_2 and NO_2

  —Shift from fossil fuel to solar, wind mill and biogas
- Depend on a sustainable urban development which

  —Promote public over private transports

—Protect farmland from urban encroachment

—Make urban and rural development naturally supporting

Depend on a sustainable rural development which

—Reduce the rate of tropical deforestation

—Reduce species extinction

—Involve community participation

CONCLUSION

If we accept the concept of sustainable development, we must accept that approach to development which does not destroy, deplete or degrade natural resources, but which conserves, augments and upgrades them. And to achieve this vision, the four most critical issues to be addressed would include economic disparity and poverty, disasters, climate change and cultural heritage. Education for Sustainable development efforts would be directed in these priority areas to enable achievement of Sustainable development objectives for the country.

REFERENCES

1. Pandey V.C, (2005) Environmental Education, Isha Books, New Delhi.
2. Gandhi, M.K. In Harijan, 20 (12), 422.
3. Sarabhai, K.V., Pandya, M and Namagiri, R. (2007) Tbilisi to Ahmedabad: The Journal of environmental education, CEE, Ahmedabad.
4. UNESCO (2005) United Nations Decade of Education for Sustainable development, International Implementation Scheme. Paris.
5. Veliappan A. (2007) Environmental Education, A.V. Parvathi Publication Pvt.Ltd, Tirunelveli.
6. Education for Sustainable Development in India: Towards Inclusive Growth - MHRD and Centre for Environmental Education (CEE), Ahmedabad.

20

Measures to Tackle Water Crisis and Healthy Sanitation Practices

M.R. HUBERT

PRESENT INDIAN SCENARIO

Rural Levels

Though India has made significant progress in terms of the GDP growth and is at the forefront of developing countries in all areas of economic development half of its people largely residing in rural areas still defecate in the open and live in unhealthy and unclean Environment. The main reason for this is due to lack of awareness amongst people regarding maintaining clean and healthy environment and personal health and hygiene.

People particularly in rural areas pollute rivers and water bodies by taking bath washing clothes and utensils throwing garbage and even defecating and urinating near water sources. This leads to not only pollution of rivers but also threatens the safety of ground water which often is the only source of drinking water in rural areas. This leads to many life threatening and preventable water and sanitation related diseases like Polio, Malaria, and Diarrhoea which most affect women and children. The improper disposal of waste water, open drains, polluted water bodies, stagnation of water around hand pumps also ruins the conditions of roads and becomes a breeding ground for all kinds of disease producing viruses. Therefore, along with provision of sanitary latrines to prevent open defecation time has come to address the problems of Solid and liquid Waste Management in villages to prevent environmental pollution and diseases

The Government of India through its flagship programme of Total Sanitation Campaign (TSC) has been able to enhance the sanitation coverage in rural areas from a mere 1% in 1981to over 54% in the current financial year. Through this programme in the year 2007-08 alone, more than 1.2 crore toilets have been constructed. The Government of India is committed to achieve cent percent sanitation coverage in all rural households by 2012 much before the Millennium Development Goal Target set by United Nations General Assembly of reducing by half the proportion of people without access to basic sanitation by year 2015. The credible point which is overlooked is does this toilets are in use and what are its efficiency situations.

Recommendations for Improvement

A system of delivery was that promotes and reinforces commitment, participation, leadership, ownership, scaling-up/innovation and preparedness for next level of response. And also was that adequate financial resources, technical resources, human resources, sustainable technologies, sustainable behavior/practices.

Adequate and sustained allocation of resources: The resources include Financial Resources, Technical Resources and Human Resources. There should be commitment and action for sustained funding at national, state level. Inputs in implementation coordination, capacity building and the focus robust monitoring/ social audit. Base should be created for human resource for current and future response

Sustainable Technologies: The technology should be affordable, available, useable, modern quality technologies. The technologies should be coupled with economic returns like in technologies like Improved leach pits Eco-san, Toilet linked bio-gas, Vermin-composting and Cleaner technologies- Carbon Credits.

Sustainable Behaviour/Practices: Sustained mobilization and monitoring for proper usage/maintenance by evolving Communication Strategy, Continuous researched/benefit inputs on sanitation and hygiene. It should be seen as new business opportunity and as a sense of modernity. It should be making glamorous to break the taboos.

Urban Levels

Sanitation is defined as safe disposal of human excreta including its safe confinement treatment disposal and associated hygiene practices. Sanitation is also depending on other elements like environmental sanitation along with the management water supply. 27.8% of Indians, i.e. 286 million people or 55 million households live in urban areas-projections indicate that the urban population would have grown to 331 million people by 2007 and to 368 million by 2012. 12.04 million (7.87 %) Urban households do not have access to latrines and defecate in the open. 5.48 million (8.13%) Urban households use community latrines and 13.4 million households (19.49%) use shared latrines. 12.47 million (18.5%) households do not have access to a drainage network. 26.83 million (39.8%) households are connected to open drains. The status in respect of the urban poor is even worse

The overall sanitation coverage in India in 2005-2006 is 44.6%. The rural sanitation is 26% and urban sanitation is 84.6% only .however field studies shown that very low usage of latrines in both rural and urban areas. 74% of people in rural India still don't have a toilet and in urban it is 16%7. There is a gradual change in sanitation coverage in India and the trend is increasing over the past two decades. But if it will take place in the same pace it may take another 200 years to get a toilet for every Indian.

India is urbanizing very fast and along with this, the slum population is also increasing. India's urban population is increasing at a faster rate than its total population. With over 575 million people, India will have 41% of its population living in cities and towns by 2030 AD from the present level of 286 million and 28%. However, most of them are not having basic facilities like drinking water and sanitation. Among the urban poor, the slum dwellers are the poorest. The very definition of slums points at acute drinking water and sanitation crisis for the slum dwellers. Slum in India is defined as a cluster inside urban areas without having water and sanitation access. Slum population is constantly increasing: it has doubled in the past two decades. The current population living in slums in the country is more than the population of Britain. India's slum-dwelling population rose from 27.9 million in 1981 to over 40 million in 2001. As per the 2001 census of India, 640 towns spread over 26 states and union territories have reported existence of slums. This means one out of every four persons reside in slums in our cities and towns. The NSSO survey in 2002 has identified 51688 slums in urban areas of which 50.6% of urban slums have been declared as "notified slums". This growing slum population and the lack of basic facilities will badly impact on India's overall target achievement in water and sanitation sector.

Social and Occupational aspects of Sanitation: Despite the appropriate legal framework, progress towards the elimination of manual scavenging has shown limited success, Little or no attention has been paid towards the occupational hazard faced by sanitation workers daily.

- Fragmented Institutional Roles and Responsibilities: There are considerable gaps and overlaps in institutional roles and responsibilities at the national, state, and city levels. Lack of an Integrated City-wide Approach: Sanitation investments are currently planned in a piece-meal manner and do not take into account the full cycle of safe confinement.
- Limited Technology Choices: Technologies have been focused on limited options that have not been cost-effective, and sustainability of investments has been in question.
- Reaching the UN-served and Poor: Urban poor communities as well other residents of informal settlements have been constrained by lack of tenure, space or economic constraints, in obtaining affordable access to safe sanitation. In this context, the issues of whether services to the poor should be individualized and whether community services should be provided in non-notified slums should be addressed. However provision of individual toilets should be prioritized. In relation to "Pay and Use" toilets, the issue of subsidies inadvertently reaching the non-poor should be addressed by identifying different categories of urban poor.

WATER CRISIS

While the world's population tripled in the 20th century, the use of renewable water resources has grown six-fold. Within the next fifty years, the world population will increase by another 40 to 50 %. This population growth - coupled with industrialization and urbanization - will result in an increasing demand for water and will have serious consequences on the environment.

AGRICULTURAL CRISIS

Although food security has been significantly increased in the past thirty years, water withdrawals for irrigation represent 66 % of the total withdrawals and up to 90 % in arid regions, the other 34 % being used by domestic households (10 %), industry (20 %), or evaporated from reservoirs (4 %). As the per capita use increases due to changes in lifestyle and as population increases as well, the proportion of water for human use is increasing. This, coupled with spatial and temporal variations in water availability, means that the water to produce food for human consumption, industrial processes and all the other uses is becoming scarce.

ENVIRONMENTAL CRISIS

It is all the more critical that increased water use by humans does not only reduce the amount of water available for industrial and agricultural development but has a profound effect on aquatic ecosystems and their dependent species. Environmental balances are disturbed and cannot play their regulating role anymore.

AN INCREASE IN TENSIONS

Water stress results from an imbalance between water use and water resources. The water stress indicator in this map measures the proportion of water withdrawal with respect to total renewable resources. It is a criticality ratio, which implies that water stress depends on the variability of resources. Water stress causes deterioration of fresh water resources in terms of quantity (aquifer over-exploitation, dry rivers, etc.) and quality (eutrophication, organic matter pollution, saline intrusion, etc.) The value of this criticality ratio that indicates high water stress is based on expert judgment and experience (Alcamo and others, 1999). It ranges between 20 % for basins with highly variable runoff and 60 % for temperate zone basins. In this map, we take an overall value of 40 % to indicate high water stress. We see that the situation is heterogeneous over the world.

CHENNAI WATER SITUATIONS

Chennai and the first thing people want to know about is the availability of water, besides the heat of course. This summer the scarcity could be the worst ever for the 55 lakh people in Tamil Nadu's capital city, not to speak of the several lakhs living in its suburbs. Chennai receives its rainfall mostly from the northeast monsoon in three or four spells during October-December. The monsoon failed in 2002 and 2003. In 2003, Chennai received only 280 mm of rain from the northeast monsoon against the normal of 580 mm, a deficit of 54 per cent. Consequently, the storage levels in the city's reservoirs - Red Hills, Poondi and Cholavaram - are the lowest in 55 years.

As on March 1, 2004, the combined storage in these reservoirs was 160.5 million cubic feet while their total storage capacity of 7,412 mc ft. Of the combined capacity, Red Hills contributes 3,300 mc ft, a Satyamurthi Sagar at Poondi 3,231 mc ft and Cholavaram 881 mcft. An official of Metro water, the body in charge of water supply in the city, called the situation "very, very bad" and said water in the reservoirs was down to the "dead storage" level. "Only groundwater can save the city," he added. In fact, it is the groundwater from the irrigation wells around Chennai that has kept the city going.

If the Tamil Nadu government/Metro water officials pinned their hopes on the Telugu Ganga project to combat the water problem in Chennai, the project flattered to deceive. The Krishna river water released from the Kandaleru reservoir in Andhra Pradesh reached the zero point near Uthukottai in Tamil Nadu, after covering a distance of 152 km, on February 16. It was to reach Poondi and then course 35 km down the Baby Canal to the Red Hills reservoir for being treated and ferried in tankers. But such hopes evaporated on February 18 with the Poondi canal remaining dry. Illegal tapping of water by farmers and the drawal of water to meet the demands of Tirupati town in Andhra Pradesh were offered as the reasons for the virtual non-arrival of the Krishna water in the Poondi canal.

The present supply to Chennai is about 103 million liters a day. The water is pumped from the well-fields at Minjur, Panchetti and other places into the system. Besides, tankers supply about 125 million liters of water a day to Chennai from private agricultural wells. With the identification of more private agricultural wells and more tankers being pressed into service, about 125 million of liters of water is being distributed in Chennai every day.

Chief Minister Jayalalithaa told the State Assembly on February 10 that a scheme was under way to ensure that Chennai continued to receive 103 million liters of water a day in the summer months. This would be done by tapping 32 million liters a day from 110 agricultural wells. Besides, 1,000 deep bore wells would be sunk in different parts of the city. This would be in addition to the existing 6,530 deep bore wells. All this would cost Rs.28.50 crores.

She said there were plans to hire about 125 field wells around Poondi and pump 30 million liters of water a day from them into the Red Hills water treatment plant. Pipes would be laid to transport this water from Poondi to Red Hills. Tankers would make several hundred more trips to supply the water to the various parts of the city. All this would continue until the end of September when the northeast monsoon sets in. These works would cost Rs.306 crores, she said.

On February 22, the Central inter-ministerial team deputed to assess the drought in Tamil Nadu visited the Red Hills and Poondi reservoirs. The Chief Minister has written to Prime Minister Atal Bihari Vajpayee requesting the release of Rs.700 crores from the National Calamity Contingency Fund to battle the water crisis in Chennai. The Centre has announced an initial assistance of Rs.50 crores.

The only hope for Chennai residents now is the New Veeranam Project in Cuddalore district, titled the Chennai Water Supply Augmentation Project - I. Jayalalithaa said the scheme would be completed at a cost of Rs.720 crores by the end of May.

But the project is mired in controversy. Leaders of the Opposition Pattali Makkal Katchi (PMK) claim that when the water in the Veeranam Lake is not enough to irrigate its own ayacut, it cannot cater to Chennai's needs. Leaders of other parties, too, share this fear.

However, according to Jayalalithaa, the scheme was being implemented without affecting irrigation in the existing ayacut. By raising the lake bund by 0.6 meters, its capacity had been raised from 930 mc ft to 1,485 mc ft, she said. This and other steps taken to augment the lake's capacity would result in the availability of water going up from 11.06 tmc ft to 14.45 tmc ft, she said. Of the additional 3.39 tmc ft, only 2.45 tmc ft would be used for the New Veeranam Project. "The truth is that agriculture will get an additional 1 tmc ft," she said. Besides, she said, her government was examining a proposal, which would be an "alternative" to the New Veeranam Project and would "strengthen" it. This would enable a supply of 180 million liters of water, she said.

Will the Tamil Nadu government use the proven expertise of the Bhabha Atomic Research Centre (BARC) at Trombay, Mumbai, to put up desalination plants, which may offer a durable solution to Chennai's water problem? BARC has erected the world's largest desalination plant linked to a nuclear power station adjacent to the Madras Atomic Power Station in Kalpakkam, about 50 km from Chennai. This plant has two sections. One section produces 18 lakh liters of potable water a day from sea water using the reverse osmosis method and the other section, which is scheduled to become operational in six months, will produce 45 lakh liters a day using the thermal method.

Ecosan is the only proven method to tackle raising water and sanitation crisis. Ecological sanitation, also known as ecosan or eco-san, is a sanitation process that uses human blackwater and sometimes immediately eliminates fecal pathogens from any still present wastewater (urine) at the source. The objectives are to offer economically and ecologically sustainable and culturally acceptable systems that aim to close the natural nutrient and water cycle.

In the event of continuing exploitation of natural recourses such as extensive use of water , polluting ground water, cutting trees , raising level of wa'er scarcity and other pollutions in urban areas play a vital role on the living condition of the people and as well as the environment. Due to virulent nature of the issues related to the Ecological Sanitation, there is a growing concern among the NGOs and Govt. of Tamil Nadu with the view to find out a long lasting solution to these issues.

'Ecosan' concept, Human waste has been identified as a valuable resource. The ecosan products like compost manure and urine has rich in essential nutrients needed for plant growth. Nitrogen (N), Phosphorus (P), Potassium (K), Sulfur, Calcium, Magnesium are the important micro nutrient component human waste stream. the remainder is in the form of ammonium or creatinine which has proven to be safe from toxins and other harmful chemical agents found in any chemical based fertilisers.

Ecological sanitation (Ecosan) is a new holistic paradigm in sanitation, which is based on an overall view of material flows as part of an ecologically and economically sustainable wastewater management system tailored to the needs of the users and to the respective local conditions. It does not favour a specific sanitation technology, but is rather a new philosophy in handling substances that have so far been seen simply as wastewater and water-carried waste for disposal. Ecological sanitation can be defined as a system that:

- Prevents disease and promotes health
- Protects the environment and conserves water
- Recovers and recycles nutrients and organic matter

Ecosan offers a flexible framework, where centralized elements can be combined with decentralized ones, waterborne with dry sanitation, high-tech with low-tech, etc. By considering a much larger range of options, optimal and economic solutions can be developed for each particular situation. Thus, the most important advantages of ecological sanitation systems are:

- Improvement of health by minimizing the introduction of pathogens from human excreta into the water cycle
- Promotion of safe, hygienic recovery and use of nutrients, organics, trace elements, water and energy
- Preservation of soil fertility
- Contribution to the conservation of resources through lower water consumption, substitution of mineral fertilizer and minimization of water pollution
- Improvement of agricultural productivity and food security
- Preference for modular, decentralized partial-flow systems for more appropriate cost-efficient solutions adapted to the local situation
- Promotion of a holistic, interdisciplinary approach
- Material flow cycle instead of disposal of valuable resources

CONCLUSION

The Ecosan would not heal the wounds of water and sanitation crisis, yet it would give a room of harmony and nature scented refreshing to the grieving community who look forward to hope.

REFERENCES

1. Front line Magazine on Chennai water situations.
2. The Sanitation programs achievements and challenges by Minister for Health–state on his Inaugural address about south India on water summit.
3. Better Agriculture Practices
4. Water Wars – Future shock, by professor dr. Alan Kendall.
5. Total sanitation Flagship – GOI declarations.

□□□

21

Role of Women in Water Management in the 21st Century : A Case Study of Suthamalli Village of Tirunelveli District, Tamilnadu

J. SACRATEES AND P. SARANYA

INTRODUCTION

Water is one of the natural resources which is essential to sustain life. Women play a crucial role in collecting and managing water for drinking and other household purposes. Goel and Patel (2002) observed that the availability of sufficient water is bound to improve sanitation, safe hygiene practices and better health standards to make India a safer place for all its citizens. Availability and access to clean water is among the most important determinants of the health and well being of any individual human being. As population grow, the average amount of renewable fresh water available to each person declines. Agarwal and Goel (2002) have considered water as the primary contributor to the control of infectious diseases through its use for personal and domestic hygiene. The large portion of tribal population is still deprived of the facility of clean drinking water. Raj Pramukh et al. (2004) emphasized that safe drinking water could make a tremendous impact on the quality of life in our villages, because availability of safe drinking water has direct impact on the working conditions and health of the people and their productive capacity.

The human being has taken water for granted and massively misjudged the capacity of the earth's water systems to sustain the demands made upon it. About 70 percent of the earth's surface is covered in water, but 97 percent of it is saltwater, which is unfit for human use. Saltwater cannot be used for drinking, crop irrigation or most industrial uses. Of the remaining 3 percent of the Worlds, water resources, only about 1 percent is readily available for human consumption. Instead of taking great care of the limited water we have, we are diverting, polluting, and depleting it at an astonishing rate as if there were no reckoning to come.

Agriculture is by far the biggest user of water, accounting worldwide for about 69 percent of all withdrawals, with domestic (municipal) use amounting to about 10 percent and industry using some 21 percent. It is important to distinguish between water that is withdrawn and water that is actually consumed. Irrigation consumes much of the water it withdraws (often half or more) as a result of evaporation, incorporation into crops and transpiration from crops. The other half recharges groundwater or surface flows or is lost in unproductive evaporation. Up to 90 percent of the water withdrawn for domestic use is returned to rivers and aquifers as wastewater. Industries typically consume only about 5 percent of the water they withdraw. Wastewater from domestic sewage systems and industries, unless treated before it is released into rivers and possibly re-used, becomes a major source of water pollution.

Many developing countries rely heavily on irrigation for agriculture. Inevitably, such intensive use of water for agriculture can strain resources. Countries are could be defined as water stressed if they abstract more than 20 percent of their renewable water resources. By this definition, 36 of 159 countries (23 percent) were already water stressed in 1998. Today, a third of the world lives in water stressed areas where consumption outstrips supply. Rapid industrialization and changes in the agricultural practices from subsistence farming to industrial and profit-oriented farming (intensive cultivation) have resulted in excessive use of water, particularly fresh water and its pollution. Pollution also further limits the amount of fresh water.

According to the estimates (NSS, GoI-1991), 84 percent of the economically active women are involved in contribution towards agriculture in India, which accounts for 87 percent of India's GNP. Thus, women play a pivotal role in agricultural development and the management of natural resources and their involvement is indispensable for the effective implementation and equitable distribution of the benefits of watershed management.

Women constitute more than 50 percent of the world population. In many communities, particularly poor women's survival and that of their households, depends on access to and control of natural resources. However, limited access to these resources like water is intensifying the cycle of poverty, gender inequalities, and poor living standard. Women and men have distinct responsibilities and different stakes in using and managing natural resources in a watershed. As economic provider, caregivers, and household mangers, women are responsible for ensuring that their families have basic resources for daily lives. They are often the managers of community natural resources, and have learned to protect these resources in order to preserve them for future generations (managers of sustainability).

Women play a crucial role in collecting and managing water for drinking and other household purposes. Goel and Patel (2002) observed that the availability of sufficient water is bound to improve sanitation, safe hygiene practices and better health standards to make India a safer place for all its citizens. Availability and access to clean water is among the most important determinants of the health and well being of any individual human being. As population increases, the average amount of renewable fresh water available to each person declines. Agarwal and Goel (2002) have considered water as the primary contributor to the control of infectious diseases through its use for personal and domestic hygiene. Raj Pramukh ,K.E.,Elizabeth and Sankar Rao (2004) emphasized that safe drinking water could make a tremendous impact on the quality water could make a tremendous impact on the quality of life in our villages, because availability of safe drinking water has direct impact on the working of safe drinking water has direct impact on the working conditions and health of the people and their productive capacity.

Water has become the most commercial product of the 21st century. This may sound bizarre, but true. In fact, the available water resources both surface and groundwater is under crisis in the 21st century. The stress on the multiple water resources is a result of a multitude of factors. On the one hand, the burgeoning population and changing lifestyles have increased the need for fresh water. For instance, the competitions among users in agriculture, industry and domestic sector are pushing the ground water table under thrust. To get a bucket of drinking water is a struggle for most women in the country. The virtually dry and dead water resources have' lead to acute water scarcity, affecting the socio-economic condition of the society.

The drought conditions have pushed villagers to move to cities in search of jobs, whereas women and girls are trudging still further. This time lost in fetching water can very well translate into financial gains, leading to a better life for the family. If opportunity costs were taken into account, it would be clear that in most rural areas, households are paying far more for water supply than the often-normal rates charged in urban areas. Also, if this cost of fetching water which is almost equivalent to 150 million women days each year, is covered into a loss for the national exchequer, it translates into a whopping 10 billion rupees per year. The government has accorded the highest priority to rural drinking water for ensuring universal access as a part of policy framework to achieve the goal of reaching the unreached. Despite the installation of more than 3.5 million hand pumps and over 116 thousand piped water supply schemes, in many parts of the country, the people face water scarcity almost every year, there by meaning that our water supply systems are failing to sustain despite huge investments.

In India, there are many villages either with scarce water supply or without any source of water. If there is no source of potable water in 2.5 kilometers, then the village becomes no-source water village or problem village. In many rural areas, women still have to walk a distance of about 2.5 kms to reach the source of water. She reaches home carrying heavy pots, not to rest but to do other household chores of cooking, washing, cleaning, caring of children and looking after livestock. Again in the evening she has to fetch water. Thus a rural woman's life is sheer drudgery.

Water is the biggest crisis facing India in terms of spread and severity, affecting one in every three persons. Even in Chennai, Bangalore, Shimla and Delhi, water is being rationed and India's food security is under threat. With the lives and livelihood of millions at risk, urban India is screaming for water. For instance, water is rationed twice a week in Bangalore, and for 30 minutes a day in Bhopal; 250 tankers make 2,250 trips to quench Chennai's thirst. Mumbai routinely lives through water cuts from January to June, when some areas get water once in three days in Hyderabad. Women have to queue up in front of the public water taps, being at the lag end of the pipeline system, they get water only after the users ahead in the pipeline finish collecting water. There are nights when water pressure dips so low that some women get it after midnight.

WOMEN'S REPRODUCTIVE AND PRODUCTIVE ROLES

Women and men assume distinct responsibilities in using and managing water and water systems. In most societies, women and girls collect every litre of water for cooking, bathing, cleaning, maintaining health and hygiene, raising small livestock and growing food. Rural men need water for irrigation and larger livestock, but women often care for the milk cattle and young animals. They also oversee family health. Because of these differing gender roles, women and men have different stakes in water use. There is a tendency to overemphasize women's reproductive roles in relation to water resource management in other words, those tasks that span providing, managing and safeguarding water for use by the family. Water is also used in building and repair work (for example, in making bricks and in plastering), for crops and food processing, and in transport. But women have pressing needs too for water to engage in economic production, including agriculture and micro enterprise. Gender disparities ensure that those needs frequently go unmet, with discrepancies in land tenure, access to water, participation, resource control, capacity and skill development, marketing and commercial linkages (GWA, 2003). Sometimes women's needs are in direct conflict with those of men: for example, food production can be an important source of family food and income for women, but women's access to irrigation is minimal (UNDP, 2002).

Gender analysis also reveals that women cope with disproportionate economic and other forms of fallout from floods, dam construction and water pollution. In 1991, after the flood action plan of Bangladesh began including gender analysis – it soon became clear that women bear a greater burden in contending with those natural disasters: not only do their normal responsibilities increase, but female-headed households are disadvantaged in terms of relief and rehabilitation. Many resort to a distinctive pattern of emergency borrowing and selling of assets, such as jewellery and utensils. Women also tend to be at greater risk of long-term economic loss than men (GWA, 2003). From a gender perspective, therefore, conservation of aquatic ecosystems can be viewed as critical in terms of improving women's access to resources essential for livelihoods, such as forests, fish species and agricultural land. This imbalance extends also to the purely domestic arena. All over the world, women and girls assume what can be the time consuming and dangerous duty of supplying the water needs of their households. Many walk long distances to fetch water, spending four or five hours per day burdened under heavy containers and suffering acute physical problems, especially in drought-prone areas. In some mountainous regions of East Africa, for example, women spend up to 27 per cent of their caloric intake in collecting water (Lewis, 1994). In urban areas, women and girls wait hours queuing for intermittent water supplies. Many then have no time for other pursuits, such as education, income generation or cultural and political activities. Since they are in regular contact with poor-quality water, women face a higher exposure to water-borne diseases. Seventy per cent of the world's blind are women who have been infected, directly or through their children, with trachoma, a blinding bacterial eye infection occurring in communities with limited access to water (GWA, 2003).

The available water is scarce; people must buy it, frequently without any guarantee of quality. High prices can swallow large proportions of family income, highlighting the importance of distinguishing between cultural and socio-economic categories, even within a gender analysis: class, wealth, age, religion and caste are important factors. Better-off women might have private wells for irrigation and domestic purposes, resources to buy safe water or treat unsafe water and domestic help to bring water from other sources. Poor women and girls do not have such options and end up with contaminated supplies. Many also lack basic education on efficient use and pollution prevention, even as they may have learned strategies to conserve water.

OBJECTIVES

1. To study how to improve the quality of life of women in rural areas by facilitating their access to water resources and by improving water resources management.
2. To study the economic loss due to fetching of water for domestic uses in the study area

3. To study the problems faced by women in the process of domestic water management in the study area
4. To suggest some policy solutions to enhance the capacities of women as domestic water managers.

METHODOLOGY

The present study is descriptive based on both primary and secondary sources of data. Primary Data are collected through questionnaire administration. The secondary data of sectoral water demand change in availability of ground water, supply demand gap in 2001 and 2050 (in TMC) and reduction in per capital availability of water has been collected from the Public Works Department. This study focused only on Suthamalli village which comes under Tirunelveli District. The other factors that are affecting due to water crisis have been collected through questionnaire survey. The relevant information pertaining to socio-economic status, available water resources for both domestic and other related purposes have been collected through field survey. The locations of the house where they are living were incorporated into the analysis. Stratified random samplings of different income categories respondents were used for different places where the water shortage acute in the village is high, medium and low. The economic loss due to fetching of water has been estimated through the questionnaire collection. The study was conducted strictly in Suthamalli village and the finding of the research work is relied only on the particular village this can be generalized across the villages in the TamilNadu. During the field survey the researcher has observed the availability of water supply sources, installation of new technology (hand pumps), and introduction of new water management strategies under State initiative. Filed work techniques such as participant observation, unstructured and structured interviews with key informants using open-ended questions and focus group discussions were used. The 100 sample has been collected within the study village. This study has been done exclusively based on field observation done among the female respondents during the period of January to March 2008. These samples have been diversified based on the various community wise populations.

BASELINE SURVEY: DATA ANALYSIS

The demographic features of Suthamalli village show some interesting trends. For instance, the number of children in the age group of 1 to 15 years is higher in comparison to adults in Suthamalli. Children constitute 24.0 per cent of the total population followed by the working population in the age groups 21-45 (35.0 %) and 46-65 (13.0). It shows that roughly every household has 1 child on average, which is in the age group of 0-14 years (Table 1). The older people above 66 years of age are only 10 (10.0%) in number, which raised questions regarding the mortality rate and life expectancy in the village. The working population (15-45 years) comprises 42 per cent of the total village population, which potentially can meet the demands of the large number of children and old people.

TABLE 1

Age wise Classification of the Respondents

S.No.	Particulars	Frequency	Percentage
1	1-15	24	24.0
2	16-20	18	18.0
3	21-25	10	10.0
4	26-35	14	14.0
5	36-45	11	11.0
6	46-55	9	9.0
7	56-65	4	4.0
8	66 & Above	10	10.0
	Total	100	100.0

Source: Primary data

The status of education in the village is still below the satisfactory level. Only 3.0 percent of the total population is educated, of which primary and secondary levels consist almost 37 per cent of the total population in the village. In absolute numbers 37 persons out of a total of 390 persons are illiterate. Only 3 persons are found professional holders among the sample total populations. This has been portraying clearly in the Table.2

TABLE 2

Educational Status of the Respondents

S.No.	Particulars	Frequency	Percentage
1	Illiterate	37	37.0
2	Primary	23	23.0
3	High school	14	14.0
4	Higher Secondary	11	11.0
5	Degree	7	7.0
6	Post Graduate	5	5.0
7	Professional	3	3.0
8	Others	Nil	Nil
	Total	100	100.0

Source: Primary data

TABLE 3

Distribution of Cultivable Land in Suthamalli Village

S.No.	Acres	No. of Households	Percentage
1	Landless	39	39.0
1	1 acre -2 acres	18	18.0
2	2 acres -5 acres	23	23.0
3	6 acres -10 acres	9	9.0
4	11 acres & Above	11	11.0
	Total	100	100.0

Source: Primary data

The above table.3 shows that the most of the households in Suthamalli village do not have adequate cultivable land. In other words, 39 per cent of households in the village are landless which indicates the existence of high level of poverty in the village (Table 3). The households having land are basically owner-cultivators most being marginal peasants. The marginal farmers constitute 18.0 per cent of the farming community having cultivable land less than 1 acre per household. It cannot be said that the distribution of land in Suthamalli is skewed, but the possession of less than 1 acre does not assure diversified agriculture in the village to serve as a potential source of livelihood. In the absence of alternative employment opportunities, especially non-farm activities, it shows the existence of structural vulnerabilities in the social and economic system in the study village.

TABLE 4

Distribution of Livestock in Suthamalli Village

S.No	Categories of Livestock	Numbers	Percentage
1	Goats	234	39.67
1	Cows	89	15.08
2	Buffalo	37	6.27
3	Bullocks	18	3.05
4	Poultry	212	35.93
	Total	590	100.0

Source: Primary data

TABLE 5

Distribution of Housing status in Suthamalli village

S.No.	Classification	Frequency	Percentage
1	Pucca	32	32.0
2	Semi-pucca	48	48.0
3	Katcha	9	9.0
4	Thatched	11	11.0
	Total	100	100.0

Source: Primary data

The livestock population in the village comprises goats, cows, buffalo, bullocks and poultry. As per the survey, households have more goats as compared to the total number of cows in the village. This may be due to the better marketability of goats and easier maintenance than cows for a supplementary source of income. The presentation of livestock data is given in Table 4. As far as housing is concerned, there are 9 *kachha*, 48 semi-pucca, 32 pucca and 11 thatched houses in Suthamalli village. Pucca houses are basically built with bricks and clay with a few of those having cement coatings.

SOURCES OF LIVELIHOOD

The village of Suthamalli is predominantly depending on agriculture for their livelihood. The total income of most of the households varies around Rs.2501- Rs.5000 per month with a few families having higher income in the range of Rs.10, 000 & above per month. Despite marginal land holdings cultivation has been the primary source of livelihood for the people in Suthamalli village. Even though agriculture is rain-fed and subsistence in nature, it provides the staple diet to the villagers. Mostly, people cultivate paddy, banana and block gram as their main crops. Besides cultivation, daily labour is the only source of income for the villagers. Only eight persons are found employed in government service. The annual income of the households in the study area from different sources is given in table 5. From table 5 it is evident that almost 66 percent of the households have monthly income in the range of Rs. 1500 to Rs. 5000, 12 percent are in Rs.5001 to Rs.7500 and 10 percent between Rs.7500 and Rs.10000 category and remaining 12 percent are having above Rs.10,001 and above.

TABLE 6

Income status of the respondents (Rs. per month)

S.No	Particulars	Frequency	Percentage
2	0-1500	29	29.0
3	2501-5000	37	37.0
4	5001-7500	12	12.0
5	7501-10000	10	10.0
6	10001 & Above	12	12.0
	Total	100	100.0

Source: Primary data

As mentioned above agriculture is seasonal in Suthamalli village during the months of June to September. For a better understanding of the daily labour disparities among households in the village based on seasonal, the distribution of households according to their labour from cultivation has done. The details are given in Table 7 around 26.84 per cent (i.e. less than Rs.1500 category) and 61.90 percent of the households earn Rs. 2501 to Rs. 5000 from cultivation during the rainy season. The low level of income from agriculture and absence of non-farm employment opportunities leads to a high incidence of poverty in the village. However, the villagers get daily employment throughout the year in the locality. As per the survey, in agricultural season (June-September) 14.29 percent of the households get income from daily labour in the range of less than Rs.1500 and 61.90 percent households are getting Rs.2501 to Rs. 5000; as their income. In lean seasons, there is not much variation in the income levels of the households (Table 7). Both men and women work during winter and summer seasons to supplement the income from agriculture.

Table 7

Distribution of Households according to Seasonal Income from Daily Labour

S.No.	Income Groups	Number of Households		
		June–September	Oct-January	Feb-May
1	Less than 0-1500	3 (14.29)	2 (5.88)	3 (6.67)
2	2501-5000	13 (61.90)	13 (38.24)	24 (54.33)
3	5001-7500	5 (23.81)	16 (47.06)	16 (35.56)
4	7501-10000	0 (0.00)	3 (8.82)	1 (2.22)
5	10001 & Above	0 (0.00)	0 (0.00)	1 (2.22)
	Total	**21**	**34**	**45**

Source: Primary data

Note: Figures in the parentheses are percentage to the total in different seasons

Drinking Water

The water sources in the village are not perennial except for one bore well for drinking water. The daily water requirements in different seasons are given in Table 8. As per the opinion of 100 households, less than 5 *Kudam* (One kudam is approximately equivalent to 10-12 litres) of water are required in rainy season (June-September) whereas in summer 6 to 10 kudam of water are necessary for daily consumption. The village women and children travel half kilometer a day during June to January for fetching water from nearby public bore wells. The situation is worse in winter and summer seasons (during February to May). On an average, they cover 4 Kms to and fro to fetch water for daily domestic requirements. Men do not participate in rainy season for fetching water; however, a thin participation is there during the months of February and May. It is obvious that the water requirement is very high during February to May. It reveals that the cost of collecting water in terms of time and energy is high in the villages.

TABLE 8

Perceived amount of Water Required per day for different Households (in Kudam)

S. No	Water requirements (in Kudam)	June-Sep	Oct-Jan	Feb-May
1	Less than 5	47	34	63
2	6-10	23	28	18
3	11 – 15	19	17	9
4	16-20	7	12	6
5	21 - 25	4	9	4
	Total	100	100.0	100.0

Source: Primary data

Therefore, necessary interventions from government and other development agencies are necessary to minimize the drudgery associated with the daily lives of the people in the Suthamalli. Even the disparity of water requirement is high among the Suthamalli village people based on caste. For example, Scheduled caste population can manage a meager amount of water during summer whereas higher community do not maximize within the availability of water requirement. Hence, from the field survey this has observed that the caste is considered the proxy of determining of water requirement in that village. However, it did not help the local people much because of its poor design and irregular follow-up by the government. There are no such efforts from District

Authorities to maintain the available water structures in the village such as bore well water is being supplying by Panchayats. This bore well water is highly significantly worsened the condition of the villagers during water scarcity.

The above table 8 clearly show that the amount of water required per day for different households (in Kudam, which means a pot, a pot, which has the capacity of 10 to 12 litres of water). Out 100 sample respondents nearly 47 percent of the respondents are needed 5 kudam water for domestic needs in the month of June-September whereas the same households needs 63 Kudam of water in During Summer (February to May) where the situation is worse with regard to acute water shortage. Most of the water bodies like bore wells and other sources like Municipal water pipes connections owned by higher caste and Scheduled caste people are denying access the available water resources frequently. Solely the higher castes and the big property owners for their benefit appropriate even irrigation facilities. As a result, the patriarchal society further oppresses the women have to travel long distances to fetch water.

TABLE 9

Caste wise Consumption of Water in Various Seasons in the Study area (in Kudam)

S.No	Caste	June-Sep	Oct-Jan	Feb-May
1	Scheduled Caste	12	8	4
2	Most Backward Class	17	14	7
3	Backward Class	24	18	8
4	Others	14	9	5

Source: Primary data

The following table 10 shows overall sectoral water demand for various needs of the people of TamilNadu have been listed in the above table. The demand for domestic needs has been increased from 78.46 (2001) thousand million cubic meters to 86.09 tmc in the year 2010. But this has been expected to raise 98.56 and 122.18 tmc in the year 2025 and 2050 respectively. Despite, the needs of irrigation do not have any changes in water demand as per the above table. However, industrial demand for water has been using rapidly from 54.91 tmc in 2001 to 70.09 tmc in the year 2050 due to vast expansion of industrial activities emerging in the era of information technology. The vast expansion of urbanization and meet the growing needs of human populations and thereby the ground water has been exploiting from peri-urban areas has led to ground water depletion. More than 60 percent of the water used in the world each year has been diverting for agricultural irrigation activities, so implementing efficient methods of delivering water to plant roots is vital. Some farmers are turning to 'surge-flow' irrigation to replace traditional flooding and channeling irrigation. Another method, which is being promoting to do, is

TABLE 10

Sectoral Water Demand (in TMC)

S. No	Classification	2001	2010	2025	2050	% of the total in 2050
1	Domestic	78.46	86.09	98.56	122.18	6
2	Irrigation	1764.82	1764.82	1764.82	1764.82	86.58
3	Industries	54.91	57.66	62.04	70.09	3.44
4	Power	4.17	4.87	5.72	6.36	0.31
5	Live stock	18.33	18.33	18.33	18.33	0.9
6	Aquaculture	0.07	0.07	0.07	0.07	-
7	Recreation	0.04	0.04	0.04	0.04	-
8	Navigation	-	-	-	-	-
9	Minimum flows	-	-	28.26	56.52	2.77
	Total	1,921	1,932	1,978	2,039	100

Source: Er.Deenadayalan, Engineer-in-Chief (Rtd.), Water Resource Organisation, Govt. of Tamilnadu.

nighttime irrigation, which reduces evaporation, improving efficiency by a factor of two to three. Industrial entrepreneurs must adopt water efficiency in their activities. This will reduce unnecessary water consumption across the nation. Thirty percent of available water in a developed country will be using for cooling purposes in electricity generating stations. Whereas in USA, the recycled water has been using for industrial purposes and thereby by 35 percent water has been saved. Every environmentalist and sociologists are discussing that, water is being treating to be a common property resources. However, today, an industrial and commercial uses of water have been given top priority over its use for human consumption and livelihood. Water bodies like rivers and lakes, etc have sold to private agencies to own and control them so that they can be in turn, siphoned off for industrial and other urban needs.

The management and distribution of water to the public is being increasingly given over to multinational water companies, which has been encouraging, by World Bank, IMF, and massive grants are given to research agencies to prove that public water distribution systems are inefficient and that they must be given over to private agencies for efficient management and distribution. The net result is that water is becoming a costly commodity beyond the research of the poor and the vulnerable. Water has been using more for industrial and commercial purposes than for agriculture. Therefore, rural poor, women, small and marginal farmers are the worst affected by these policy shift. Whereas if urban people under thrust, the government immediately take some policy initiatives to supply water for their domestic needs through any schemes like seawater desalinatization or pumping water from rural to urban through lorry tankers. Nevertheless, this would not be possible in rural areas, even if the people are affected, government will not do anything immediately for the betterment of the rural livelihoods.

The table 11 shows that overall economic loss of the Suthamalli village has been estimated amount of about Rs.6320 loss from irrespective of all caste throughout the year based on the sample respondents. This has been calculated based on the wage rate of women labourers in village. The overall man day's loss in the village is 158 days in a year of about 100 sample respondents. In fact, this has happen more in Schedule caste people those who depend on daily wages.

The quality of ground water is depends upon the water intensive mono cropping and cash cropping, seeds and crops and agricultural practices. The increased quantities of water for industrial purposes and

TABLE 11

Economic Loss due to fetching of water in Suthamalli Village

Caste	Time spending for water collection (in Hours) per day			Total hours loss due to water collection per day	Wage Loss per day in all seasons (in Rs.)
	June-Sep	Oct-Jan	Feb-May		
Scheduled Caste	2 to 3 (26%)	1 to 2 (26%)	4 to 6 (26%)	286 hours (36 man days loss)	1440
Most Backward Class	2 to 3 (24%)	2 to 3 (24%)	3 to 5 (24%)	264 hours (33 man days loss)	1320
Backward Class	3 (26%)	5 (26%)	5 to 7 (26%)	374 hours (47 man days loss)	1880
Others	2 to 4 (24%)	3 to 4 (24%)	4 to 6 (24%)	336 hours (42 man days loss)	1680
Total	100.0	100.0	100.0	1260 hours (158 man days loss)	6320

Source: Primary data

Note: (within brackets percentage of the respondents)

TABLE 12

Change in Availability of Ground water in TamilNadu

S. No.	Year of Assessment	No. of District	Total no. of Blocks	Categorization of Blocks				
				Dark (85 - 100%)	Grey (65- 85%)	White (65%)		
1	1987	19	378	41	86	251		
2	1992	22	374	89	86	209		
				Over exploited (> 100%)	Critical (90% - 100%)	Semi-Critical (70%-90%)	Safe (<70%)	Saline
3	1998	28	385	135	35	70	137	8
4	2003	28	385	135	37	105	97	8

Source: Er.Deenadayalan, Engineer-in-Chief (Rtd.), Water Resource Organisation, Govt. of Tamilnadu

water overdraft with little attention to recharging have all led to depletion of ground water resources and consequent drought like condition affecting the livelihood of village people. Water has been increasingly become polluted because of the release of industrial waste into water bodies and also chemical fertilizers and pesticides. The major rivers and lakes are becoming sources of death due to increasing aquaculture, soft drink companies and other industrial establishments are polluting local water bodies. The worst sufferers are in village level is Scheduled caste and Scheduled Tribes communities. Drudgery of women has been increased, as they have to travel long distances to fetch clean water for their daily domestic requirements.

The domestic water supply sector is also affect by the various anthropogenic activities. Domestic water supply includes the potable (drinking and cooking) and non-potable (bathing, washing, flushing and gardening) use of water. As far as Suthamalli village is concern that the ground water potential is highly depleted and even the available water is salt content and not fit for domestic use. According to Jacob et al., (1999), "it is significant to note that the level for certain physio-chemical parameters like EC, TDS, Chloride, Sulphate Hardness, Sodium BOD, and COD of ground water exceeded the permissible level prescribed by the Bureau of Indian Standards and World Health Organization standards for drinking water". Therefore, the village of Suthamalli has been relied largely on ground water to meet their domestic water requirement. Since 1995, the ground water potential has been deteriorating due to several activities. People are using more ground water for agriculture, and constructions purposes. Even little more, the ground water has been extracting for urban needs. Ultimately, more stress has been experiencing on the available local source of water. The water, which is being supplying by local Panchayat, is not sufficient for the growing domestic needs of the village. The well or bore well water quality have been deteriorated day by day due several human pressure. Since the municipal water supply is insufficient to meet the growing household requirements, people are about to purchase water. The amount spent for the water purchasing varies from Rs.200 to Rs.600 per month per households. This is high even in metropolitan cities like Chennai, Calcutta, New Delhi, Bombay, Hyderabad and Bangalore. They have been spending more than Rs.2500 to Rs.4000 per month for water. Whereas in villages people do not spend, any money with regard as far as drinking water is concerned. Instead of that, they have been losing their money income (opportunity cost) due to fetching of water from far away (where the drinking water quality is good). They may not go for job at right time, they have to allocate one, or two days in a week for water collection for their domestic needs. Sometimes, people may loss job from their masters due to late attendance. In some cases, people are awake early in the day and sleep in late night due to collection water and completion of their domestic work; this led to several health problems in due course. This study shows very clearly that there is a good positive relationship between the water quality deterioration and money income lost for water collection in the village.

TABLE 13

Supply Demand Gap in 2001 and 2050 (in TMC)

S. No	Supply/Demand	2001	2050 (If there is no improvement)
1	Total Water Resource	1643.51	1643.51
2	(i) Agricultural Demand	1764.82	1764.82
	(ii) Non-Agricultural Demand	155.98	273.58
	(iii) Total Demand	1920.91	2038.51
3	Gap	277.39	395.00
	Gap percentage	16.88	24.03

Source: Er.Deenadayalan, Engineer-in-Chief (Rtd.), Water Resource Organisation, Govt. of Tamilnadu

The above table 13 reveals that total water supply in Tamilnadu in the year was 1643.51 tmc. Out of which, agriculture demand is expected to be 1764.82 tmc in the year 2050 but whereas the non-agricultural demand for water supply has been shifted from 155.98 tmc in the year 2001 to 273.58 tmc in the year 2050. The total water supply shortages is 117.6 tmc will be occur in the year 2050 when compared to the water demand in the year 2001. The overall water supply gap will be 395.00 tmc in the year 2050 as in terms 24.03 percent, which is being considered to be the gap as per the year 2050.

TABLE 14

Reduction in Per Capita Availability of Water in TamilNadu

Year	Population in Millions	Total water Resources	available per annum**	Surface water availability
(1)	(2)	(3)	(4)	(5)
1951	30.1	44.923	1492	803
1961	33.7	44.923	1333	717
1971	41.2	44.923	1090	586
1981	48.4	44.923	928	499
1991	55.9	44.923	804	432
2001	62.1	44.923	723	389

Source: Er.Deenadayalan, Engineer-in-Chief (Rtd.), Water Resource Organisation, Government of TamilNadu

TABLE 15

Source-wise Net Area Irrigated in Tamilnadu

Year	Net Area Irrigated (Lakhs in Ha.)				
	Tanks	Canal	Wells	Others	Total
1960	9.36	8.82	5.98	0.46	24.62
1970	8.98	8.84	7.75	0.35	25.92
1980	5.90	8.89	10.67	0.24	25.70
1990	5.31	7.69	10.58	0.14	23.72
1997-98	6.76	8.63	14.12	0.19	29.45
1998-99	6.90	8.34	14.77	0.18	30.19
1999-00	6.33	8.67	14.54	0.18	29.72
2000-01	5.89	8.33	14.49	0.16	28.87

Source: Er.Deenadayalan, Engineer-in-Chief (Rtd.), Water Resource Organisation, Govt. of Tamilnadu

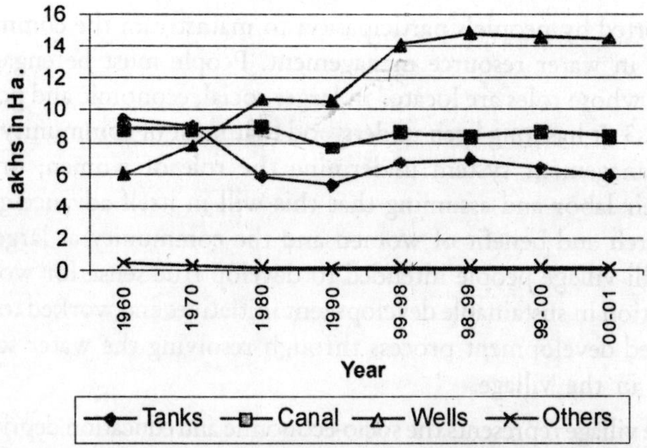

Chart : Source-wise net area irrigated (Lakhs in Ha.) in TamilNadu

This above chart shows that the majority of the land has been irrigated based on the well irrigation, which comprises 5.98 (lakhs in Ha.) in the year 1960 to 14.49 lakhs in ha in year 2000-2001. Tanks and Canals are almost reveals the same level of irrigation in Tamilnadu.

FINDINGS

- The village people are highly depending on Bore well (27.54%) and Municipal water (71.01%).
- The quality of bore well water is poor, dirty, saline and it has little turbidity
- Women and Girl children have to make at least three trips a day
- Total distance traveled is 2- 3 kilometers in normal period, during summer it may reach more than 7 kilometers
- Average time spent for a day is 3 hours for fetching water from public bore wells
- The estimated amount of about Rs.6320 loss from irrespective of all caste throughout the year based on the sample respondents.

The overall man day's loss in the village is 158 days in a year of about 100 sample respondents. Based on the above findings an important insight that has emerged is technological interventions must be supported by people's participation to mainstream the community concerns in water resource management. People must be engaged as partners, whose roles are located in larger social, economic and political structures3. It has long been understood that most of community based water management system undermine the role of women; drawing upon their labor and assuming that this will in itself advance goal of the research and benefit of women and the community at large. The Suthamalli village people intended to develop true sense for women's participation in sustainable development initiatives and worked towards a gendered development process through resolving the water scarcity problem in the village.

The village represents the socio-economic and education deprivation of the scheduled caste is under thrust. Water is the lifeline for human life. While most people in the urban areas take clean and pure drinking water for granted, there are many villages in the country, where availability of drinking water is a luxury. Even if there is a available good water resources in the village level, this has been transported to urban needs and therefore the rural needs to be denied. This district has abundant water resources but due to mismanagement and poor conservation techniques faced severe shortage of water post-monsoon and the women have to walk almost 3-4 km for fetching drinking water daily. The study shows that most of the families are landless and work as laborers for a major portion of the year. The Government has been neglecting to address the basic issue of the illiterate marginalized section. Therefore, the Government of TamilNadu has to realize the consequences of neglecting these problems evolved a strategy to resolve the water problem by providing an appropriate technology through forming of Water Committee at the state level to look into the problem facing by rural poor pertaining to drinking water problem. Government can make use of the people participation to construct check dams in the available water sources as for their community sensitization and community building. People from the Suthamalli village are ready to work for conservation of water resource management. However, since they did not have the necessary technical and financial expertise, so that government has to make some necessary arrangements to provide technical and other assistance along with the village people, the resources will be restored without any further degradation.

At large, if this would happen in the village no longer has subject to the vagaries of the monsoon; the future of the well-being of the village people looked bright. By helping to harvest rainwater for domestic and irrigation purposes, check dams can also help to improve livelihoods, particularly by providing a source of water for livestock. Women too benefit from access to more water. The time saved in fetching water from distant sources has been reduced to spend pursuing other income-generating and household welfare enhancing activities. A more stable income means better nutrition and education opportunities for the children and an overall improvement in the daily life of the entire family. Establishing the Water Committee helped to make key leaders from within the community with maximum active participation of women. The involvement of the Water Committee in the entire check dam construction led to people realizing the value of credibility and that is how the trust building of the village community developed unity in the village. The simple regular dialogues with women made them realize their inherent potential to contribute economically, socially and politically; an important result was that women formed a self-help group to enhance their livelihoods. Women in the hamlet also gradually realized that the need of water and women's role and status in society are related to each other. Based on an assessment, the following recommendations are needed to be strengthened while restructuring water resource management.

RECOMMENDATIONS

- Elicit adequate participation of rural women in decision making and action with respect to water resource management
- Fulfilling of holistic gender-based water needs at family level
- Availability of safe drinking water for all
- Indigenous knowledge to be encouraged among the village people
- Local, social and cultural conceptions, beliefs etc. linked to water resource management
- Research should be encouraged on the quality of ground water
- To bring effective water resource management system in rural India

- Water efficiency in the home should be encouraged
- Restore all the water resources through conventional methods
- Extension of rainwater harvesting system at village level properly
- Proper water conservation measures should be adopted
- Training and awareness should be given to rural people, more preciously women about the water resources management
- Panchayat Raj Institutions are to be strengthened to maintained water resources.
- Involvement of Self-Help Groups in the water resources management
- Women should be trained as water mangers for the better utilization of water
- Banned Private water business people
- Metering of water is seen as an essential tool in making consumer aware of their water use
- Encourage people to harvest rainwater for garden watering and for washing paths and vehicles.

Despite, in India the long-term adverse impact of drought, increasing numbers of marginalized farmer's suicides across the country is due to there is no proper management of water in rural areas. At one end the landlords or big farmers (and urban middle classes are able to access water sources on a large scale. On the other hand, small and marginal farmers do not have access to minimum water resources. The new National Water Policy does not take into account the local needs and participation.

CONCLUSIONS

Women are the water provider in India. In most of the villages, women walk long miles and wait long hours to bring water for the drinking and domestic needs of their families. The water crisis translates into an increasing burden for women as water providers. And with increasing water scarcity and water pollution, water related diseases increases among women and exclusively for female children between the age group of 14 and 18. To get a bucket of drinking water is a struggle for most of women across the country. The virtually dry and dead water resources have lead to acute water scarcity, affecting the socio-economic condition of the society. The drought conditions have pushed villagers to move to urban centres for their life bread. Women and girls are trudging still further in collection of water for domestic uses. The time which they lost in fetching water can very well translate into financial loss of the family. Therefore, this study will reveal the economic loss due to spending more time for fetching water in Suthamalli village in Tirunelveli district.

Women are most often responsible for domestic and community water management in developing societies, being in charge of determining sources, quantity and hygienic quality. Often they travel great distances in search of water, which limits their time for other activities, including growing and preparing food and income generating work. On average women and children, travel 10-15 kilometers spending eight or more hours per day collecting water and carrying up to 20 kilos or 15 litres per trip. The economic value of this unpaid contribution is enormous: In India, it has been estimated that women fetching water spend 150 million workdays per year, equivalent to a national loss of income of 10 billion rupees.

Water is critical for household care and nutritional health. It is generally agreed that a minimum of 20-40 litres of freshwater is required per person, day to meet minimum drinking, and sanitation needs. When women's access to water is restricted due to distance, time constraints or economic factors, they are often obliged to accept lower quality water. This is a particularly frightening alternative given that 80 percent of all illnesses have been transmitted by contaminated water. The Convention on the Elimination of All forms of Discrimination against Women (CEDAW) Committee has underlined that the health of rural women often crucially depends on adequate and non-discriminatory access to water.

REFERENCES

1. Srivastava, Surira, (2003), "Going Parched in the Land of Troubled Waters" Shara Times, 18th May 2003, New Delhi.
2. Pandya, Rameshwari, (2002), "Role of Home Scientists in Water Management", Kurukshetra, Vol.50, No.11, Sep 2002.
3. Chand, Dinesh, (2003), "Towards Sustainable Rural Water Supply", Kurukshetra, Vol.51, No.3, Oct 2003.

4. Singh, N., Bhattacharya, P. & Jacks, G. (2002) Women and Water: The relevance of gender perspective in Integrated Water Resource Management in rural India. In: *Proceedings: of the 3rd International Conference on Water Resources and Environmental Research* (ICWRER) 22-25 July 2002. (Volume 3).

5. Singh, N., Bhattacharya, P., Jacks, G. & Gustafsson, J-E. (2003) Women and Water: A policy review. Water Policy 5: 289-304.

6. Singh, N., Bhattacharya, P., Jacks, G. & Gustafsson, J-E., (2003) Gender Concern in Global Water Policy: An insight from Local Perspective. XI World Water Congress, Water Resources Management in the 21st Century, Madrid, October 5-9, 2003.

7. http://www.arts.mcgill.ca/152-497.b/h2o/water/gwater/wfacts.htm

8. Bulajic Borjana, Women's Roles – a policy overview, Waterline, Vol.17, No.1, July, 1998.

9. Maude Barlow and Tony Clark, Water Apartheid, The Nation, 15 August, 2002.

10. As reported in Jal Swaraj Abhiyan (Campaign for Water Liberation), NAVDANYA/ Research Foundation for Science, Technology & Ecology.

11. According to UN Economic and Social Council Report

12. Committee on Economic, Social and Cultural Rights for the Covenant on Economic, Social and Economic Rights, General Comment No.15 E/C, 12/2002/11, Geneva 26 November 2002.

13. Report of the Special Rapporteur on the Right to Water, UN Doc. E/CN.4/Sub.2/2002/10 (2002), para.33.

14. Water Resources: Agriculture, the Environment, and Society. – David Pimentel et al., BioScience, Vol. 47 No.2; February 1997.

15. World watch – journal of World watch Institute USA – Sept. 04 – D. Pimentel

16. Living Planet Report. 2006 – WWF (Worldwide Fund for Nature), Zoological Society of London, and GFN (Global Footprint Network).

17. New Scientist: Dismay over call to build more dams. - Fred Pearce. March 2003.

18. Localisation: A Global Manifesto. - Colin Hines, Earth scan, 2000.

19. Thirsty Planet; Strategies for Sustainable Water Management. Constance Elizabeth Hunt. Zed Books, 2004.

20. Our Planet, UNEP, volumes to March 2005.

21. Nature February 2006.
22. American Association for the Advancement of Science Web bulletin - February 2007.
23. Investment research paper, Robin How, November 2006.
24. United Nations, "*State of the Environment in Asia and the Pacific*", Chapter Four. Prepared by ESCAP with ADB. UN, New York, (2000).
25. Asian Development Bank."*Bringing Water to the poor*", Selected ADB Case Studies, ADB, Manila Water for All Series no 8. (2004).
26. World Bank, Washington DC. "*User organization for sustainable water services*" edited by Ashoke subramanian, N. Vijay Jagannathan and Ruth Meinzen-Dice, (1997).
27. Frans, Dirk and John Saussan, "*The water and poverty initiative*". Water for All series 3 Asian Development Bank, Manila. (2004).
28. Poney N and Others, Aspects of Environmental Impact quoted in UNCHs, '*Issues in the integrated planning and management of river lake basins and costal Areas*', Nairobi, (1996).
29. Falkenmakr, Malin. "*Water Management and Ecosystems*", Living with change. TEC Background paper No.9, Global Water partnership, Stockholm. (2003).

PART-V
HEALTH VARIATIONS IN INDIA

22

Mentally Retarded Children's Real Life in the Coastal Villages, Kanyakumari District, Tamilnadu

C. CHIDAMBARANATHAN

INTRODUCTION

It is a shocking and alarming fact that approximately 2.5 to 3% of the total population are mentally retarded which in most cases is a lifelong condition. Mentally retarded children at homes are lifelong pain for parents. Proper handling and treatment can make them to live self sufficiently. Mental retardation is a developmental disability that can appear from the very birth of a child. People who were mentally retarded function at an intellectual level that is below average and have difficulties with learning and daily living skills. It is a misconception that mental disabilities are related to gender or race. Conceptual skills like language, social skills like interaction with others and practical skills like self care are lacking in people classified as mentally retarded. Children labeled as such need special care to overcome social, intellectual and physical disabilities.

"Care for Mentally Retarded Children" by Saneesh states that it is a less suggestible I idea that you separate retarded child from family. In the presence of loving parents retardants have double chances of picking up fast. When educating your child prepare a special curriculum tailored to his needs. Involve your mentally challenged child in extracurricular activities to foster social interaction. If your mentally retarded child has a language development disability, try using sign language to communicate. The aim of the training given to a retardant is to make him/her self dependent. Therefore more than bookish knowledge gives importance to teach them day today skills. A retarded child should never feel that he is neglected or avoided in his family. Help them to be a part of family occasions and get together's. Never shut them in a room for life long. Let them live in touch with the outer world; take them for a walk or shopping. Teach siblings to see the retarded child as their own brother or sister. Never feel ashamed of a retarded child as he/she is also your child with all the rights for your love and care.

Tehal Kohli, had analyzed in his study on "Family and community intervention services through self help groups (CBR) for enhancement of development of mental retardates" that any type of disability/ handicap is stigmatization. This stigmatization can be removed if the attitudes of the Society towards disabilities/handicaps become favourable. Society can only then take initiate of organizing community based programmes for training, education and welfare of the disabled, especially mentally handicapped children. The National Policy on Education (NPE, 1986) and its modification (1992) has laid a lot of emphasis on the education of the mentally handicapped. It is emphasized that mentally retarded individuals should be provided with equal educational opportunities as others, with the aim of developing in them the self-confidence, courage and integrating them into the mainstream of community as equal partners.

There are various helping strategies to promote education among mentally retarded children such as special education, integrated education, and community based rehabilitation programmes which include home-based early intervention programme such as portage rural based District Rehabilitation Centre Scheme, Vocational training and self-help groups. Intervention through self-help group's programme cares and provides training and education to all levels of mentally retarded individuals according to their individual rehabilitation plans. Services are delivered to urban and rural population. Parents are involved directly in the training and education of their mentally retarded children. National Policy on Mental Handicap (1987) reported that the self-help group movement is an expression of the potentials for helping each other among families with a mentally handicapped individual. This movement allows for services to develop within home; and in small communities without excessive amounts of professional inputs. Studies by Balgopal et al. (1986), Banerjee (1986), Pamer (1987), Halperin (1987). Rao (1987, 1988, and 1990) reported that self-help group has become an increasingly important vehicle for providing educational and mental health services for this population and is highly cost effective.

The mining and processing of beach sand along the coastal villages near Manavalakkurichi could fetch foreign exchange for India, but contributes definitely too a little known fact that people in this region are affected by deadly diseases such as cancer and mental retardation. Radioactive sand along the Kanyakumari coast, which has heavy minerals like Limonite, Monazite, Zivon, Silliminate and Garnet, is the reason for the high incidence of mental retardation and cancer in the region. Among these heavy minerals, Monazite contains four to eight per cent Thorium Phosphate, an alpha ray emitter, and is significantly on the increase, mainly due to its use in the nuclear technology and power generating industry.

The NGO, Conservation of Nature Trust's report revealed that radioactivity along the southwest Tamil Nadu coast is around 200-235 mentally children per year and they accelerate mutation at nucleotide positions. Cancer and mental retardation cases' are found in several hamlets of Manavalakurichi panchayat, including Periyavilai, Chinnavilai, Puthur and Kottilpadu.

Objectives of the Study

1. To find out the causes and problems of the respondents
2. To bring out the remedial measure taken by their parents
3. To analyze about their daily life styles

Significance of the Study

Modem world was so fast and all values were decreasing slowly. Many kinds of homes and institution were functioning for all people towards their need and problem. Family's role was distributed to the above mentioned institutions. In this stage, the mentally retarded children's life was in puzzle manner. To realize about this problem many real incidents should be explored in an analytical way towards the people. The held based study will be more worthful than the others to help these children.

Scope of the Study

This study covers the socio economic condition of the respondents such as age composition, sex composition, family background, and economic condition of the family etc. Beside these, causal factor for mental retardness, their problems and real life condition were analyzed in this study.

Selection of the Study Area

The investigator had selected the Colachel and ChinnaMuttom coastal villages of Kanyakumari district for this present study. There are 46 coastal villages in Kanyakumari district in that; Colachel and Chinna Muttom have high number of mental retardation cases. It is because of radiation and other socio environmental factor. So the researcher has selected these areas for this present study.

SELECTION OF SAMPLE

Due to the time construction the researcher had selected two coastal villages mental retarded children for this present study. To know about their causes and problems, we had to study all the respondents. So census study method was the more appropriate one for this study. The sample size was 36 (i.e. Chinna Muttom -12 and Colachel- 24).

Tools

To know the social problem the case study method would be the right choice. For this type of studies it will give us real and descriptive picture of the selected problem. So the researcher had used case study method for collecting the data.

Findings

The mentally retarded children's problem and risk are studied in the two coastal villages. The most important findings are given below.

The mentally retarded children's problem varies from the socio-economic status of their family. Only below 14 age group only taken for this study. 0-5 and 6-8 age groups are high in number. Most of the respondents belong to fishing community (Paravar or Fernandez). And their income is determined by the season. Because, in the season time, they were get plenty of fishes and variety of fishes. Whereas, in the non-seasonal time, they were struggle to get fishes. Beside this, rain also interfaces their fishing. So, their income is unpredictable and most of their income is below 2500 per month. And all the respondents were living in the coastal region.

The blood relationship of the parents before marriage, pregnancy period of the mother, delivery period and initial period of the infant all are important factors which influence for the mentally retardedness. Many respondents affected by mentally retardness from birth itself. First we analyze the causes for this disease. Many respondents' medicinal reason or biological reason was nervous problem. But it was identified that age at marriage, pregnancy health disorder, delivery risk, infant illness, weight of the infant during birth and month of the delivery also reflects in the mentally retardedness.

Low birth weight, premature baby, brain fever, no crying during the birth etc also resu1t in mental retardedness. In the family, many of the children's parents early marriage, marriage within blood relation, pregnant illness, and malnourished during pregnancy were the prime one. Moreover, few children are affected due to human loss in the family. Poor economic condition, birth interval and abortion also cause for this stage of their children.

PROBLEMS

These children's problems can be dividing into four stages. They are, 1. Physical

Problem, 2. Family problems, 3. Problems in society and 4. Other problems.

1. Physical Problems

Many of the children's who had mentally retardness often suffer from fits. Atleast once in a month they had fits. They also cannot spend or play in sunlight. They cannot sleep well without the help of tablet. They cannot eat and even they need support for going to toilet. In the house, many of them were cared by their grand parents. If they didn't take regular medicine, it will result in other harmful effects. Importantly, their physical growth and strength of the baby was very poor. These children are also affected by some infectious diseases.

2. Family Problems

Many parents cannot do their work unless those were cared by others. All the time, any one of the family member have to take care of this children. Family function, social function, festival days and other religious days were not happily celebrated by these families. Mainly these parents suffer a lot with these children. Their younger or elder children's imitate or make fun on these children's. All the time family members have to be very cautious.

3. Problems in Society

Many children of this type had stopped their education due to fear by other children's in the school. And this children's performance was sometime cruel in the school. In the special school, most of the children are often affected by fits. Some kind of improvement found in the special school. But poor economic conditions not favour their parents offer in special school. In the public places these type of children often smiles or frequently cry while seeing the crowd. Some small kids beat these children. Many complaints about these children were consistently heard by their parents.

4. Other Problems

Their future itself darkened due to this problem. Many of their parents' feel that their children cannot marry, cannot go for good job, cannot get a good life.. .etc. They were very slow comparing to others. Their survival also limited due to various reasons. Very few children are come forward from these struggles.

Caring

Parents and grand parents took care of these children in many families. Moreover, special schools also take care of them. Many families had tried lot of things to change their children. They also tried in medical, religious and other means to solve their children's problem. Most of the parents and grand parents spend their full time even without sleeping, eating and working for these children. Often once in a month, they only take them to the hospital. These parents give regular medicine, food, bathing and other work of the children. Some doctors advice these parents to give exercise and some tips to care their children. Many difference found by their parents about their children from school to house.

For the financial assistance, government and NGO helped once in a while. Now, many of them not received any financial assistance from any sector. Unmarried girls, who suffered from this type of problem, are eligible to get Rs. 500 per month which is given by the government. Yoga, exercise and other type of educational training programme were given by some schools and NGOs.

Some Important Cases

Case 1

Arnold was 12 years old. He was suffering from mentally retardedness by birth. His family was a low-income earning ~ He was fully cared by his parents and grand mother. His parents were illiterate. So they didn't aware about the less physical growth and mental growth of their child. After 5 years only, they came to know about the problem of their son. Often their child suffered from fever and diarrhea. Beside these, they came to know the lack of WBC reduced the level of blood in their child's body. Due to low-level of blood, there was no strength and protectiveness in the body. This child had lost his education and life due to this problem. The doctor had asked 20 lakhs to cure this problem. But the poor fisher parents manage to collect 8 lakhs with the help of non-governmental sector and from their relations. This child is at heavy risk in continuing his life.

Case 2

Brito was 13 years old boy whose life is started with fits. This boy often suffers from fits. His parents had only one child. During the delivery, the mother suffered from piles problem which leads to some nervous problem *for* the infant at the delivery. So the infant had no function in the right hand. His physical and mental level made him as slow runner in the society. While comparing the age and growth of the boy, he was very backward in the physical as well as mental growth. His grandmother only takes care of him and he also never allowed going outside lonely to any places. The peer group of his area makes fun and irritates him. In some occasions, he had beaten and bitten the young ones *for* such incidents. He cannot spend more time in the sunlight, due to his physical health condition and nervous problem. He also become unconscious and behaves like. ~ mad. He had no assistance from both government and private sector. Without medicine he cannot survive in this world. So he should take the medicine regularly. If he fails to take it, then it will result in fits or other health problem. Atleast 2 to 3 hours the fits attack his body.

He also stopped his education due to this problem. His life was a questionable one.

Case 3

Daisy was very young child of 5 *years* old. She was very different from other mentally retarded children. She suffers from the mental illness from the 8th month of her birth. She was affected by this illness after the brain fever. She also often imitates others and repeats the behaviour and attitude of others. In short she reflects her activities based on others. So she had no way *for* going to school. She found difficulty in sleeping even in the night also. She used to cry and felt uneasy in the crowd area. She used to beat her head on the floor when she gets angry. Her parents took her too many churches to cure her problem. Yet now, she was suffering from the mental illness.

Case 4

Jasmine was 9 *years* old. She couldn't talk upto 7th age. She also suffers from deaf condition. Major reason for her stage was said by physician that her parents married within their blood relation and her mother fails to take the necessary medicine regularly. But she was admitted in special school which turns her life slowly. Her teachers helped her to talk and train her with some physical exercise as well as yoga practice also relaxed her mind. Though there were few changes still she was in a miserable position. She also has the problems from the neighbours and other children. She felt very comfortable in the school than in the house. Moreover, she found similar children living with her in the school.

Case 5

John Brisco was 12 years old. He was behaving like 8.5 years old boy. His physical as well as mental growth was very slow. He was taken to various special hospitals but no improvement in his life till now. He also went to both regular as well as special school for some period. It also stopped due to his unconsciousness and fits in the educational institution. The parents told that during his birth, he never cries for some hours and he is a premature baby with low birth weight. He couldn't eat and do his work without the help of others. Every time some person should watch his activity. Now also his speech was not clear and correct. He used to be very calm and quite in the public places. Totally he lost his health, education and even the future.

Case 6

Salia was 6 years old. Her one leg and hand was not functioning from the birth itself. Always her saliva comes out of her mouth. She used go for toiler suddenly without informing to others. More than half an hour she had fits once in a week or thrice in a month. Often she was ill the hospital due to the illness. One day in the school van she had fits and she struggled a lot. Fortunately her teacher took her to the hospital at the right time. But that made her school life end. In many occasions even the doctor had no hope for her survival. Her parents borrow money and taking treatment for her. Because she was the only child they have. They are in a sorrowful manner.

CONCLUSION

Young children's life in our world is to be protected for the next generation. Mentally retardedness is making the life of the children very slow. Many policies, programmes are going with the help of government and non government sector for the welfare of the children. To make fruitful towards the children the reality should be known and it will change the scenario.

REFERENCES

1. Radioactive sand causes cancer, disabilities in children in India.
2. Express Buzz in Tamil Nadu, India: December 8, 2008.

23

The Challenge of Naturopathy on Malnutrition

B. JEYASURESH AND V. IRUDAYARAJ

INTRODUCTION

Malnutrition, as most people understand it, is a disease due to the insufficient, excessive or imbalanced consumption of nutrients[1, 2] and it continues to be a major public health problem throughout the developing world, particularly in southern Asia and sub-Saharan Africa[3–7]. A number of different nutrition disorders may arise, depending on which nutrients are under or overabundant in the diet causing ailments like hypoglycemia and hypothermia, dehydration, septic shock, infections, vitamin deficiency, severe anemia and heart failure etc.[8] These diseases are by no means restricted to frail, delicate people, but those of apparently good health are often unconscious victims of it.

Malnutrition increases one's susceptibility to severity of infections, and is thus a major component of illness and death from disease[9 -11]. It is consequently the most important risk factor for the burden of disease in developing countries[12]. The risk of death is directly correlated with the degree of malnutrition[13–18]. Mortality due to malnutrition accounted for 58% of the total mortality in 2006: In the world, approximately 62 million people, all causes of death combined, die each year. In 2006, more than 36 million died of hunger or diseases due to deficiencies in micronutrients[19]. There were 923 million malnourished people in the world in 2007, an increase of 80 million since 1990[20]. FAO estimates that[21] percent of India's population is chronically undernourished. But recent on-the-ground surveys paint a more accurate and desperate picture: 49 percent of adults and 53 percent of children in India are underweight, a proxy measurement for hunger[21].

An expense to treat and prevent mal-nutrition goes roughly $300m of aid each year, less than $2 for each child below two in the 20 worst affected countries[22]. In contrast, HIV, which causes fewer deaths than child malnutrition, received $2.2 billion—$67 per person with HIV in all countries[22].

MANAGEMENT OF MALNUTRITION

Data from 67 studies worldwide show that the median fatality rate has not changed for the past 5 decades, and one in four severely malnourished children died during treatment in the 1990s[23]. Severely malnourished children die in the hospital of four main causes: hypoglycemia, hypothermia, cardiac failure from over hydration and electrolyte imbalance, and infection[24]. The available treatments for malnutrition are mainly composed of Composition of mineral mix, Composition of vitamin mix, Drugs for treatment of infections in severely malnourished persons. While the treatment schedule is followed, a severely malnourished individual without complications should show definite signs of improvement within short span of period. Failure to achieve this initial improvement causes failures in regaining appetite, losing weight, losing oedema, gaining weight and so on[8].

IMPACT OF NATUROPATHY ON MALNUTRITION

Naturopathy answers to this challenge. Naturopathy is a distinct system of treatment by itself just as there are other systems of treatments. This system is a science of disease elimination without drugs. It is based on the principle of cooperation with the natural laws of life which are forever working within, as well as outside the body, and it makes use of only the natural agencies like fruits, vegetables, greens and others like water, air, light, heat, exercise, etc., for the purpose of curing disease. This system of naturopathy is now a thoroughly developed and organized system, the principle of which may be grasped by any intelligent person and utilized to a most useful extent in dealing with every known malady.

DIET THERAPY

Naturopathy deals with diets in populations there are frequently deficient in macronutrients (protein, carbohydrates and fat, leading to protein-energy malnutrition), micronutrients (electrolytes, minerals and vitamins, leading to specific micronutrient deficiencies) or both[25,26]. Diet-based strategies are probably the most promising approach for a sustainable control of micronutrient deficiencies. Increasing dietary diversification through consumption of a broad variety of foods, preferably from home gardens, is effective[27, 28]. Foods with a high content of absorbable micronutrients present in the fruits and vegetables are considered the best means for preventing micronutrient deficiencies[29]. The role of diet in the etiology of most non communicable diseases is well established. The shifts towards highly refined foods and towards meat and dairy products containing high levels of saturated fats, i.e. the nutrition transition, now increasingly evident in middle income and lower-income countries, have, together with reduced energy expenditure, contributed to rises in the incidence of obesity and non communicable diseases[30, 31]. Besides over a large part of the world the dietary patterns of people are determined by food materials which are freely available in their respective regions[32].

Diet is being recognized as the most important single factor for promoting either health or disease. Apart from infections and accidents, 90 percent of the remaining illness and death are due to defective food habits[33] Natural food, properly selected, scientifically combined and judiciously administered, have true medicinal value for curing many diseases by supplying the necessary elements in organic form. The organic elements in food preserve the tissues from degeneration and putrefaction. A diet in which there is abundance of these physical and regenerative elements will bring back vitality glowing health and the joy of living[34]. Raw foods are the only foods which carry 100% nutrition with full quota of vitamins and the specific cure for malnutrition. This cannot be truthfully stated of foods which have been cooked[35]. To correct this undernourished, condition the patients should be put on a rich, nourishing diet of plenty of green fresh raw vegetables and fruits will supply the deficiency of mineral salts, and the copious use of water internally will oxygenate and expand the dried tissues. Fresh air and sunlight, with as much sleep as it is possible to get at least ten hours each night, will go far towards effecting a rapid recovery and the establishment of sound, vigorous health[35].

The share of over nourished adults who jumped by more than half—from 9 percent to 15 percent—between 1989 and 1992. In several Latin American nations, such as Brazil and Colombia, the prevalence of overweight people—at 36 and 41 percent, respectively. In these and more and more developing countries, it is not uncommon for the overweight population to exceed the underweight population[36]. Naturopathy answers through raw foods as the greatest value in breaking down unhealthy fat tissue and replacing it with firm flesh, the amount of which may be easily regulated. Raw, green vegetables and juicy fruits are the certain enemies of flabby, diseased flesh, and the unsightly rolls of fat on the shoulders, abdomen and hips, as well as girth of waist, will be rapidly reduced on a diet of raw foods. Effective reducing is quickly accomplished with raw foods without sustaining the sunken-faced, hollow-eyed look which usually characterizes the man or woman who attempts to reduce by starving himself on a meager diet of cooked foods which, when eaten plentifully, carry the minimum amount of nutrition. When that minimum is cut, slow, starvation sets in[35].

Along with the above dietary treatment healthful exercise, sleep and as much fresh air as possible will aid materially in overcoming the most stubborn cases of malnutrition. Traditional diets associated with little nutrition-related illness and lengthy adult life expectancies are generally plant based— rich in whole grains, vegetables, fruits, and nuts— and supplemented by sparing amounts of animal products[37]. Naturopathy advices conditions like one must eat any food materials slowly, masticating the food completely. Too many varieties of food are not mixed at one meal. Eat moderately and avoid over eating. Avoid the mixing of incompatible food items. Avoid eating when emotionally and mentally upset. Select natural and wholesome food and restrict the use of common salt, sugar, ice water and too hot food items. Also must be avoided alcoholic beverages, and the regular use of spices. Should prefer absolutely vegetarian foods and restrict or avoid the use of non-vegetarian foods, because our body construction is strictly obeying the principles and structure of vegetarian beings. The structure of the digestive system of the human beings is like that of herbivorous animals and not that of carnivorous animals.[38]

CHANGING THE DIET

Sudden changes of diet particularly when attempting to use raw food to the exclusion of all else, may have serious results; the age, physical condition, susceptibility to food reactions, and the general nerve conditions must all be considered. It is safe to change the diet gradually. If a person has been eating principally meat and potatoes, eliminate the meat and substitute a vegetable and a salad, or if cannot abstain totally from meat cut it down to two to three times a week until gradually break away from it. Meanwhile cultivate and encourage a taste for the various vegetables, particularly those which are ordinarily eaten uncooked. Many people are not naturally fond of salads, lettucc, tomatoes, etc, and for these people the raw diet represents a great problem. If meat has already been eliminated then the progress is more rapid, for every vegetarian knows how much better he has felt since he ceased to eat flesh.

CONCLUSION

Health is a state of physical, mental and social well-being and not merely the absence of disease. It is a positive state of well-being in which every organ of the body functions in perfect condition. A person who falls ill naturally wishes to become well again as quickly as possible. This instinctive desire leads people to use any curative method that promises speedy relief. Unfortunately people resort to treatment that may cause irreparable harm to the body and mind. There is a widespread belief among people that disease can only be cured by the use of powerful drugs. So, contrary to the laws of nature, we usually endeavor to suppress the symptoms by means of pernicious drugs. It militates against the nature of the body. The toxic over load of drugs may lead to dangerous degenerative diseases. Hence the remedy becomes worse than the disease itself. Here, the real health can be achieved by following the diet of clean, wholesome foods, eaten in their natural live state.

REFERENCES

1. Sullivan, Arthur; Steven M. Sheffrin *Economics: Principles in action*. Upper Saddle River, New Jersey 07458: Pearson Prentice Hall 2003, pp. 481.
2. Corinne Cataldo et al., *Nutrition and Diet Therapy: Principles and Practices* (Belmont, CA: Wadsworth Publishing, 1999.

3. Schofield C, Ashworth A. Why have mortality rates for severe malnutrition remained so high? *Bull World Health Organ* 1996; 74:223-9.

4. World Health Organization. World health report. Geneva: The Organization; 2002.

5. Brabin BJ, Coulter JBS. Nutrition-associated disease. In: Cook GC, Zumla AI, editors. *Manson's tropical diseases*. London: Saunders; 2003. pp. 561-80.

6. World Health Organization, United Nations Children's Fund. Joint statement on the management of acute diarrhea. Geneva: The Organization; 2004.

7. Food and Agriculture Organization of the United Nations. Undernourishment around the world. In: *The state of food insecurity in the world 2004*. Rome: The Organization; 2004.

8. *Management of severe malnutrition*: a manual for physicians and other senior health workers World Health Organization Geneva 1999

9. Murray CJL, Lopez AD. Global mortality, disability, and the contribution of risk factors: Global Burden of Disease Study. *Lancet* 1997; 349:1436-42.

10. Rice AL, Sacco L, Hyder A, Black RE. Malnutrition as an underlying cause of childhood deaths associated with infectious diseases in developing countries. *Bull World Health Organ* 2000; 78:1207-21.

11. Black R. Micronutrient deficiency — an underlying cause for morbidity and mortality. *Bull World Health Organ, 2003*; 81:79.

12. Nemer L, Gelband H, Jha P; Commission on Macroeconomics and Health. *The evidence base for interventions to reduce malnutrition in children under five and school-age children in low- and middle-income countries.* CMH working papers no WG5:11. Geneva: World Health Organization; 2001.

13. Black RE, Morris SS, Bryce J. Where and why are 10 million children dying every year? *Lancet* 2003; 361:2226-34.

14. Chen LC, Chowdhury AKMA, Huffman SL. Anthropometric assessment of energy-protein malnutrition and subsequent risk of mortality among preschool aged children. *Am J Clin Nutr* 1980; 33:1836-45.

15. Pelletier DL, Frongillo EA, Habicht JP. Epidemiologic evidence for a potentiating effect of malnutrition on child mortality. *American Journal of Public Health* 1993; 83: 1130-3.

16. Van den Broeck J, Eeckels R, Vuylsteke J. Influence of nutritional status on child mortality in rural Zaire. *Lancet* 1993; 341:1491-5.
17. Man WD, Weber M, Palmer A, Schneider G, Wadda R, Jaffar S, et al. Nutritional status of children admitted to hospital with different diseases and its relationship to outcome in The Gambia, West Africa [published erratum appears in *Trop Med Int Health* 1998; 3:854]. *Trop Med Int Health* 1998; 3:678-86.
18. Fernandez ID, Himes JH, De Onis M. Prevalence of nutritional wasting in populations: building explanatory models using secondary data. *Bull World Health Organ* 2002; 80:282-91.
19. Jean Ziegler, *L'Empire de la honte*, Fayard, 2007 ISBN 978-2-253-12115-2 p.130.
20. Food and Agriculture Organization Economic and Social Development Department. "The State of Food Insecurity in the World, 2008: High food prices and food security - threats and opportunities". *Food and Agriculture Organization of the United Nations*, 2008, p. 2.
21. FAO, op. cit. note 12; Lisa Smith, *Can FAO's Measure of Chronic Undernourishment Be Strengthened?* Food Consumption and Nutrition Division (FCND) Discussion Paper No. 44 (Washington, DC: IFPRI, May 1998.
22. *The Economist* (US) Article date: January 26, 2008.
23. Schofield C, Ashworth A. Why have mortality rates for severe malnutrition remained so high? *Bull World Health Organ* 1996; 74:223–9.
24. Ann Ashworth, *J Pediatric Gastroenterology Nutrition*, Vol. 32, No. 5, May 2001.
25. Pinstrup-Andersen P, Burger S, Habicht JP, Peterson K. Protein-energy malnutrition. In: Jamison DT, Mosley WH, Measham AR, Bobadilla JL, editors. *Disease control priorities in developing countries.* 2nd ed. Oxford (UK): Oxford University Press; 1993. pp. 391-420.
26. Millward DJ, Jackson AA. Protein/energy ratios of current diets in developed and developing countries compared with a safe protein/energy ratio: implications for recommended protein and amino acid intakes. *Public Health Nutr* 2004; 7:387-405.
27. Nemer L, Gelband H, Jha P; Commission on Macroeconomics and Health. *The evidence base for interventions to reduce malnutrition in children under five and school-age children in low- and middle-income countries.* CMH working papers no WG5:11. Geneva: World Health Organization; 2001.

28. Tontisirin K, Nantel G, Bhattacharjee L. Food-based strategies to meet the challenges of micronutrient malnutrition in the developing world. *Proc Nutr Soc* 2002;61:243-50.

29. Gibson RS, Yeudall F, Drost N, Mtitimuni B, Cullinan T. Dietary interventions to prevent zinc deficiency. *Am J Clin Nutr* 1998; 68(2 Suppl):484S-7S.

30. Popkin BM. Nutrition in transition: the changing global nutrition challenge. Asia Pacific Journal of Clinical Nutrition 2001; 101:S13-8.

31. Thomas malicka, *Bhakshanam marunnanu* (Food is Medicine), Nature cure hospital Moozhikulam, 1987, p.14

32. Jussawalla, JM, *Prevention is better than cure*, Jaico Publishing House Bombay, 1961, p.37.

33. Jussawalla, JM, *Natural way of Healing*. Vikas Publishing House New Delhi, 1974,p.1

34. Benjamin, Harry, *Your diet in health and disease.* Wilco publishing House, Bombay, 1992, p.2.

35. St.Louis A. Estes, *Raw Food and Health*, Ivanhoe Printing Co. New York, 1963, p.23.

36. U.N. survey from Flores, op. cit. note 5; China data from Catherine Geissler, "China: The Soya Pork Dilemma," *Proceedings of the Nutrition Society*, May 1999, and from Barry M. Popkin et al., "Body Weight Patterns among the Chinese: Results from the 1989 and 1991 China Health and Nutrition Surveys," *American Journal of Public Health*, May 1995; Brazil and Colombia from WHO, *Obesity*, op. cit. note 5; overweight exceeding underweight from Flores, op. cit. note 5.

37. Ibid.; traditional diets from a multiyear international conference series, "Public Health Implications of Traditional Diets," organized by Oldways Preservation & Exchange Trust, Cambridge, MA, <www. oldwayspt.com>, viewed 31 January 2000.

38. *Your Family Friend*, New Delhi, May 2000, p.180.

24

Social Neglect in the Path of Women Health in India

I. JENITTA MARY AND C. CHIDAMBARANATHAN

INTRODUCTION

World health organization has defined health as a state of complete physical, mental, and social wellbeing which is necessary for leading a productive and fruitful life. Health is a basic human right and women right. If the women assess nutritious food, appropriate medicine for illness, clean water, safe housing, pollution free environment and health services, then they can attain and maintain their health very well. Thus women's health is determined by such forces like working homes, working places, society and the state.

According to Dr.Amartya Kumar Sen, "Burden of hardship falls disproportionately on women" due to six types of inequality.

- Mortality(due to gender bias in health care and nutrition)
- Natality (sex selective abortion and female infanticide)
- Basic facility (education and skill development)
- Special opportunity (higher education and professional training)
- Employment (promotion)
- Ownership (home, land and property)

NUTRITION

Balanced diet containing carbohydrate, protein, vitamins and minerals make a healthy body and healthy mind. Only 10% of women are fortunate to have the privilege of nutritious diet. Majority of women in our country work more than men and for longer period but eat less the last and the left over of poor quality of food. Their energy expenditure is not compensated by intake of diet and lacks in Nutrition. India has the highest prevalence of iron deficiency anemia in the world, 87% of pregnant women, about 68% in the reproductive age group and about 60-70% of adolescent girls in our country anemic. This is the major reason for high level of morbidity among Indian women.

COMMON ILLNESS

Women's specific common illness are aches/pains (back, head, stomach, uterine), weakness, fevers, respiratory problems, gastro-intestinal problems, skin, eye, ear problems and reproductive problems such as reproductive tract infection, white discharge, endometriosis. CEHAT study reveals that morbidity is much higher among than men. Middle-aged women have arthritis, menopause related hot flushes and uneasiness, osteoporosis, migraine and swelling of legs. In both rural as well as urban areas, a proportion of physical immobility is higher among elderly women than among elderly men. Women are last one to taken to a doctor and they have least access to rest, healthy recreation, exercise and sports. All these combined together aggravate the situation and future deteriorates women's health.

Availability of Health Care

Women avail four types of health services. First of all, the majority of women try home remedies, falling which they approach either a homeopath, Ayurvedic doctor, unanihealer or the allopath. Those who can afford private practitioner's health care center's (PHCs) or the health care facilities provided by the non-government organizations. During the last decade, yoga, meditations have become extremely popular among the middle and upper class educated women, while the poor women approach witch doctors.

Attitude towards Women's Health

Social discrimination against women results into systematic neglect of women's health, from womb to tomb. Female infanticide and female feticide are widely practiced in Bihar, Madhya Pradesh, Rajasthan, Uttar Pradesh, Punjab, Haryana, Himachal Pradesh and Gujarat. As per 2001, census, there were only 933 women per 1000 men and there was a deficit of 3.5 crore women. Sex ratio is as a result of selective abortion of females fetuses after the use of ultra-sound techniques to determine sex of the fetus. As a result of sex-determination and sex-preselection tests, sex ratio of the child population has declined to 927 girls for 1000 boys. Negative attitude towards women's health is the major reason for high levels of prenatal mortality and morbidity including low birth weight babies.

Vicious Cycles and Poor Women

The vicious cycles of poverty generates vicious cycle of ill health. For mother, poverty leads to low intake of food and nutrients which results in under nutrition and repeated insults from nutrition related disease and infections, which affect them in terms of stunted development and growth faltering, hence they have small body size as adults, which impairs productivity as a result they have low earning capacity. The end result is poverty.

For a girl child, poverty gives three options-child labour, child marriage and child prostitution. Poverty gives coupled with control over women's sexuality, fertility and labour is manifested in neglect and discrimination of a girl child, she remains a malnourished girl, early marriage maker her pregnant and she is an impoverished mother who produces low birth weight baby. If the baby is female, she faces discrimination, repeated low birth weight baby. If the baby is female she faces discrimination, repeated pregnancies/ deliveries to get son results in maternal mortality.

Miserable profile of reproductive health of Indian women is due to octopus clutches of early marriage and pregnancy, high prevalence of reproductive tract infection, ignorance, high infant mortality rate, no control over contraception and repeated pregnancies. As per UNICEF in 1995, there were 453 maternal deaths per 1000 births in India. Nutritional needs of lactating mother demands urgent attention.

Violence and Health Issues of Women over the Life Cycle

As unborn children, they face covert violence in terms of sex-selection and overt violence in terms of female foeticide after the use of amninocentesis, chorine villaibiopsy, sonography, ultra sound imaging techniques. IVF (In Vitro Fertilization) clinics for assisted reproduction are approached by infertile couple to produce sons. Doctors are advertising aggressively, "Invest Rs.500 now, save Rs. 50000 later" i.e. If you get rid of your daughter now, you will not have to spend money on dowry.

As girls less than 5 years of age women face neglect of medical care and education, sexual abuse and physical violence. As adolescent and adult women in the reproductive age-group, they face early marriage, early pregnancy, sexual violence, domestic violence, dowry harassment, infertility, if they fail to produce son, then face desertion, witch hunt. The end result is a high maternal mortality. Causes of maternal deaths in our country are haemorrhage, abortion, infection, obstructed labour, eclampsia (blood pressure during pregnancy), sepsis and an anemia.

Sexual harassment at work place should be treated as an occupational health hazard as it causes damage to both physical and mental health of women. Even in the medical profession right from medical students to other women health workers face this problem.

Home and Work Conditions Affecting Women Health

Pollution of air and water, noise pollution and chemicalisation of environment affect every body. Scarcity of fuel wood, fodder, water and herbs as a result of deforestation has taken heavy toll of women's health. Rural and tribal women have to walk for miles for these basics survival needs of human beings and domestic animals. Floods crease deaths, destruction and epidemics. Global warming has resulted in resurgence of older epidemics such as cholera, typhoid, malaria, degut and hemorrhagic fever. Burgeoning sex-trade have made 2 million sex-workers potential ariels of HIV, STD, and AIDS. More over women in prostitution may suffer from T.B other STD's, malnutrition, malaria and skin diseases. At present, there is an evidence of rising HIV rates among young married women who are infected by their husbands. Modern life style and environment has increased breast and uterine cancer among Indian women. Techniques meant for detecting cancer are rarely used by women. As a result detection of cancer and its treatment at earlier stage is impossible.

MENTAL HEALTH

The most neglected area concerning women has been well mental health. Stress generated due to major life events such as breakup of marriage, widowhood, illness in the family, financial hardship and substance abuse destroy psychiatrists are approached by husbands to issue "mentally unfit" certificates. So they can flash them in court of law to demand divorce. Relatives do not want to keep mentally ill women in the family.

There is a need to situate women's health in overall macro parameters. Gender divide in the access of health care and health cost is so sharp that women have to access informal provides and informal care. Gender audit in health should be done on the basis of identifying issued for reorientation at each stage of women's life cycle and focusing on the problems of each age group of women. To address the problems concerning women's health, a holistic life span approach is needed. Women as a growing human beings, home makers, and workers, mother and elderly citizens face different type of health related issues.

Women's health is determined by the material reality generated by socio-economic, cultural forces as well as gender relations based on sub-ordination of women. It is important to make men aware about women specific health needs. Improvement in women's health is a precondition for development of her family.

CONCLUSION

The health problems of women in our country are primarily related to their social status in society. This factor of social status is important irrespective of the economic group to which women belong. In the case of women from poor families the risks due to being female are added to the already presents risks of poverty. The medical profession gives little importance to both the economic as well as the social factors which determine the health status of women. By focusing merely on their reproductive function, the medical profession neglect, the far more important causes of morbidity among female population.

REFERENCES

1. Amartya sen, "Many faces of Gender Inequality", New Red Cliff Institute, Harwad University, 2001.
2. Sunil Nadaraj and Neher Madhiwalla, "Women and Health care in Mumbai". Mumbai: CEHAT, 2002.
3. Iqbal Grewal and Manju Purohit, "Women's health-A complete Guide". Delhi: Gyan Sagal Publications, 1999.
4. Vibhutipatel, "Women's challenges of New Millennium". New Delhi: Gyan Publishing House, 2002.

❑❑❑

25

The Problems of Elderly Persons in Rural Society : A Sociological Analysis

D. THIRUMALRAJA AND I SINGARAM

INTRODUCTION

Academicians have defined old age from various angles. One of them is from biological view point. Biologists refer to ageing as 'senescence' this is general term which is used to describe decrease in the efficient functioning of an organism with age. It is important to remember that senescence is a natural process which must be distinguished from abnormal processes which bring about pathology and disease. Biologists consider that ageing is the change which occurs in the post reproductive phase of life, resulting in a decrease in the survival capacity of the organism which brings about a decrease in its adaptive capacities.

Another view point of defining old age is through chronology. Chronologists suggest that calendar is frequently useful to define the onset of old age. Their opinion is that ageing is based upon the cultural ascriptions of the society. The age at which old age is thought to start varies in different cultures for example in some primitive and tribal society's old age starts at 60 and in most western industrial countries it starts at 65 to 70 years. The third approach of defining old age is through economic dependency. This approach considers that the experience of ageing and late life can best be understood b looking at the position of the elderly in relation to the labour market and the relationships and social structures that this produces. Emphasis is given to the peripheral status of the elderly in society as dominant age cohorts assume their economic functions.

Ageing entails two types of dependency: Intrinsic and Extrinsic. The intrinsic dependency results from disability or incapacitation and is simply the direct need for support experienced by those who cannot care for them. In contrast extrinsic dependency refers to the elderly who are made dependent by 'artifacts of our culture'. They are not disabled yet, because of social and economic roles, are in position, where they are incapable of supporting themselves at most fundamental level. Extrinsic dependency emerges with the development of an industrial economy as either social groups or economic sectors are excluded from full and equitable resource exchange in the market place.

AGED IN RURAL INDIA

Ageing is not only physiological or chronological but also a social and cultural phenomenon. It is frequently assumed that ageing is more a passive and positive experience in rural cultures based on agriculture, rearing animals etc. although several cultures have extremely harsh attitudes towards the old and the aged were killed or allowed to die when they were no longer productive, most of the rural cultures resorted a reverent attitude and held the aged with high esteem prestige and privileges. These variations are marked even in rural India until recently. In rural India, the traditional joint family system and the closely knit community structure maintained mutual harmony, between

Life E..pectation of at Ages 60 and 70 for India (in %)

Year	Male		Female	
	60 yrs	70yrs	60yrs	70yrs
1971	13.80	8.57	14.75	9.10
1981	14.25	8.83	15.31	9.42
1991	15.01	9.27	16.23	9.97
2001	15.74	9.70	17.05	10.45
2011	16.29	10.03	17.75	10.87
2021	16.75	10.32	18.18	11.14

Source: Irudayarajan et.al. (1999)

the young and the old. But with the drastic changes in the family structure and functioning of the communities, the elders are left with multifaceted problems. They suffer from loss of status and authority, lack of attention, in security and the old are alienated with an undignified existence.

STATUS OF ELDERLY UNDER CIVIL CODE

Sections 877(1) of the civil code provide that person indirect lineal line ad siblings are mutually responsible for helping each other. There fore children or grand children are obligated to take care of and support their aged parents or grand parents. In contrast, 820 of the civil code must be read together with the section of the civil code. Section 820 states that the person who holds parental power, shall have the right and duty to protect and children. Thus the relation and obligation of a person towards his or her children is much stronger then towards his or her parents. His is significant since the supplementary benefit act, which is the basis for welfare or for helping the aged, stipulates that those who are obligated to support others by law shall be primarily responsible to guaranteeing the livelihood of those who should be cared for and that all available sources related to them shall be utilized before they are benefits.

PROBLEMS OF ELDERLY PERSONS

Problems Faced in the Transitional Society

The problems faced by the elderly in transitional society are as follows:

- Lack of homely atmosphere in families
- Segregation of age from social contact
- Lack of social relationship in relatives due to the problems
- Negligence by youngsters in the family
- Lack of love and affection on elderly by their own family members
- Physical inability to move around
- Inadequate are by their own daughters and sons
- Suppression of their voice by dominant persons
- Feeling of disrespect of dishonour

- Inadequate medicine
- Loss of mental balance and other physical problems by ageing
- Generation gap between seniors and the juniors

OLD AGE IN PRESENT-DAY SOCIETY

It is common knowledge that the condition of old people today is scandalous. Before examining it in detail, we must try to understand how it comes about that society puts up with it so easily. As a general rule society shuts its eyes to all abuses, Scandals and tragedies, so long as these do not upset its balance; and it worries no more about the fate of the children in state orphanages or of juvenile delinquents or of the handicapped, then it does on the face of it seen more astonishing, since every singly member of the community must now that his future is in question and almost all of them have close personal relationships with some old people.

A society is a whole made up of individual parts. Its members are separate. But they are united by the need for reciprocal relationships. The individuals understand one another, not inasmuch as they are all men in the abstract, but by means of the variety of their praxis. 'The basis of comprehension is a fundamental is a fundamental association in all undertakings; all ends, as soon as they are announced, emerge from the organic whole composed of all possible human ends'.

Up to a certain point this state of the aged person is analogous to that of the child, with whom the adult does not establish any reciprocal relationship either. It is not mere chance that makes families speak of a child who is. 'Extra ordinary for his age' and also of an old man who is ' extra ordinary for his age': the extra ordinariness lies in their behaving like human beings when they are either not yet or no longer men. We have seen that in many primitive communities they belong to the some age-class, and that throughout history the general attitude of the adults has been much the same towards both, but since the child is a potential active member, society ensures its own future by investing in him, whereas in its eyes the aged person is no more than a corpse under suspended sentence.

The idea of non-reciprocity is not adequate for a positive definition of the relationship between the adult and the aged. This depends upon the relationship between children and parents, and above all-since we live in a male world and since old age is primarily a male problem-upon the relationship maintained with their mother.

According to Freund a characteristic feature of this relationship is its ambivalence. The son respects his father, admires him, would like to identity himself with him and even take his place; this last wish gives rise to hatred and fear. The heroes of myth always rise up against their father and end by killing him. In real life the killing is symbolical. The father-image is stripped of its glamour, and when this is done the son can be reconciled with him but the reconciliation is complete only when the son has fact taken the father's place. Thus says Freund, in Christianity there was a recondition that ended with the dethronement of the father, Christ having become the person of the greatest importance. Where the antagonism exists, it is not mutual it is active in the son, taking the form of aggression and resentment, but generally speaking it does not appear in the father. This aggressive sexual resentment undoubtedly provides the framework for the developments of the one-way relationship of the young with the old. (When resentment of the young by the old occurs it is no more than a secondary reaction) the father is killed by being depreciated; but for this to be brought about, old age as such has to be discredited as well.

Major Problems of the Elderly in Present Scenario

- Economic problems include such problems as loss of employment, income deficiency and economic insecurity
- Physical and physiological problems include health and medical problems, nutritional deficiency, and the problem of adequate housing etc
- Psycho-social problem which cover problems related with their psychological and social maladjustment as well as the problem of elder abuse etc

This study focused about Physical and Psycho- social problems of rural elderly persons in present society. Elderly persons mostly affect by nature in the way of biological problems than the psychological problem. Following health and mental problems faced by the rural elderly persons.

Common Minor Health Complaints of Elderly

Hearing impairment

The loss of hearing occurs progressively over many years as the person ages. There are different causes for this. Sensory-neural deafness is particularly common and important. This is due to a combination of degenerative changes in both the cochlea and the auditory nerve. It typically results in preferential loss of high frequency hearing, which is particularly important in understanding speech (Bagga, 1998). Presbycusis is another very common type of hearing loss in older people (Rao,1990). Changes in the delicate structures of the inner ear lead to difficulties in understanding speech and possibly an intolerance of loud sounds, but not total deafness. Just as graying of hairs occurs at different rates, presbycusis develops differentially from persons to person. The other types of deafness are conductive deafness and central deafness. Hearing problem hinders communication with others, limit social activities and reduce constructive use of leisure time. Such people often withdraw from others to avoid frustration. Occasionally they become suspicious of relatives and friends (Rao, 1990).

Cataract

These are major causes of disability in older people, especially in developing countries where there are fewer resources for prevention and treatment. At present, about 25 million older people are blind; the number is expected to double by 2020 (WHO, 1998). There is a gradual increase in the incidence of eye ailments with increase in age. The ability to discriminate fine details decline slightly from 20 to 50's and accelerates thereafter. Reduction in the size of the pupil is also noticed. Ability to change to focus near and far objects is common. Increase the rigidity of lenses and also reduces the night vision. The most common eye problems among the aged are:

It is a very common eye change in old age. It is the occurrence of opaque areas in part of the lens or whole of it in the eye. Cataract can occur in one eye or both eyes. When it forms, light cannot easily pass through the lens and this affects vision. Cataract may develop without any sign of pain, redness and tears etc. in the eye. Some of them remain small and do not affect the vision seriously. Surgical removal is necessary when the cataract become larger in size or is denser.

Glaucoma

It results from too much pressure inside the eye from the fluid within, which damages the eye and causes a loss of vision. This relates to deficient drainage of aqueous humour. As the process progresses, the angle of vision becomes increasingly narrower, until the victim is effectively looking down a narrow tunnel. Because details in that tunnel are clearly seen the patient can manage to lead a normal life, until a critical point of visual loss has passed when it is too late to regain lost vision.

Excessive Tears

It may be caused due to a sign of increased sensitively to light, wind or temperature changes. Protective measures such as sunglasses may help the patients. Sometimes eye infection or a blocked tear-duct may also cause excessive tears and need treatment.

Excessive Dryness

Dried eyes result from the tear glands producing too few tears. It causes irritation, burning of eyes or a poor vision.

Retinal Defects

It results from Senile Macular Degeneration, Diabetic Retinopathy and Retinal Detachment.

Senile Macular Degeneration

It is a condition in which macula (a specialized part of the retina, responsible for sharp, central and reading vision)loses its function. The early signs of causing it are-blurring of reading matter, loss of central vision, a dark spot in the center of field of vision and distortion in vertical lines.

Diabetic Retinopathy

It is a serious complication in the elderly. The vessels that nourish retina fail to do so or there may be a leak from the blood vessels, which interfere with vision. In latter stages new blood vessels may grow and release blood into the centre of the eye resulting in serious loss of vision.

Retinal Detachment

It is a separation between inner and outer layers of retina. Detached retinas can be surgically reattached with a good or partial restoration of vision.

Blood Pressure Changes With Age

The systolic and diastolic blood pressures generally increase with age.

Hypotension

Distributions of autonomic functions are common in old age and postural hypertension is common. It is often worse in the morning and occurs when the person stands up from the sitting or lying position. Its onset is favoured by exertion such as walking. The initial blood pressure may be raised on to normal but falls to levels where cerebral perfusion is adversely affected and giddiness, vertigo, faintness and even transient syncope result and the patient exhibits pallor and a thin pulse that may become virtually undetectable. Postural hypotension is favoured by prolonged recumbence. In addition many other factors may operate, important among them are conditions leading to impairment of cardiac output such as salt depletion, aortic stenosis, etc. (Bagga, U.G.C.Minor Project Report).

Hypertension

High Blood Pressure (BP) is called hypertension. It tends to rise with age although the rate of increase seems to fall off beyond 65 years of age and may even be reversed in the oldest age groups. It is not possible to give a firm ruling as to what should be accepted as a normal blood pressure in old age. A diastolic level of 110 mm Hg or more can be taken as hypertensive if this is sustained under conditions, which do not produce stress or anxiety. (Hokinson, 1981).

PROBLEMS ASSOCIATED WITH CARE GIVING

Stress and Caring

The role of accumulated consequences of acute and chronic stress over the life span for health problems in later life is an extremely complex issue which is largely unresolved. Key components in stress reaction include both psychological mechanisms (Cognitive appraisal of the significance of stress stimuli, preferred coping strategies, and repertoire of behavioural responses) and physiological mechanisms (internal stimuli and body changes, emotional states, and physiological responses). Feedback loops connect these components and their elements, and there are pronounced individual differences in the expressions of response to stress.

Stress and caring approximately needs a lot of understanding and patience especially with regard to care giving for the elderly people. Stress is also experienced by the family and friends of disturbed older people, and the appraisal of such burden (summed objective problems) and strain (overall subjective awareness of being overloaded), is well developed. The rapidly developing body of investigation into carer support should assist in understanding the gross discrepancies between burden and strain that are sometimes reported. The model of family-oriented community care for other people is influential in practice. The most noxious product of stress is abuse of old people by careers or of careers by old people.

Even though there are difficulties and limitations of family carers in the process of care giving and it is very stressful for the majority of carers, it is essential to care over elders and give respect for them along with love and concern. But the care giving process is sufficiently stressful for the majority of carers. They can be given some form of professional intervention, based upon developing a shared commitment to the supervisory and supportive aspects of caring at a rate which permits the principal carer to maintain their caring role as they have the desire and resources to do (Garland,1993).

Gender is one of the reasons care giving has received so little attention. Legislatures are dominated by men and for the most part they are not as involved in care giving. Women need to make alliances with male care givers and use their power to make this everybody's issue. The rewards of care giving are so enormous, that this is such as profoundly moving experience that nothing else compares. It is a romanticization of care giving, an indirect way of saying to women that they are better off going back to this role because of the spiritual rewards. It feeds into a backlash to return women to the home and is something to watch.

Unfortunately, caregivers rarely have time to ponder political imperatives, grappling instead with the day-to-day realities of work, family obligations and personal needs. Helping families carry the financial burden of care is by far the most important issue. But families also need support services and respite care. Caregivers need to know that self-help groups are essential. There is a magic in getting people who are in the same boat together. It can be so supportive, and transformative. And then there is respite care, something experts consider the most important form of caregiver assistance. There are variety of services, form adult day care that affords caregivers a modicum of leisure, to holiday or weekend retreats, to in-home nursing or therapeutic services only in the major cities. There are also very few privately funded respite programs across the country.

WELFARE PROGRAMMES FOR ELDERLY PERSONS

Poverty Target Programmes for the Elderly

Free time the needs and problems of the elderly vary significantly according to their age, socio-economic status, health, living status and other such background characteristics. Perhaps the most important problems confronting India's elderly are financial. Mass poverty is the Indian reality and the vast majority of the families have incomes far below the level which would ensure a reasonable standard of living. The Ministry of Social Justice and Empowerment, in its document on the National Policy for Older Persons (1999), maintains that 33% of the general population live below poverty line and that one-third of the population in 60-plus age group is also below that level. On this basis, there are 23 million poor older persons. As people get older, they need more intensive and long-term care, which in turn may increase financial stress in the family. Inadequate income is a major problem facing the elderly in India.4 The most vulnerable are those who do not own productive assets, have little or no savings or income from investments, have no pension or retirement benefits, and are not taken care of by their children, or live in families that have low and uncertain incomes and a large number of dependents. Nearly half of the elderly are fully dependent on others, while another 20% are partially so.5 For elderly people living with their families - still the dominant living arrangement - their economic security and well-being are largely contingent on the economic capacity of the family unit. Particularly in rural areas, families suffer from economic crisis, as their occupations do not produce income throughout the year.

Welfare Policies and Programmes for Elderly

Across the globe, steps have been taken by various countries to provide social systems for the elderly and other disadvantaged groups. Such systems ensure that senior citizens are not deprived of their most basic needs when they lack the resources to fulfill them. The policies and programmes of the Indian government for the elderly are presented for a deeper understanding;

- National Policy on Older Persons (NPOP)
- National Social Assistance Programme (NSAP)
- The Indira Gandhi National Old Age Pension Scheme (IGNOAPS)
- Insurance Coverage
- The Indira Gandhi National Old Age Pension Scheme (IGNOAPS)
- Jan Arogya (People's Health) of SEWA
- Annapurna Scheme

CONCLUSION

Healthy ageing is the development and maintenance of optimal physical, mental and social well-being and function in older adults. It is most likely to be achieved when physical environments and communities are safe, and support the adoption and maintenance by individuals of attitudes and behaviors known to promote health and well-being; and by the effective use of health services and community programs to prevent or minimize the impact of acute and chronic disease on function. Hence, we have numerous welfare programmes for elderly. They giving the economical support and social assistance to improve the social status of elderly, but there were not much welfare programmes for related to health development of elderly people. So government take initiate some welfare programmes for development elderly health.

REFERENCES

1. Amesur, C.A. (1959), Welfare services for the Aged and the Infirm journal social work 20 (3) 157-162.
2. Deasi, K.G. Naik. R.D. (1971) Problems of retired people in greater Bombay, Tata Institute of Social Science. Bombay.
3. Anderson John. E., (1960) Researching on Ageing, In E.W.Burgers Ageing in western societies, Chicago Press, Chicago University.
4. D'sauza, V.S., (1969) 'Changes in Social structure and Changing Roles of older people in Indian', proceeding of 8th international congress on Gerontology, Washington.

5. Frank, L.K., (1946) 'Gerontology, Journal of Gerontology, vol.1 Nov.2, July 10.

6. Kreps, J., (1963) 'Employment income and retirement, problems of the age', Durham, North Carolire Duke University.

7. Rowos, I., (1967) 'Housing and social Integration of the aged', Free Press, New York.

8. (1994), Health Status of Elderly Women in Maharashtra: Ageing and Society, 4.3-4.11:11.21.

9. 'Mobility Sedentary Opposition: A Case Study among the Nomadic Gadulia Lohars'. In Joseph Berland and Hatt T. Salo, eds *Peripatetic Peoples*. Special Issue of *Nomadic Peoples*, Nos. 21 and 22

10. "Ageing and Mental Health of Older Women" (1996-2000), UGC's Major Research Project Report, Pune.

11. "Ageing and Mental Health of Older Women" (1996-2000), UGC's Major Research Project Report, Pune.

12. http://www.islamset.com/healnews/aged/economichtml

13. http://www.deccanherala.com/contest/july72007/wring2007070611326.asp

14. www.Planningcommission.nic.in.

15. http://www.globalageing.org/health/world/2006/indiapop.htm

□□□

26

A Comparative Study Between the SHG and Non-SHG Women Members on the Health Status and Decision Making

S. SAMPATH KUMAR AND V. VIJAYALAKSHMI

INTRODUCTION

Rural women in India are among the most disadvantaged people in the world in terms of their health status and access to accurate and appropriate health information and comprehensive, adequate and affordable health services. Gender beliefs and practices define roles, opportunities and limitations for women and men, greatly influencing life in all societies. Aspects of daily life shaped by gender include use of language and means of self expression, dress and appearance, education, work opportunities, family structure and size and each individual's health. (Susan Paulson, 2005)

Closely related to this, are the personal, relational and institutional barriers to rural women achieving their fundamental sexual and reproductive rights, their right to exercise control over their bodies and sexual and reproductive lives, which encompasses their right to decide upon such issues as contraception, marriage and abortion. Further, their overall health status is diminished by the lives they are forced to lead – lives that pivot around the harsh realities of malnutrition, illness, injury, and fatigue, frequently the consequence of long hours of demanding physical labour in unhygienic and dangerous conditions; the strains of childbirth and caring for multiple children; and not having enough to eat, which is often the result of more and better food going to male household members.

A gender sensitive approach emphasizes the need to probe deeper into sector such as health, nutrition, immunization, family planning and population and identify what are women's and men's realities, perspectives and needs and evolve strategies to integrate these into macro and micro planning and the implementation process. (Reproductive Health Programming from gender perspective, 2009).

Rural women are especially vulnerable to pregnancy- and childbirth-related deaths. According to recent WHO estimates, Asian maternal mortality ratios (maternal deaths per 100,000 live births) are among the highest in the world: 500 in Pakistan, 740 in Nepal, 540 in India, and 650 in Laos PDR, with most of these deaths being concentrated among rural women. In Nepal, only 10.2% of rural women giving birth are attended to by a skilled birth attendant, compared to 51.1% of urban Nepali women. 90% of maternal deaths in Nepal happen in rural areas, and it is estimated that for every death 30-40 women suffer from life-long disabilities.[3] In Pakistan, home births are more common among rural (76%) versus urban (54%) women, with only 30% of first time deliveries at home having a skilled attendant present, demonstrating rural women's greater risk In China, too, the rural-urban inequities are pronounced, as rates of maternal death in rural western China are four times those in urban areas

The process of empowerment should start from our own home. Women's position in the household determines women's autonomy in the family. It is worth to examine whether women can decide about household matters like buying jewelries, having access to money, having mobility to go to market or relatives' house or getting health care facilities.

In India the study of women's empowerment is scanty. The study on its regional variation is also very rare. On the basis of women's decision making power in different sphere of life, women's autonomy has been judged in three-fold ways in this paper: Firstly, to investigate the percentage involved in decision making power of women in socio-cultural, socio-economic and health aspects of their own lives; Secondly, the assessment of regulatory factors or ability to formulate the decision making power and thirdly, the comparative account of women's empowerment and its associated factors through the comparison between working (paid and un-paid workers) and non-working women.

In this paper we have found the state wise variations in the percentages of women who are involved in the household decision making power and have examined whether levels of education, types of occupation, working status of women etc., and the other characteristics of the household like standard of living, sex of head of household etc. have positive influence on the empowerment. Data from NFHS-3 Survey conducted in 2004-05 have been used for the analysis.

The degree of women's decision making power is not same over the different aspects of life considered here. Women are almost the sole authority to decide about cooking and have access to money but can rarely buy jewelry of its own. Less than one-third of women can decide about health care or get permission to go to relative's house or market.

The study reveals the women's autonomy through the decision making power on different aspects of life such as household, access to money, self-health care and freedom of movements to relative's house or to the market. It covers women of reproductive age (15-49) of different states and zones of India. The study also provides socio-cultural and socio-economic variations in the level of empowerment. The empowerment of women increases with the age of women and remains almost same among different occupational groups. Husband's education or occupation does not contribute much to the empowerment. Working women have distinct advantage as against non-working or unpaid working women. Though maximum percentage of empowered women has been observed about cooking but its nature is different from others. Unlike others, this percentage decreases as SLI increases, is less for literate women and female headed households. Behaviour of North-East region is also a bit different due to matriarchal societal norms from other regions in India which becomes evident if one compares the coefficients of the logistic regression.

Our result indicates that there exists a great regional variation in the levels of women's autonomy. Highest autonomy in household such as cooking has been seen in North-east zone and lowest in North zone. In state-wise distribution, greater autonomy has been seen in women of Nagaland, Karnataka and Tamil Nadu in case of cooking and Goa, Kerala, Tripura, West Bengal and Tamil Nadu in case of buying jewelry. And lower percentages have been found in Jammu, Kerala, Uttar Pradesh etc. for cooking and Nagaland, Punjab in buying jewelry. South zone and North zone show highest and lowest autonomy in buying jewelry respectively. In regards to economic aspect, i.e. access to money, highest autonomy has been seen in West zone and lowest in Central zone. State wise the higher degrees are found in Meghalaya, Goa, Himachal Pradesh and Tamil Nadu and lowest in Nagaland, Assam etc.

State wise distribution of health care autonomy of women for themselves shows high percentages in Kerala, New Delhi, Assam, Tamil Nadu etc, and less in Nagaland, Manipur, Orissa etc. Highest empowerment is seen in West Zone and lowest in East zone. Greater freedom of movements is found in West zone and the lowest is in Central zone. When seen State wise, greater mobility is found in Goa, Gujarat, Maharastra, Tamil Nadu etc, and it is lesser in Jammu, Uttar Pradesh, Assam, Nagaland, Orissa, West Bengal etc.

The striking feature is that among the paid workers, decision making power in spending the earnings are seen to be high in Jammu, Goa, New Delhi and low in Nagaland, Mizoram, Orissa, Madhya Pradesh etc. Zonewise, highest degree is found in North zone and lowest in Central zone. Women's autonomy through the comparison among three working categories viz. non-working, working (paid) and working (unpaid) is seen to vary in different spheres of cooking, buying jewelry. Earning women have greater access to decision making power. But in case of access to money, there is no significant difference between non-working and working (paid) women. Among the other two of decision makings such as mobility and health care, non-working women shows lesser ability in mobility. In health care ability, lesser autonomy is found among the working (unpaid) women than non-working and working (paid) women. In India, rural women show less autonomy than urban women. Age-groups and educational attainment has a positive relation with the increment of autonomy.

Working status (paid), better nutritional status, standard of living index, and female headed household act as a stimulator for the enhancement of autonomy. So it is proved that higher female earnings make women unambiguously better off giving them more power in household decision making, health care and mobility. A striking feature is that household and domestic female workers have greater decision making power than paid workers. Thus improvement of household wealth may not enhance female autonomy rather it may reduce the autonomy of female. It also supports the view that women's education helps to increase the autonomy. To sum up, to answer the question why women's autonomy varies over different regions/states, the analysis through the above depicted explanatory variables is not enough. One has to have an in-depth knowledge about the cultural beliefs and practices that exist in the different zones and the states and also among different castes and religious groups.

BARRIERS OF CULTURE AND SOCIETY

Culture and society play a significant role in rural women's health status and access to services. Socio cultural norms shape beliefs and attitudes and condition human behaviours in ways that can be damaging to one's own or another person's health and well-being. Longstanding and entrenched gender inequalities impact rural women's health in Asia. Rural communities adhere more rigorously to customary laws and norms of social stratification that perpetuate biases against rural women – biases which impact the allocation of assets, power, rights, status, and opportunities. Rural women have less access to basic resources (e.g. social, health, educational, and agricultural service systems) compared to their male counterparts. Moreover, biases result in rural women being treated with contempt, humiliated, violated, and discriminated against, which leads to their lowered self-esteem and feelings of fear and loneliness.

The violence that many rural women face at the hands of their husbands and other family members is one of the most physically and psychologically damaging experiences faced by many rural women. The degree of acceptance of such behaviours in many rural communities, combined with the women's powerlessness to stop such actions, including the lack of someone to turn to for help, all compound to keep rural women in abusive relationships and limit positive behaviour changes on the part of men. Stressful circumstances appear to intensify the abuse of rural women.

Women's lack of decision-making power is apparent in their

inability to control when and to whom they will be married. Early marriage is more common in rural areas and unfortunately this can negatively impact their health and well-being. Women who marry at a young age, who often drop out of school, also have less of an opportunity to learn about their sexual and reproductive health and rights and how to access related services. With minimal education and limited access to reproductive health services, they are left on their own to manage their fertility and sexual and reproductive health and well-being. Religious and political conservatism, which influences many elements of society, including government, also negatively impacts rural women. Socio cultural norms also influence health seeking behaviours and health delivery. For example, male village-level health providers in India report that taboos prohibit them from conducting physical examinations or invasive diagnostic and therapeutic procedures on rural women, a situation that results in them providing care that is ineffective and more expensive (e.g. pills and shots) and can delay correct diagnosis and access to appropriate facility-based care One of the strategies identified for advancing these goals was the establishment of Self-Help Groups (SHGs) , particularly in rural regions especially to eliminate the social exclusion of poor women. In India, SHGs are usually oriented to the needs and interests of women, with most of their activities concentrated on economic empowerment by providing financial savings and credit activities apart from specifically designated activities focusing on health, personality and educational attainment.

The influence of society over the range and exercise of choice also means that if it should seek to promote empowerment, it must also consider factors affecting women's status and rights as a group. Although many microfinance programs promote social solidarity at some level, most microfinance organizations tend to focus their attention on promoting changes at an individual level—a woman who, for instance, is now able to send her children to school, negotiate lower prices for her raw materials, or even dream bigger dreams for herself, her family, and her business. The achievements of individual women can have a powerful impact on the way women are perceived and treated within their communities, but the levels of empowerment individual women may achieve are usually limited if women as a group are generally disempowered. For that reason many organizations also include elements designed to uplift women and communities as a collective rather than just as individuals.

Seeking to enable the poor to become agents of change in their communities, our approach encompasses social, economic, political, and spiritual empowerment within the individual, household, business, and community. The empowerment of women at the individual level helps build a base for social change. Movements to empower women as a group increase opportunities available to individual women, and economic empowerment can increase women's status in their families and societies. Practically speaking, the interrelatedness of different aspects of empowerment and between empowerment and development makes it very difficult to move far ahead in any one area without corresponding changes in other areas.

While health is obviously an integral component of women's well-being and empowerment, it is also organically linked to their empowerment within the household and the society. It is in this context, that SHGs is expected to play the important role of ensuring good health for the women through empowering them within the household as well as within the society.

There is a common perception in development literature that the increased participation of women in savings and credit activities, or economic attainment, will empower women by helping them to access and utilize better health services and facilities, and by elevating the health, nutritional, and educational status of their families, in particular that of children. One of the major consequences anticipated to result from this empowerment is the enhancement of women's welfare, particularly in relation to their health. The underlying approach to women's participation in micro-finance programmes, then, has been highly instrumental, not only in terms of their own socio-economic well-being but in relation to that of their families as well. Numerous studies have shown, however, that while women may be empowered in one area, this does not necessarily translate into empowerment in others. This is attributable to a number of factors but fundamental to the constraints on interventions such as SHGs are structural inequalities.

However, till date, the functioning of SHGs has been viewed only from an economic perspective. The existing approach emphasizes economic development of people and women in particular, in case of women SHGs. However how these economic benefits are being translated into change in women's status, particularly their health status has not been explored.

In this backdrop, the present study explores the extent to involvement of SHGs in attaining women empowerment in decision making and better health for them and also attempts to bring out a comparison between the autonomy and decision making power in health aspects between women of two different regions having similar socio economic background but with a comparison between women of Self Help Groups and Non Self Help Group members. The study tries to reveal the health status of women with regard to the decision making power in rural villages of Tamilnadu and Pondicherry.

Objectives of the Study

- To analyze the participation of women in decision making particularly with their reproductive health.
- To identify the change in status of women with respect to their autonomy in decision making through the Self Help Groups

MATERIALS AND METHODS

The sampling process involved selection of one village panchayat from each blocks of Coimbatore as first stage and selection of households from the sample frame as second stage through a systematic random sampling method. Out of the selected household, randomly 173 respondents were chosen and systematically interviewed using structured interview Schedule. Similarly in Puducherry, among the three blocks, Villianur block which is a rural block is taken for the purpose of sampling. The Self Help Group members in that block registered under District Rural Development agency (DRDA) were selected randomly as samples. Thus a random selection of 167 respondents was chosen and was interviewed under structured interview schedule. Few focussed group discussion were conducted to identify the reality.

RESULTS AND DISCUSSION

The present study is made in a systematic approach to find out the role of women in decision making and also to identify her position in the family in the process of family building.

The findings of the study reveal that the decision on reproductive health of the respondents was made by both the respondent and her husband in 50% of the households. In more than two fifths of the cases, the husbands were the sole decision makers. A Western Guatemale study by Becker et al (2006) and the Colombian Demographic and Health Survey by Pallitto (2004) also brought out similar findings. The results of both studies show that men prefer to see themselves as the senior partners in all decisions including reproductive health decision making and further they say lack of communication between partners as a reason for low decision making role of women.

With regard to the household work performed during pregnancy, the vast majority of the respondents (95.5 percent) were doing all the household works till the last stage of pregnancy. A few less than half of the respondents were cared by their mothers during pregnancy; about one third of the respondents were cared by their husbands. The vast majority of them were discussing their health status during pregnancy with husband. About three fourths of them had taken rest during pregnancy. More than two fifths of them stopped doing heavy work just one month before delivery; one fourth of them were working till the very end of their pregnancy. A study conducted in rural China disagree with study findings and reveals that women's position within the family is positively associated with the likelihood that a woman receives prenatal examinations, stops heavy physical work before birth (Li J, 2004). With respect to immunization status of the respondents during pregnancy, almost all the respondents were immunized.

With regard to the nature of care received by the respondents during pregnancy, majority of the respondents consulted with doctors 9 to 10 times. Three fifths of the respondents were accompanied by their husband to hospital for regular checkup during pregnancy while three tenths of them were taken by their mothers. With regard to diet during pregnancy, about three fifths of them had special diet and more than two fifths did not have special diet due to poverty though they desired to have, very small number of them felt that special diet was not needed and they eat whatever available. In the case of nine out of ten respondents, were visited by the health workers when they were pregnant, since visiting mothers during pregnancy is mandatory that every village health worker should visit each house periodically to give them education about the diet during pregnancy and the importance of regular health checkups and taking immunization.

The above findings in relation to the reproductive health status of the women clearly show that the women do not have any great say in determining their health during pregnancy in which the space is occupied by the husband. The contraceptive awareness is very low among the respondents. The reasons citied by them are menstrual problems, spousal disapproval, and lack of necessity. The contraceptive behaviour of the women is a major determining factor of the composition of the population of the country which in turn influences the health status of the children as well as their own.

India's goal for achieving replacement level of fertility is in the year 2010. While Tamil Nadu has achieved zero population growth in 1991 and replacement level of fertility in the year 2000. This has been accomplished through the efforts of a concerned and committed family planning program, improvement in maternal and child health care, girl children's prolonged stay in school , which in turn delayed their marriage and exposure to conception, near universal immunisation coverage, more than eighty four percent institutional deliveries and hundred percent antenatal registration (Aiyer, 1993).

Though Tamil Nadu considered as a one of the model state in providing maternal and child health care through different levels of health care delivery system, the cultural barriers, patriarchal family system, and second grade citizenship of women put women in the darkness of ignorance, which further not allowing them to raise voice against the age old system. The major responsibility lies on the health care providers, especially nurses in bringing women into the main stream of decision making process by making them to understand that the reproduction is the biological responsibility of women.

As far as SHG women members were considered, Structured interview schedule was based on several health indicators on which the Health empowerment of the women were analysed. The indicators were categorised under three broad headings

- Impact of SHG on Women Empowerment
- Impact of SHG on Health Knowledge and Awareness
- Impact of SHG on Women's Health Perception and Behaviour
- Impact of SHG on Empowerment and Health

Mainly for analysing all three aspects, more than 30 indicators are used. The respondents were interviewed on the basis on the indicators on the above Four categories.

The first objective on the impact of SHG on Women Empowerment focussed to find out the overall empowerment level of respondent with regard to SHG. Though the respondents feels that the SHG gave them a stand in their economic level, by increasing their income through employment opportunities, still others factors like family empowerment, importance in family and community, health awareness are still having a long way to go.

Similarly, the second objective on Impact of SHG on Health Knowledge and Awareness clearly depicts that the SHG has not brought any change in their knowledge level as well there is no awareness about Child Care, family planning methods, contraceptive usage, post natal care which are more crucial for nation development. Thus SHG's role in transforming and generating the health knowledge among the women is minimal.

Our third objective of research, on the Impact of SHG on Women's Health Perception and Behaviour clearly summarises their perceptions towards Health. Respondent's opinion on sickness is very unique and different. Self Medication found in major cases. If in need of a treatment, the first level contact for care is Primary Health Centre, Villianur. Very rarely the respondents opt for Private clinics, since it's too expensive. Also, since first deliveries are not undertaken in that PHC, due to lack of facilities, those cases would be sent to Government Hospitals for further treatment.

The final objective of exploring the Impact of SHG on Women Empowerment and Health shows that the health awareness and the knowledge of women are much less. The women SHG members are not that exposed to Health schemes of the Government as well as other bodies. On the whole, The Health Empowerment of the Women through SHG is very low.

All the above aspects were similar in the case of both women in the two regions. There was not much a difference between their autonomy in decision making irrespective of the SHG membership. Rather, a higher majority of the respondents didn't receive any knowledge from the SHG in respect to health. The indicators looked in to the respondents on health were awareness on hygiene, vaccination, contraceptive usages, care during pregnancy, knowledge on family planning and awareness on available health care services. But neither the BDO nor the NGO focused on the health related aspects in detail, but had a one day session in general. Thus the respondents requests the respective organizations to concentrate on the health awareness and extent to which SHGs can be involved in attaining better health for women.

Women from rural areas needs specific empowerment programme to enable them to be more autonomous in the household decision making. Women's autonomy by education, wealth quintile and development region needs a further social science investigation to observe the variations within each stratum. A more comprehensive strategy can enable women to access community resources, to challenge traditional norms and to access economic resources. This will lead the women to be more autonomous in decision making in the due course.

Although SHGs were expected to play a significant role in women's health and empowerment, basic need of food, shelter and work came out as primary to their life and well being and without achieving or fulfilling these basic primary needs of food, shelter and work, one cannot empower the women or provide better health and life. The study further explores that women's economic empowerment through micro-credit programmes doesn't have a direct impact on women's health. However, there may be indirect positive impacts on health but ultimately there has been a lag in the implementation of SHG when empowerment in the Health of the Women is concerned, which has to be taken under consideration by the policy makers

REFERENCES

Ahuja, R. (2005). Universal Health Insurance Scheme. Yojana. Vol. 49, July 2005. New Delhi. Ministry of Information and Broadcasting:

Goetz, A.M. and Sen Gupta, R. (1996) 'Who takes the credit? Gender, power, and control over loan use in rural credit programs in Bangladesh' World Development 24(1):45- 63.

Hashemi, S.M.; Schuler, S. and Riley, A.P. (1996) 'Rural credit programs and women's empowerment in Bangladesh' World Development 24(4):635-53.

Hashemi, Syed and Sidney Schuler. (1993). Operationalising Indicators of Empowerment: A Methodological Note. Dhaka: Unpublished mimeo in Goetz, Anne Marie. 2001. Women Development Workers: Implementing rural credit Programmes in Bangladesh pp. 44 New Delhi: Sage Publications.

Jing, Fang. 2004. "Health Sector Reform and Reproductive Health Service in Poor Rural China." *Health Policy and Planning.* 19 (Suppl. 1):140-149.

National Policy for Empowerment of Women. (2001). New Delhi: Department of Women and Child Development. Ministry of HRD.

Nayar, K.R.; Kyobutungi, Catherine; Razum, Oliver. (2004). Self-help: What future role in health care for low and middle-income countries? International Journal for Equity in Health 2004, 3:1

Shah, Sirjana; Thapa, Muno; Niraula, Chitra; Pradhanang, Shilpa, Sing, Sewa. 2005. *SRHR Country Position Paper, Nepal.* Kathmandu, Nepal: Beyond Beijing Committee. (unpublished)

Sultana, Munawar. 2005. A Brief on Reproductive Health of Adolescents and Youth in Pakistan: Culture of Silence. Islambad, Pakistan: The Population Council.

[1] **Learning Ladder**- The education kit developed by Rishi Valley Rural Education Centre consists of graded cards supported by a pictorial 'achievement ladder'. These cards represented a breaking down of the learning process into smaller units. Groups of cards are then assembled into a set of 'milestones', which lead students from level I to level V in the areas of language, mathematics and environmental science.

[2] The term is borrowed from Donald Schon [1971: 123]. In this context, it means the idea that is implemented and institutionalized.

❑❑❑